As one of the blues world's most respect

men, Holger Petersen has won the trus

women, the roots rock musicians inspired by the blues, and the record producers who captured this music for posterity. As a result, he's able to evoke fascinating information in these interviews, giving the reader new perspectives on the Delta blues tradition, and how the blues grew from its Southern birthplace to become a worldwide phenomenon. With Holger's incisive questioning, the artists illuminate the blues before the world discovered it, early recordings, the beginnings of the British blues boom and how it converted a generation of American kids to the blues and blues/rock. Whether you're a knowledgeable blues fan or a newcomer to the music, you'll find *Talking Music* to be a truly enjoyable read."
—Bruce Iglauer, President and Founder of Alligator Records/Co-founder of *Living Blues Magazine*

Musicologist, broadcaster and entrepreneur Holger Petersen is a true Canadian treasure. Widely-respected as the pre-eminent blues and roots music authority, Holger has an innate ability to draw out the most fascinating insights and personal anecdotes from his decades of interviews, as evidenced by those included in this engaging volume. They're all here, the movers, shakers, innovators and trailblazers from skiffle to blues and roots revivalists, all at ease in conversation with Holger. Enjoy!
—John Einarson, author of *Four Strong Winds: Ian & Sylvia* and *Randy Bachman: Still Takin' Care of Business*

I have known Holger Petersen for almost 40 years.
That is over a century in Canadian time.
Holger Petersen is taller than Leonard Cohen.
Holger Petersen weighs more than Shania Twain.
Holger Petersen is seen in public more than Joni Mitchell.
Holger Petersen should be called "The Great One" but another Canadian got that name first.
So Holger Petersen is "The Pretty Good One."
I am honoured to speak on his behalf.
—Dick Waterman, author of *Between Midnight and Day: The Last Unpublished Blues Archive* and photographer

Talking Music: Blues Radio and Roots Music is a welcome addition to the literature on North American and British roots musics. Holger Petersen's love and knowledge of his subjects' music permeates these conversations. The result is a wonderful collection of interviews that range from Honeyboy Edwards' first-hand account of the death of Robert Johnson to Bonnie Raitt's and Maria Muldaur's moving recollections of meeting and working with Sippie Wallace. I couldn't stop turning the pages.
—Rob Bowman, Music Department, York University

I know of no other Canadian who is such an enthusiastic authority on Blues than Holger Petersen. His Saturday CBC Radio show is legendary, his record label is legendary in presenting true authentic roots and blues music and he himself is a delight. I am happy to call him a friend for many decades. For him to put some of his past chats into book form is a must for all music fans to read. An insight into the hearts, souls, minds and lives of the music legends is a must for everyone. So get the book and let it take you on a journey you'll never forget. That's what I'll be doing!
—Randy Bachman

Frank Zappa rightly said that writing about music is like dancing about architecture. But talking about music—when it's two or more people who know what they're talking about—is likely to be not only fascinating, but educational in a way no mere essay can be. *Talking Music* is an absorbing compilation of working-man's interviews by Canada's Mr. Roots Music, founder of Stony Plain Records and host of the longest running blues radio program anywhere, Holger Petersen, speaking intimately and at length with...well, just look at the table of contents; you won't believe me if I tell you. True gods and goddesses of The People's Music, veterans of the road, pivotal avatars of blues, soul, rock, jazz, country and/or R&B—and for lagniappe, the field's first scientific student, the legendary Alan Lomax. Holger asks the right questions, listens hard to the answers, then thinks up even better questions. Often, he gets answers a civilian might not have been given. His first book is a treasure-chest bursting with swag, a priceless opportunity to be a fly on the wall for some of the most authoritative, revelatory, and purely entertaining discussions of the nature and history of music that have ever occurred.
—Spider Robinson, author of *Very Hard Choices*

Hi Linda,
Thanks for everything you do for CKUA and for this great music.

talking music

Holger Petersen

INSOMNIAC PRESS

Library and Archives Canada Cataloguing in Publication

Talking music : blue radio and roots music / Holger Petersen.

Collection of radio interviews.
ISBN 978-1-55483-033-6

1. Blues musicians--Interviews. 2. Country musicians--Interviews.
3. Folk musicians--Interviews. I. Petersen, Holger, 1949-

ML3470.T146 2011 780.92 C2011-905412-4

The publisher gratefully acknowledges the support of the Canada Council, the Ontario Arts Council, and the Department of Canadian Heritage through the Book Publishing Industry Development Program.

Author photo by Darren Jacknisky, Bluefish Studios. 2010

Printed and bound in Canada

Insomniac Press
520 Princess Ave.
London, Ontario, Canada, N6B 2B8
www.insomniacpress.com

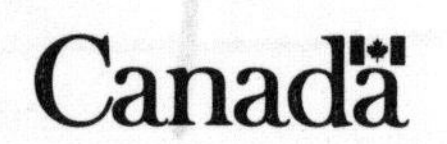

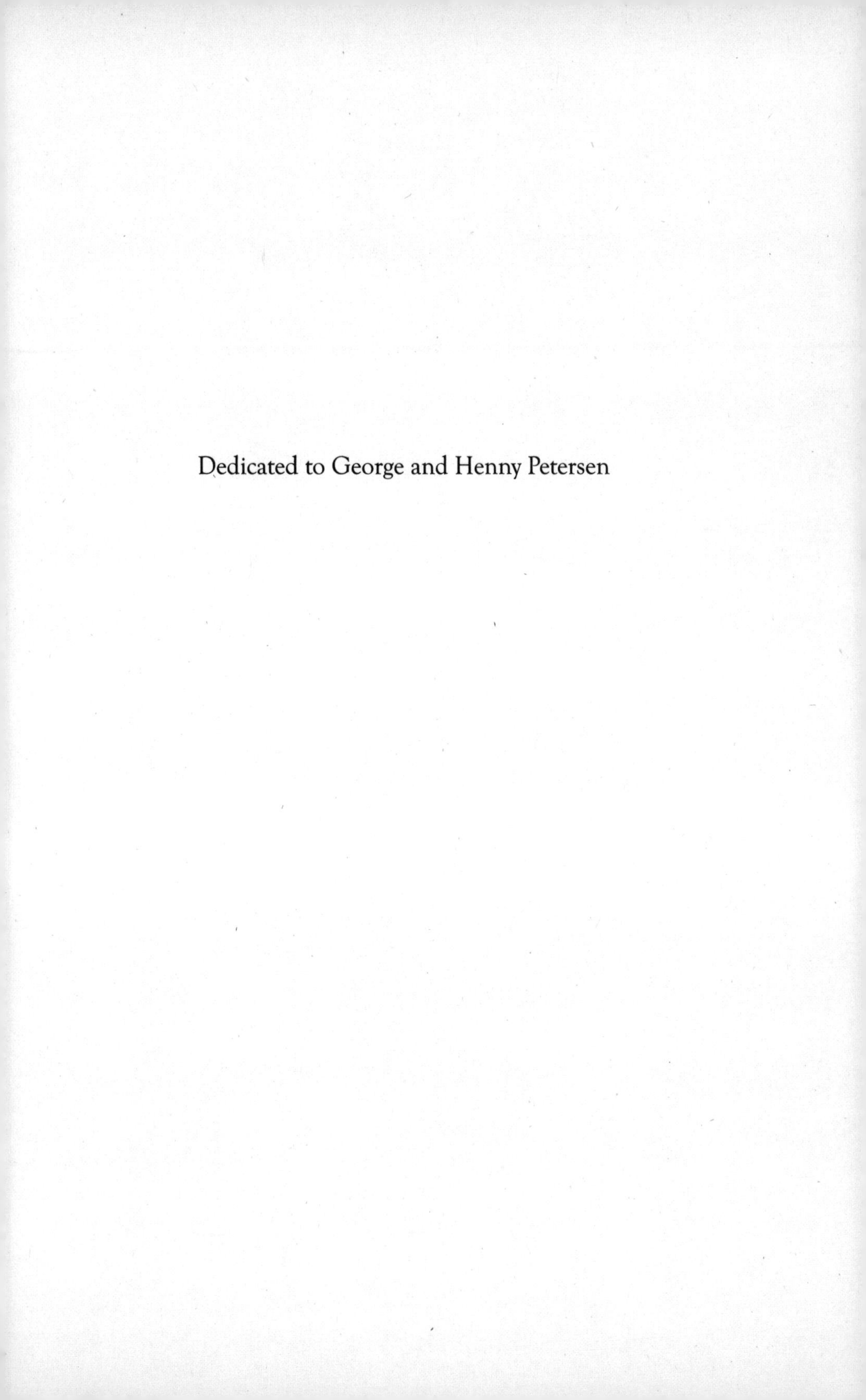

Dedicated to George and Henny Petersen

Acknowledgements

Going through the interviews included in this book has reminded me of how fortunate I've been to be in the good company of so many amazing artists.

I'm grateful to have spent time with them, for their generosity, and to the people around them who provide support.

Brian Wood's encouragement and perseverance got the ball rolling. Mike O'Connor from Insomniac Press shared the vision and Gillian Urbankiewicz lent her patience and editing talent. Most of the interviews were transcribed by Jennifer Burns. Mark Dutton at Halkier & Dutton Design did the wonderful front and back covers. Thanks to each of you for your enthusiasm, support, and for making this fun.

Many of the interviews have been broadcast on my CBC Radio show *Saturday Night Blues* and are reprinted here with CBC's permission. Thanks to Dan Cherwoniak, Chris Martin, Steve Glassman, Don Marcotte, Mark Steinmetz, Denise Donlan, and Chris Boyce. Since 1989, I've had the pleasure of hosting the program and working with past CBC producers Bill Law, Rick Fenton, Rayfield Rideout, Al McLennan, Richard Craig, Ron Yachimec, Eitan Cornfield. I've learned from each of you and am grateful.

The interviews with Bill Wyman, Ry Cooder, and Alan Lomax were first published in *Penguin Eggs* magazine. Thanks to editor Roddy Campbell and to Megan Campbell who transcribed them.

The CKUA Radio Network in Alberta has played a major role in my life since 1969 when I first started my ongoing show *Natch'l Blues*. Thanks to my fellow announcers for constant inspiration, to all the volunteers, staff, and to Brian Dunsmore, Katrina Regan-Ingram, Sharon Marcus, Joan Patton, and Ken Regan.

I'd like to acknowledge my mentors Richard Flohil, for your huge role with all aspects of this project, and to Bob Hunka for all your support, guidance, friendship and for setting the bar high in everything that you do. Peter North, Ron Dezman, Jim Yanaway, Thomas Fenn, Rob Edwards, Yehudi Altman, and Larry Reese–thank you for your friendship.

I'm grateful to the Galaxie Network for allowing me to program the BluesTime Channel and be part of their service.

Thanks to Terry Wickham and everyone involved with the Edmonton Folk Music Festival. I'm so proud to have been a part of it and continually admire what you've done for the music and the community.

I'm fortunate to have many friends in the music industry; friends whose love of music and commitment to bettering the industry has been a constant inspiration. You know who you are and I thank you.

I'd like to acknowledge the following music writers for their research, insight, and inspiration–John Einarson, Dick Waterman, Larry LeBlanc, Rob Bowman, Dave "Daddy Cool" Booth, Colin Escott, Peter Guralnick, Paul Myers, Denise Tapp, J. Marshall Craig, Art Tipaldi, Jeff Hannusch, Joe Boyd, Bob Mersereau, Julian Dawson, Jim O'Neal, Joe Nick Patoski, Chuck Haddix, John Broven, Dick Shurman, John Swenson, Cindy McLeod, Richard Wagamese, Peter North, Roger Lavesque, and Spider Robinson.

Working at Stony Plain Records is my day job. Alvin Jahns has been my partner at the label since day one and deserves huge credit for his work and for making it possible for me to live my dream by working on productions with some of the most talented artists in the world. Alvin has been my close friend since we both started playing music together in garage bands. We've had many talented and dedicated people working with us since 1976. A special thanks to Peter Chapmen for also helping me with this book and to Julie King,

Crystal Sherris, Angeline Cumings, Mark Pucci, Steve Kane, David Kerr, Philippe Langlois, Alain Rivey, Ulrich Schulze-Rossbach, Lynne Tattersall, Kent Sturgeon, Al Chapman, Bert Pijpers, Don Hargrove, Michael Burke, Tommy Banks, John McCullough, Al Mair, Bill Wax, and Jay Sieleman of the Blues Foundation for your support.

Finally, the biggest thanks of all go to my family, extended family, and especially to Anne Green for her love, inspiration, and encouragement.

Table of Contents

Foreword
by Richard Flohil

"Writing about music is like dancing about architecture."

So, apparently, said Frank Zappa, Elvis Costello, Martin Mull, Steve Martin, Hunter S. Thompson, and several others. Who said it first is cheerfully discussed by smart people who think the quote is funny, or apt, or a brilliant non sequitur, and nobody has yet attributed the line to any of the above (and more) with any certainty.

In any event, it's silly, inaccurate, and meaningless.

Writing about music, in fact, illuminates the joy we feel when we hear it, it tells us about the people who wrote and performed it, and it places the music in the contexts in which it was created and performed.

And how about talking about music? This is the way people who love music get other people to join the discussion, lead listeners in new directions, help them discover new music, and remind them of the great music of the past.

Who better to talk about music than the people who make it? Leading them, questioning them, and getting them to open up has been one of Holger Petersen's passions for four decades. This collection of interviews puts a bright light on the musicians and the music they made—music that helped shape the lives of anyone who cares about the roots of popular culture.

Holger Petersen has had a remarkable impact on music in Canada—his story is not easily summarized. He has been collecting records since he was a boy. He has been a radio personality for more than forty years. He has built a record company that has won numerous awards and still continues, thirty-five years on. He helped found what is now Canada's largest folk music festival.

At an early age he was a radio junkie. One of his earliest memories is listening to country music on his folks' radio, thinking that the singers and players were actually, somehow, inside the radio itself. Later, there were camping trips from his family's Alberta home into the mountains, where his parents would let him sit in the car, late at night, and listen to the radio—but only for an hour, before the battery ran out.

He bought his first record in junior high school in Edmonton, Alberta, in 1961. (It was Bob Luman's "Private Eye," an undistinguished novelty song by a popular country singer of the day.) With his weekly allowance and some money earned delivering flyers for a grocery store, he bought used records from local jukebox operators.

Music films such as *A Hard Day's Night* with the Beatles, or *The T.A.M.I. Show* (with James Brown and the Famous Flames, Chuck Berry, Marvin Gaye, and the Rolling Stones) added a visual dimension to the music on the singles. And magazines like *Rolling Stone, Creem*, and even the slim Canadian music trade magazine *RPM*, suggested new music, new artists, and new records to explore.

But it was the Stones, the Animals, the Yardbirds, Manfred Mann, the Kinks, and many other "British Invasion" bands that initially led Petersen to the blues. Reading the small type of songwriting credits on record labels took him to the music of Howlin' Wolf, Muddy Waters, Bo Diddley, Chuck Berry, Little Walter, Otis Rush, and countless others.

This was the strongly beating heart of American music, taken across the Atlantic, and returned with thanks to capture a young new generation of North American teenagers. Holger Petersen was among them.

A two-year Radio & Television Arts course at the Northern Alberta Institute of Technology led Petersen to the student radio station where he hosted a weekly show (heard, he recalls, only by students in the cafeteria). And since nobody else wanted the job, he became the station's music director.

From there, the suggestion to the editor of *the Nugget*, the student newspaper, that he write record reviews, cover concerts, and perhaps interview visiting artists was an easy jump. The first interview was with Spencer Davis, whose band was a significant part of the British rock scene.

Prepared, ready with dozens of written questions, the conversation was less of a success than he hoped. Others, with the gentlemanly Roy Orbison, the flamboyant Little Richard, and down-home bluesman Bo Diddley were more successful, and Petersen over time learned not only the need for preparation, but the art of setting the mood, listening, and asking the right questions.

In 1968 he began to listen to CKUA, the provincial radio network then funded by the Government of Alberta. It has the distinction of being Canada's first public broadcaster. This was free-form FM eclectic radio in its infancy, when listeners could hear Mozart and Muddy Waters on the same program.

The people involved with the station were all characters: independent, smart, quirky, and rebels in many ways. But it was their passion for music – and the station's massive record library – that resonated with Petersen.

A Saturday night program host asked if some of the *Nugget* interviews could be used on air, and an invitation to talk about recent blues recordings led—in early 1969—to a weekly forty-five minute program named *Natch'l Blues* after a currently popular Taj Mahal recording. (The program continues to run on CKUA forty years later.)

The record-collecting contributor to a student newspaper was becoming a radio personality.

Meeting visiting artists, listening to concerts (often from backstage), writing articles, and broadcasting interviews led to the next step: producing records. In 1972, learning as he went, he recorded Walter "Shakey" Horton, a grizzled, reclusive blues harmonica player from Chicago. Then over the next few years New Orleans pianist Roosevelt Sykes, and Johnny Shines, a rural blues singer who had travelled, in his youth, with the legendary Robert Johnson. He also produced sessions with Paul Hann, a country folk artist who called himself the Cockney Cowboy, Irish folk legend Liam Clancy, and Saskatoon's Humphrey and the Dumptrucks.

From there, the creation of Stony Plain Records in late 1975 with Alvin Jahns, was a logical progression. Petersen had licensed his first productions to other record companies; surely it made more sense to release them himself.

Three years later, with a dozen releases under his belt, Petersen—following the advice of other independent record companies—tested the international waters by attending MIDEM, the annual music industry conference in Cannes. In the years since he has only missed the conference once.

MIDEM is now a sophisticated, intense, technologically savvy affair, held in the same massive concrete structure—the Palais des Festivals—that houses the Cannes Film Festival and many other events. In the late '70s and early '80s, however, it was held in a decrepit convention centre. It was loud, boozy, free-spirited, and fuelled by excessive major record company parties, star-studded live concerts, and late, late night gatherings in the bar at the Martinez Hotel. MIDEM not only put Petersen in touch with like-minded music industry people who shared his enthusiasm, it also put Stony Plain on the international map. Stony Plain picked up the Canadian rights for labels such as Rounder, Folkways, Blind Pig, Sugar Hill, and others; in turn Stony Plain's productions were now being released around the world.

The little record company from Edmonton was becoming, in music business parlance, a significant "player."

In the mid-eighties, Stony Plain Records was very much a going concern. Veteran folk singer turned Alberta rancher Ian Tyson, who wanted to make "just one more record—for the cowboys" delivered *Cowboyography* to the label, and it went on to become Stony Plain's first platinum record and revived a career that is still going strong.

The sheer variety of the music on the label was already astounding as Stony Plain marked its twentieth anniversary in 1996. At that time the roster included transplanted British artist Long John Baldry, political folkies Spirit of the West, Edmonton punk country band Jr. Gone Wild, guitar heroes Amos Garrett and Ellen McIlwaine, San Antonio's Doug Sahm (initially famous as the front man in the Sir Douglas Quintet), and Canadian blues stars King Biscuit Boy and the Downchild Blues Band. There were more Ian Tyson albums, a couple by his former wife Sylvia Tyson, and the initial release of Steve Earle's remarkable comeback album. There were also albums by Robert Cray, Ricky Skaggs, and the first of half a dozen records by Maria Muldaur (three of which have been nominated for Grammy Awards).

A chance meeting at the Winnipeg Folk Festival had led to an ongoing relationship with American guitarist Duke Robillard—who in the years since has released more than a dozen albums on the label and produced others by a wide range of other artists.

As the label prospered, Petersen continued *Natch'l Blues* on CKUA, featuring regular interviews and music from a record collection that was slowly taking over most of the downstairs rooms in his suburban Edmonton house.

And, in addition to his work with CKUA and the record label, Petersen was asked to chair the board of a new venture, the Edmonton Folk Music Festival. Getting the first Edmonton event off the ground in 1980 was difficult, and even more so when the initial festival lost some $70,000. After five years, Petersen, reluctantly, agreed to be the festival's artist director, responsible for choosing, booking, and programming some sixty artists over the three-day event. It was a job he did for three years; the festival turned around, became profitable, and was described by *Rolling Stone* as "the summer's hippest music festival."

And then, almost out of the blue, another opportunity presented itself.

Bill Law, an Edmonton-based CBC radio producer, came up with an idea: What about a regular national blues show within the Corporation, Petersen was excited by the idea, and a pilot program was assembled—and rejected.

But the door had been opened, and finally a third revised proposal was accepted. In December 1986, *Saturday Night Blues* went on air for the first time, coast to coast. It was the first national radio network blues show in Canada. And, more than twenty-five years later, the show is now a key part of CBC's Saturday evening programming on Radio One and Radio Two.

In 2008, the Memphis-based Blues Foundation named Petersen Public Broadcaster of the Year as part of the Keeping the Blues Alive award.

Holger Petersen's interviews have always been a key part of his radio shows, and the trial-and-error lessons he learned four decades ago still stand: Always make your interview subject feel at home and relaxed. Always be prepared; do your research. And know your subject's music—and background—like the back of your hand.

This book collects nineteen of those interviews, complete with Petersen's notes about each of them. The first ones are all with British artists—the people who turned Petersen on to his music career in the first place—all of whom played a major part in making American blues popular on a world-wide basis. Chris Barber, the jazz trombonist who brought Muddy Waters, Sonny Boy Williamson, Louis Jordan, and many others to Britain for the first time, talks about the skiffle craze he helped pioneer—and which, in turn, led to the rise of the Beatles and countless other bands.

Long John Baldry, who had given Elton John his name and who

had discovered Rod Stewart, recalls the early days of British blues. The Rolling Stones' bassist Bill Wyman remembers the days when his band did more than 350 gigs a year. Two other prominent British blues figures—Fleetwood Mac founder Mick Fleetwood and the Animals' front man, Eric Burdon—both tell fascinating stories.

The second group of interviews brings the music back to North America, threading the stories of folklorist Alan Lomax, who recorded many great artists (and many unknowns who made great music), with those of Honeyboy Edwards, the last living artist who helped create early Mississippi Delta blues.

Sam Phillips, the founder of Sun Records and who gave the world the first records of Howlin' Wolf and Elvis Presley, has stories to tell, as does Ike Turner, who went on to become one of the most popular rhythm and blues artists before his career imploded. Finally, you'll get to meet Rosco Gordon, whose influence far exceeded his mainstream acceptance.

The third section consists of meetings with a group of artists in various genres, all of who made records for Stony Plain. Kansas City pianist Jay McShann, who mentored jazz legend Charlie Parker, recalls the time and the place where jazz and blues melded. Maria Muldaur—still remembered for "Midnight at the Oasis," recorded in 1974—talks with her old friend Bonnie Raitt. One of the fathers of the American folk boom of the early sixties was Leon Bibb, a great friend of Paul Robeson; he reminisces with his son Eric about the blues artists who became part of the folk scene.

Duke Robillard, one of the most gifted—and prolific—guitarists, bandleaders, and producers on the scene today talks about collecting records and guitars and his friendships with peers such as Ronnie Earl and Jay Geils. And Jeff Healey, the stellar guitar player who played driving blues-based rock and roll, but who also loved the music of Louis Armstrong and hundreds of now-forgotten dance bands of the twenties and thirties, talks about his reluctance to become a rock star.

Ian Tyson's story has been well told—his autobiography *The Long*

Trail was being written when he was interviewed. Not surprisingly, Tyson talks about horses, the Greenwich Village folk scene, and the artists and photographers who documented the realities of cowboy life in the West's glory days.

To round out this unusual collection, you'll get the opportunity to meet singer-songwriter Lucinda Williams, who talks about the blues roots of her music and Mavis Staples, who continues the gospel traditions she learned with her family group.

Finally, there's an extended interview with Ry Cooder, the one-time session guitarist who became known for his solo records, eclectic productions, and numerous film soundtracks. Rarely interviewed, he talks about the development of roots music in California.

Record collectors have a reputation of being obsessive, compulsive, and almost cult-like in their devotion to their hobby. On-air broadcasters are regarded as loud, brash, relentlessly cheerful, and mile-a-minute talkers.

Holger Petersen is neither.

All these years later, he still hears music that surprises and delights him; the cynicism that's part of so many people in the music industry just isn't part of the man's make-up. He's still thrilled to have the opportunity to meet his heroes.

And more than forty years after his first interview, he's delighted to share some of them with you.

Writing about music—and talking with musicians—is still the best way to spread the word about good music. May your discoveries be as exciting as the ones Petersen has made.

Richard Flohil is a Toronto-based writer and music promoter who has worked for more than thirty years with Stony Plain Records. As a publicist, he has worked with artists as diverse as k.d. lang and Loreena McKennitt, Downchild Blues Band and Serena Ryder, Ian Tyson and Nana Mouskouri. As a concert promoter he's worked with Muddy Waters, Benny Goodman, the Chieftains, B.B. King, Miles Davis, and Buddy Guy.

Introduction

The sequence of interviews in this book roughly follows my own discovery of blues and roots music after being exposed to the British Invasion bands as a teenager. My hope is that the interviews in the first section help capture the time when blues and R&B exploded in Europe and inspired the British Blues Revival and so many fans like me.

The material recorded by those British bands leads us to Chicago, which in turn points blues lovers south to music from the Mississippi Delta, Memphis, and other American regions. The second section of interviews takes us back to the thirties with first-hand accounts of the Delta and some of the country blues legends from that era. That music leads us down the path to the origins of rock and roll and even ska and reggae music.

It was my love for blues and roots music, and my desire to work with artists to help their music gain exposure, that led me to start Stony Plain Records. In my thirty-five-plus years of working at the label I've been involved in releasing close to four-hundred records. In the third section of interviews I talk with some of the artists I've worked with. As a long-time record collector, I wanted to track down everything available by these artists and to learn as much as I could about their roots. In each case it's been an ongoing, first-hand, learning experience and a rare privilege to work and hang out with them. Each chose a different musical path and has contributed greatly to the body of work available in various music genres.

I called the final section "Bonus Tracks" because both Mavis Staples and Ry Cooder are important multi-talented artists who have contributed not only to music, but also to awareness of social, political, and cultural issues. Both are passionate and generous with great stories to tell. Two of my favourite interviews.

The interviews in this book only really scratch the surface; little is included about music from Louisiana, Texas, Toronto, or Vancouver, for example, and you can never get enough Chicago blues. Perhaps that will be for another day. The interviews have been condensed and edited.

Holger Petersen
July 2011

Robert Plant and Holger in Edmonton, 1969. Photo: Doug Cole.

Part 1

British Blues Revival

Chris Barber
(Born 1930)

Before the first wave British Invasion of the sixties, there was a skiffle craze in the UK launched in the mid-fifties by Lonnie Donegan and Chris Barber. Most British blues-, folk-, and rock- influenced artists who were part of that invasion credit skiffle as an inspiration, including John Lennon and Paul McCartney, who were members of the Quarrymen in 1957 pre-Beatles Liverpool. It was fun, party music, easy to play for beginners, and anyone could join in on cheap kazoos, washboards, jugs, or homemade bass guitars.

Skiffle grew out of the traditional jazz scene in the UK and musicians' desire to play material first recorded by American jug bands and blues artists like Lead Belly and Gus Cannon's Jug Stompers. Ken Colyer's Jazzmen were the first. By 1954 Colyer had left the group, which then became Chris Barber's Jazz Band. That band, with front man Lonnie Donegan, had a massive hit in 1956, recorded for the British Decca label under the name Lonnie Donegan's Skiffle Group. "Rock Island Line," a Lead Belly song, with "John Henry" on the B-side, kick-started the skiffle craze. That single (with Chris Barber on bass) went on to sell a million records worldwide. Several other skiffle hits followed. So popular was skiffle music in the UK that it's estimated there were tens of thousands of bands playing the music by the late fifties.

Chris Barber's Jazz Band is also credited with helping to introduce traditional New Orleans jazz, ragtime, blues, and swing to British audiences. They had a #3 single in the UK with a cover of Sidney

Bechet's "Petite Fleur" in 1958. With the band's success came the opportunity for Barber to invite some of his favourite artists to tour Europe. Muddy Waters and Sonny Terry and Brownie McGhee first played Europe as Chris' guests. He later brought over and recorded with Louis Jordan, Sonny Boy Williamson, Howlin' Wolf, Champion Jack Dupree, Jimmy Witherspoon, Sister Rosetta Tharpe, and Dr. John. These performances were issued on CD for the first time in 2008 as part of a series called *Chris Barber Presents the Blues Legacy: Lost & Found*, a three volume set. Chris joined Van Morrison and Lonnie Donegan for the recording of *The Skiffle Sessions: Live in Belfast 1998*. Now in his early eighties, Chris remains incredibly active with his big band and various projects and looks forward to invitations to perform in North America.

His generous spirit for collaboration and love of blues and jazz led Chris to become aware of Jeff Healey's Jazz Wizards. He called Jeff in Toronto and both artists discovered much in common. As serious record collectors, they shared incredible knowledge of obscure 78s that included sidemen, label matrix numbers, and endless detail. After Jeff signed with Stony Plain Records in July of 2005 he wanted to record a live album with the Jazz Wizards and Chris Barber on trombone and vocals as his special guest. With the help of Richard Flohil, we recorded the album *It's Tight Like That* at Hugh's Room in Toronto over two nights. Jeff had hoped to perform in Europe with the Big Chris Barber Band, but his schedule and then failing health unfortunately prevented him.

This interview took place August 22, 2005, at a Toronto hotel while Chris Barber was in town performing and recording with Jeff Healey and the Jazz Wizards.

Chris Barber, Toronto, 2005. Photo: Holger Petersen.

Chris Barber and Jeff Healey, Toronto, 2005. Photo: Holger Petersen.

Chris Barber and Jeff Healey, Toronto, 2005. Photo: Holger Petersen.

We were talking about your inviting Jeff Healey to perform some concerts with you in England in the future. Inviting blues and jazz artists to perform with you is something that goes back to the nineteen-fifties. Were you hoping it would turn a new audience onto what you do and vice versa?

Certainly that's a nice thing if you can get it, but the reason we did it in the first place was rather more because we were the first band to be professional in a full time, straight nothing-but-jazz-and-blues band in '53 really, and we began to feel rather isolated. We felt we were a part of this jazz and blues music. To us, it felt like we had joined the family, you know? Some other people in Britain tend to play it, "Oh, we're British—we're different and we're not part of it." But I said, "We are part of it." But we felt very isolated because whereas a youngster in New Orleans who bought a trumpet could play along with the parade band, and maybe get to the age of twenty and get to join an established band. He could learn and enjoy being a part of this whole music—we couldn't do that. Plus our musicians' union at the time wouldn't allow Americans to play in Britain and the AFM [American Federation of Musicians] wouldn't allow British bands to play in the USA either and that had to be got over eventually. So we discovered, by chance, that there was something going on here that the musicians' union did not reckon to deal with. Singers were variety artists; they belonged to the American Guild of Variety Artists or the British Variety Artists Federation who didn't mind in the least if American singers came and sang in Britain provided they paid the union dues—two percent of their fee, which is a lot of money—and it was all right if they accompanied themselves on musical instruments—it didn't make a difference. Although, when Louis Jordan toured with us in '63, the local union representative came to our concert, said he enjoyed it, marvellous music and so on and so forth, however, two weeks later I got a letter from the headquarters of the union saying, "We understand that Mr. Louis Jordan played an instrumental piece. Next time you'll need an exchange for that." Oh, God, you know, but that's our stupid union: It's hopeless.

Apart from the union problems for you in bringing people like Muddy Waters, *Sister Rosetta Tharpe, Lonnie Johnson, and Sonny Terry and Brownie* McGhee, *what were the other obstacles that you as a band leader faced introducing these talents to the UK for the very first time?*

None, really, because we always paid them. Luckily we were popular enough that we could afford to pay them, so we did. Probably the only obstacle was that the promoters who organized the concerts where we played throughout Europe, not just Britain, said: "Look, we're charging as high a ticket price as we can for your band from your fans already and you're already getting the lion's share of the money coming in to the point where our profit is just acceptable. How can we give you more for anybody else, if you have Muddy Waters who we've never heard of by the way? So if you want him on the concert, you pay him." So we did. As simple as that. So not only did we provide the young Eric Clapton or whoever else with Muddy Waters to hear, we paid Muddy Waters a lot of money as well. I'm not looking for a medal for it. It was the obvious thing to do and I would do it again, of course, and we've done it in other situations, too. You have to do it and I must say it doesn't happen very often I've noticed. I was so impressed and pleased in '78 when Eric Clapton took Muddy Waters as a support band on his European tour and paid him to do it. Not only that—Muddy was on first and Eric got up and played with him every night before he did his own spot and *that* is absolutely...in show business, people don't do that. Eric Clapton made sure that Muddy Waters got that and that to me was putting your money where your mouth is and quite right. And that was one great mark in Eric's favour, as if he needed it. He doesn't need it from me because he can do what he can do, you know, but there are a lot of people who sort of say: "Oh, yeah, we saw Muddy Waters," but what do they do about it? Not much. They just say it. Some of those guys who they liked were really still starving, close to starving, in America. They didn't do much about it really. I mean, they could have—they've got enough money to do an awful lot about it. There you are.

It was wonderful that you also had a chance to record with some of these artists, I'm thinking of Louis Jordan, Sonny Boy Williamson, Lonnie Johnson...

Sonny and Brownie, of course, and Rosetta Tharpe. We wanted to record with them. Our recording manager (producer) at that time was a man named Denis Preston. He was the first man to persuade major record labels to accept a lease tape deal as a recording manager in Britain. In the USA, it started with...I don't know...people like Norman Granz and people like that. Later on, some new people started record companies, that's different, but I don't think that RCA and CBS and so on actually accepted deals where they bought the tape and the tape was entirely in the control of some independent recording manager. Sometimes, they signed deals with artists and gave them that privilege, but not recording managers. But Denis Preston got this deal so he got us good things, too. But the whole [skiffle] record thing was difficult because he was of the opinion that I went in on the recording day and recorded three or four tunes in three hours and I'd say, "I want to do that one again. It's not right." And he'd say, "Dear boy, sit down, don't worry about it. In twenty years' time, you and I will sit down, playing our Duke Ellington records and having our brandy, and we shan't care about all this rubbish. Don't worry, play whatever the fans like in the clubs." So I persisted and said, "No, I'm going to play the best that I can and work at getting it right." But there wasn't a very positive attitude, you see, so when Big Bill Broonzy was with us, I said, "Well, we must record Big Bill with Lonnie Donegan with our skiffle group. We can make Big Bill a lot of money because he'd be wonderful with that, you know. We're doing his music, he's in it so much." "Oh, no," he said. "I shouldn't play with Big Bill. He plays with good musicians, right?" So Denis organized a recording date with Big Bill with some English modern jazz musicians who, for a start, didn't recognize he was playing thirteen-bar blues, they played twelves and that sort of stuff and the backing is awful. It's an attempt at a sort of Harlemy sort of sound, but people didn't play it that way, you see? And it just sounds wrong.

And when Rosetta Tharpe was in a year or two year after that, I said, "Can we record with Sister Rosetta? It's fantastic music. Can we record that?" And he said "Oh, no, she has a contract." She hadn't, she had no contract, but he just didn't believe that we should be messing with that. We should just be content to remain these English boys who played this funny music that people seemed to like and when this all stopped it'll be, "Oh, it'll all be over and we'll all have a drink and forget about it."

But then he didn't like black music and, I mean, he's not alone in that. People who are a little bit—what would you call it?—Jim Crow in their attitude or the other way around, you get people who say that. And the blacks were put down for so long it's hardly surprising that some of them want to put us down. I don't blame them; I'm not surprised. The American music, the American people we dealt with—musicians, gospel singers, blues singers—all of them were nothing more than welcoming. They admired and welcomed our attempt or our way of playing their music, absolutely. They had nothing but praise and nothing but enjoyment for it, so it was fantastic. There was no difficulty in any way. I remember the first time we were in Chicago. Muddy toured Britain in October '58 and following it we went to America for the first time with the band on one of these exchange things and we did real gigs in America, you see, unlike some of the other bands who were doing so-called exchanges. Musicians who sat in a hotel in New York and sent postcards home and then the cost of sending them there went onto the bill for the American band the people in Britain wanted to hear, you see. But we did tours over there and we got to Chicago in February '59. which was the first tour (the tour in which we played Massey Hall) and we went down to Smitty's Corner to see

Muddy Waters, which was marvellous. Muddy Waters and the band that recorded Muddy's *At Newport*. Beautiful band, and it was great. Of course, Muddy said, "You've got to play." Well, we didn't have the horns with us—they were in some van/truck somewhere—but, of course, Ottilie Patterson, our singer at the time and my then-wife (was asked to sing a couple), which she did. She got up and she sang very well—it's as much her music as mine and theirs. And we came back there about a year later and now outside the front of Smitty's Corner were two hefty policemen, and we got out of a cab—a year later—and the policeman said to Ottilie: "Are you going to sing 'Careless Love' again?" I mean, he heard it once. If you can do that, you're all right. It makes me cry to think of it. So sad that people should think anything different. If you're going to do the music, do it right and if you do it right, they accept you because they know you're trying to do it right—that you believe in it. What the hell, that's it.

I thought you made some wonderful recordings with Ottilie Patterson singing. I know she was your featured vocalist for about ten years and the diversity of material, from country blues and gospel and covers of Memphis Minnie and Muddy Waters. Those were great recordings. I especially like "Trombone Cholly."

Yeah, the Bessie one, "Trombone Cholly." It's a good record that is, I like that. People request it all the time and I said I know the trombone bit, I can't do the singing bit.

And the material that she recorded with you and so much of that obscure material that you recorded with Chris Barber's Jazz Band, how did you find that material?

Old records or new records, I mean, records really. Just knowing the music, I guess. It's all derivative. Let's think of a good example. Sonny and Brownie do these things. They pinched songs from somebody else, like Tampa Red and Georgia Tom. They didn't get away with too much stealing from them, but they tried. Brownie's pretty good at putting his name to everything or used to be and in a sense there's an argument that says that all those songs are public property, really, and you could only really own your version of it. But that is not how copyright law works. But they all did it. Sonny and Brownie. It carries on, you know. Sonny Boy Williamson #1 [John Lee Williamson] was completely different than Rice Miller [Sonny Boy Williamson #2]. Leroy Carr and Scrapper Blackwell. We'd pick up a Bessie Smith song and we'd find out that the way we did it was kind of more thirties/forties-ish and then we'd find out Memphis Minnie had done the same thing to that same song, but differently, but you do it because it's a heritage. And the thing is to play this music—jazz and proper jazz or what I call real jazz and blues, gospel—you have to make it your heritage. I don't have heritage in English music at all. In fact, my only heritage is, I guess, American black music really so that's what I did because I love it and so I listen to it. I've heard it and I know what it is and how it is and I can't do it as well as I would like because I don't have the right kind of voice—I haven't a voice at all, really. I can sing in tune and in time, but I haven't got a nice tone...no tone control, which annoys me intensely.

To me, what I'd learned about jazz, I think I really first got a hold of—getting into jazz properly—was when I bought "Weary Blues." I got that when I was about thirteen years old and that was it! It's a very charismatic...it's not factually accurate entirely but it's got the psychology, the feel of the whole of the music right. What it is and why it's there and so and so and once you get that, there's no other way of doing it. You want to do it right and that's more important than anything else for me.

Chris Barber's Jazz Band with Lonnie Donegan was responsible for the skiffle movement in England, which paved the way for so many other forms of popular music, especially a blues revival and the British Invasion ultimately—effects that are still felt today. Can you define what skiffle is and how the term skiffle came about?

I only called it skiffle because we had a record on the Paramount label made in 1929. It's called *Hometown Skiffle*, which was kind of a sampler (and the only time I've seen them do it). They had actually dubbed half a side of each of their current latest release of four records on the two sides of the 78. So it had a minute of Charlie Spand and a minute of Blind Lemon Jefferson, and a minute or so of probably Charlie Jackson or whoever it was, whatever the current releases, and with kind of a spurious party atmosphere going on. A bit like, what's that amazing album, *Trini Lopez Live at PJ's* where there wasn't such a place, right? Just party noise put on in the studio, right? So it was the same thing as that, you see, so it gave the impression and they called it *Hometown Skiffle*. The name just sounded good fun, you know, good time music. It's kind of blues and jazzy bluesy stuff and, you know, a bit folky blues and so on and Blind Blake and all that, so we called it that. And there was one other use of the phrase by Dan Burley, who played the piano and edited the *Amsterdam News* in the thirties, and he called his group his Skiffle Boys. I think he only made two records as far as I know. But it was the old record that caught our attention because it was reissued. *The Hometown Skiffle* was reissued by one of the early jazz and blues reissue labels in Britain, so we had that record, you see. I had the Paramount anyway, the original one, but it doesn't make a difference, the point was still there. So we called it skiffle.

At first, we didn't say skiffle. When we made the record *Rock Island Line*, it didn't say skiffle, it just said Lonnie Donegan (or even Tony Donegan. I'm not sure, it may have said Tony Donegan, which was his real name, of course), Chris Barber, and Beryl Bryden. It didn't say skiffle on that. But then we'd been calling it skiffle music for some time before that, meaning kind of a general party, like rent party music roughly speaking. We could have called that "rent party music," but it didn't seem quite so charismatic, so we said skiffle and that was it.

So there isn't anything to define because it wasn't a form of music in the sense. It was an absence of form almost, just songs that could have been anything from the sort of popular songs that Bill Broonzy always liked to sing like "When Did You Leave Heaven?" and "I'm Looking Over a Four Leaf Clover," which he much preferred singing than singing the blues really because he was always singing those to himself. So that was the stuff and the word just caught on. Marketing is a strange practice and a charismatic logo or title or name makes all the difference, hence the reason why Tommy Steele is called Tommy Steele and not Tommy Hicks, you know? That's about the size of it. But it did catch on and, of course, the music caught on because when Lonnie and I started doing that music, we were trying to do Lead Belly, maybe a bit towards. There are a couple of albums on Folkways with Sonny Terry and J.C. Burris and I think Brownie and other guys were on it, which was more or less like our skiffle group, and then Lead Belly things and the Blind Blake ones on Paramount where there's a clarinet and a washboard or something on it. It was all a mixture of those things, but I think the basis of it all was like Lead Belly.

Now people used to rather knock Lonnie Donegan's singing and I could never think why. It was a very amusing thing. Our first EP we did with the band was recorded in Denmark in '54. Lonnie sang "Precious Lord, Take My Hand," which we did slow first and then double tempo up. The sleeve notes on the EP were written by Alexis Korner, a friend of mine. He was in my first band playing a guitar and so on and so forth in 1949 and I went to school with him, but he spent half of the sleeve note denigrating Lonnie's singing on Lonnie's record. Now, I mean, wait a minute–this is absurd. You don't have to say he's greater than Caruso, but you say he's the best so and so that does...you know, there's ways of putting it. You're paid to write a sleeve cover–you don't put in *that*, which he did. Alexis hasn't got a voice either, you know, what the hell? Charismatic? Yes. But Lonnie's charismatic as hell which is...Lonnie was good.

But what I was going to say is: when Sonny Terry and Brownie

McGhee came in 1958, Ottilie and I were married at that time and we used to invite the guests up to the house and play records and have a meal, you see, and I put on one of the earliest concert recordings I had from '54, which (it might have been re-released later) but it wasn't skiffle at that time, it was just Lonnie on the guitar and me on the bass and Lonnie sang a number called "Leaving Blues," which is Lead Belly from 1931…"I'm leaving in the morning, ain't got nowhere to go"…I played it for Sonny Terry and I said, "Who is that?" He said, "That's Lead Belly." Now Sonny, if he thought that was near enough to Lead Belly so that he didn't notice it wasn't, then Lonnie must be doing something right.

It's the same thing when we were at a concert in England in '59. We were the support band with the Louis Armstrong All Stars and Ottilie was singing the blues, probably one of the Bessie Smith ones, and Louis said to a friend of mine, "That gal put me in mind of Bessie Smith." Well, if putting him in mind of is near, and that was the thought, he wasn't meaning "She shouldn't cover Bessie Smith, she's a white girl she should sing different." He just said that she put him in mind of Bessie Smith. Anybody in their right mind and who can would want to sound like Bessie Smith—perfectly great.

Long John Baldry
(1941–2005)

We were incredibly fortunate when Long John Baldry decided to relocate to Canada in 1978. Although he had recorded a couple of important blues albums in the sixties, he was much better known in North America for his *It Ain't Easy* gold album (1971). That was a payback project produced by two artists that John had mentored. One side was produced by Elton John (who had changed his name to John in tribute to Long John Baldry) and the other by Rod Stewart (discovered by John at the age of eighteen). As a record collector, I knew of John's love of the blues and that he was considered one of the "founding fathers of British Blues" in the early sixties. However, it wasn't until I saw him perform on his first Canadian tour in 1979 that I understood the depth of his talent and dedication. Much of his set was blues, including several solo acoustic Lead Belly tunes played on twelve-string guitar. He had one of the richest voices to come out of Britain and had total command of the stage. At 6'7", immaculately dressed, spontaneous, and with his very British sense of humour, John was a fun loving theatrical showman who brought out the best in musicians. After interviewing him on that first tour, we kept in touch. He would often co-host blues radio shows when he came though. I loved going to his gigs and hanging out with John and the wonderful group of people in his band, which included the amazing singer Kathi McDonald and John's long-time guitar player, Papa John King. It seemed that after each one, I'd be driving home at sun-up thinking, "I just had the best time of my life."

John's career started in the late fifties when he began playing acoustic blues, although he started playing blues much earlier than that. In 1962 he was a member of Blues Incorporated, the first blues band in Britain. The group included Alexis Korner, Cyril Davies, Mick Jagger, and Charlie Watts. His early bands included Jack Bruce, Ginger Baker, Brian Auger, Julie Driscoll, Nicky Hopkins, Jimmy Page, as well as the previously mentioned Rod Stewart and Reg Dwight (a.k.a. Elton John).

In 1967 John had a #1 record in the UK with "Let The Heartaches Begin" followed by another hit a year later "Mexico." These slick, pop ballads had nothing to do with his real love of the blues and ultimately branded him as a tuxedo wearing lounge singer in the UK, which was an image that he regretted and was uncomfortable with the rest of his life. It was that pigeonholing that eventually led John to relocate to Los Angeles. Several tours took him through Eastern Canada where he found a welcome fan base and a recording contract through Dean Cameron at EMI Canada.

John had several Canadian hits during the late seventies and eighties and continued to lead great bands. He was a generous bandleader taking pride in featuring the players on stage. In addition to his music career, John was also in demand doing voice-over work for commercials and animated television series. He was the voice of Dr. Robotnik in *Adventures of Sonic the Hedgehog* and was a spoken word Grammy nominee for *The Original Story Of Winnie The Pooh* in 1997.

Our friendship grew over the years and in 1991 John signed with Stony Plain Records. I wanted to record his underrepresented blues and roots music sides. We recorded six albums together before his death including the Juno Award winning *Right To Sing the Blues* and his last album, the one he was most proud of, *Remembering Leadbelly*. John is also heard joining his old friend Jimmy Witherspoon and the Duke Robillard Band on a live album we recorded in Vancouver.

I interviewed John many times over the years and always appreciated his generosity and memory for detail and dates. This interview was done in Edmonton in August of 1996 and is included as a "bonus track" on the CD *Right To Sing The Blues*.

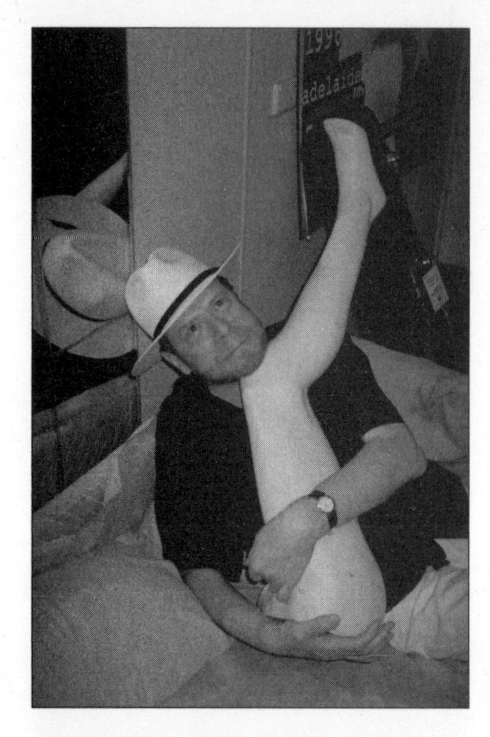

Long John Baldry, Australia, 1997.
Photo: Holger Petersen.

Holger and Long John Baldry, Edmonton, April 2002. Photo: Neil McBain.

Long John Baldry, Australia, 1997. Photo: Holger Petersen.

John, when did you first discover the blues and what sparked that initial interest?

Well, I suppose 1953 saw my first exposure to the blues. I had heard blues music back in 1949, although at that time I wasn't aware what it was. To me it was something very, very unusual–the particular song I heard, it was "Fox Chase" from Sonny Terry. In fact, what it had been used for was for a dance piece in which, I guess, they had just invented the blue light so that dancers would wear black costumes with skeletons painted on the front and all you'd see were the skeletons jigging around and they were jigging around to "Silver Fox Chase." Of course, I was eight years old at the time and didn't know it was the blues, but felt that it was something very different. But '53 came along and that was when I heard Big Bill Broonzy for the first time and just fell in love with the music and wanted to play and sing it for myself, so I nagged my parents into getting me my first guitar. I had toyed with the banjo, but it didn't quite work–it never has worked for the blues–so when I got my first guitar I rapidly started to learn parrot fashion because back in those days there was no one to teach you.

Did you start working with any blues artists during the fifties?

Yes, a lot of blues piano players were coming over to England. People like Champion Jack Dupree, Memphis Slim, Roosevelt Sykes, oh, the list goes on and on. And because I was basically the only person around, except for Alexis Korner, really playing blues guitar around England. Not that I was that good, but they very often invited me when they couldn't get Alex to accompany the piano players on guitar because a lot of these guys were used to acoustic guitar players playing with them.

What a great opportunity for you to get to know these people. Did you go on tour with them?

Yes, with Slim and with Champion Jack Dupree. We played many cities right through England in a concert situation as opposed to nightclubs and I enjoyed it very much. Of course, it helped me learn so rapidly.

When you were playing with these established artists, were you playing twelve string?

Yeah, in fact, one of the concerts I did with Jack in 1958 in a place (that sadly now they've pulled down in Bradford, Northern England) called The Mechanics' Institute, a really nice theatre, I was billed on a huge great poster outside "The World's Greatest White Twelve-String Guitar Player." That was because I was probably the only one they could think of who was playing twelve string at that time.

Did you have a hard time even finding a twelve-string guitar in England during the fifties?

My first twelve string was made by a cabinet maker who I'd met in 1956 maybe going into 1957, a man by the name of Anthony Zemaitis who, of course, went on to become a world famous guitar maker/luthier. But he was an exquisite cabinet maker (I mean, not him being exquisite, his work was exquisite) and he made my first twelve-string guitar much in the same way he would construct a piece of very fine furniture and it really was an amazing sounding instrument. Sadly, it got stolen the same night as the Sharpeville Massacre occurred actually. We'd all gone down to South Africa House in Trafalgar Square to protest (that was the beginning of what would become the Anti-Apartheid movement in England) and I'd left it standing in the corner as I was busy protesting and somebody made off with it and that really, really upset me. Tony has built a couple of guitars for me subsequently, but, of course, he's built many of Keith Richards', Eric Clapton's, and Ronnie Wood's guitars.

There have been a few recordings of Cyril Davies and Alexis Korner from the late fifties that show a skiffle kind of a band emerging before the blues band that you were a part of later. The skiffle thing was pretty unique to England, wasn't it?

That's right. The style was kind of based on the old jug band thing of the twenties like Gus Cannon's Jug Stompers and they could include guitars and banjos and mandolins, usually someone playing a washboard, and in most cases where people could not afford to buy an upright bass or a bass guitar (they were very new back then—bass guitars), they'd use a tea chest with a broom handle and the broom handle being able to be tightened or loosened as you would and attached with a strong cord to the tea chest so you would thump away at that string and, depending on which way you were pulling the broom handle, you'd get a note of sorts out of it. Some of them actually became quite musically proficient on this strange looking instrument. Then, of course, Jesse Fuller came up and changed everybody's idea of how it should be done because he had this—actually for that time—very sophisticated thing that he called the fotdella, which was an old coffin (or looked like it) that actually had several strings on it operated with his toes.

Being a twelve-string player, I'm sure that Lead Belly had a great effect on your music. Do you remember the first time you heard Lead Belly's music and the impact that it had on you?

Well, I guess it was round about 1953 or '54 when I heard Lonnie Donegan doing Lead Belly songs. It was two sides of a single that was enormously successful for Lonnie in England when the skiffle craze started. And Lonnie chose the "Rock Island Line" for one side (enormous hit) and Lead Belly's version of "John Henry" on the back. And when I saw the name Lead Belly in there, I thought: "Hmm, let's find out more about this man." So there were a few recordings of Lead Belly that started to become available at that time in the fifties and I gradually started assembling a collection of Lead Belly stuff including some vinyl material that I still have, the Folkways/Ramsey recordings of Lead Belly's *Last Sessions*, which I recently acquired (thanks to your good self) in the CD format. But I'm still very proud of the vinyl set that I've got and it's still in relatively mint condition, which is something when you consider that the albums came out in 1953, I think it was. And over the years, of course, I've built up a massive collection of Lead Belly stuff. I don't think there is any recording of Lead Belly's that I haven't got.

One of the Lead Belly tunes you recorded, I think back in 1971, was "Black Girl." Did you hear another cover version of "Black Girl" before your own?

I never heard it done by anyone else before I did it. That's not to say that other people hadn't done it. The only version I knew, at that point, was Lead Belly's own version—well, he recorded it several times over the course of his life. No, I can't think of anyone else who did it. Now, people have done it subsequently, of course, including Kurt Cobain from Nirvana. Now, whether he was influenced by my recording or Lead Belly's recording to do that tune, I really don't know. And, of course, he's not telling anyone now.

What is it about Lead Belly's music that touches you?

Well, I think it was the very strength of the man and getting back to what I was saying earlier about the depth of his guitar playing, because his guitar was tuned so many keys down from what is normal concert pitch.

Would it be safe to say that without Lead Belly's music there would have been no skiffle and no blues revival in England?

I think it's safe to say that if there had been no Lead Belly and if there had been no Big Bill Broonzy and, of course, Muddy Waters as well, there wouldn't have been that initial thing to capture us, to drag us in which happened with so many of the people I was growing up with. And, of course, the people who came a little later like Keith Richards and Mick Jagger and the Davies brothers from the Kinks and the list just goes on and on. But Lead Belly and Bill Broonzy were the major catalysts.

What were some of the other components that led to that revival in England at that point?

Well, it was a thing that happened more around the London area. It was very, very odd because many of the students in art colleges scattered around London were very enamoured of the music of Big Bill Broonzy and Muddy Waters and many other blues artists and none of us knew each other at that particular time but we came together in the seeds of a movement. Let me see, Eric Clapton, actually I'd met a little bit earlier than 1962; I think it was either '59 or '60. I was playing at a folk club in Richmond, which is to the west of London, and he came down to see me. He's gone on record as saying that this particular evening prompted him to learn to play guitar.

You mentioned the movement. Other people, of course, who initially came out of that movement would have included Cyril Davies and Alexis Korner.

Cyril and Alexis, yeah, I'd know them as far back as '57 (although it may have been '56) when they had a folk club in a pub on Waldorf Street (in a room above a pub, actually) and the pub was called the Round House and the club they ran every Thursday evening was called the Blues and Barrel House Club and many of the people who performed there were, like me, solo acoustic guitar players and singers.

People like Rory and Alex McEwan who were the most fabulous guitar players you've ever heard, they played in that Blind Gary Davis style of what, I guess, they would call the Piedmont Blues/Rag stuff. They were often up there with Cyril, of course, playing twelve-string and later, harmonica. Alex played mandolin and guitar. Bill Colyer, Ken Colyer's brother, played washboard. And then, of course, all the visiting American artists would look in there as well, like Big Bill Broonzy and Jack Elliott, Muddy and Otis Spann when they came over initially in 1958, and all the piano players I mentioned earlier were all up there because it was a good, fun place at the bar there and everything. No microphones or anything, but the acoustics of the room were such that you could be heard—the guitar could be heard and the voice could be heard.

I want to ask you about Alexis Korner's Blues Incorporated, the first electric blues band that came out of England that you were part of. When was that?

That was 1962. That band had its initial unveiling in March of 1962 and the line up at that time of the Alexis Korner's Blues Incorporated was Alexis Korner on guitar, naturally enough, Cyril Davies on harmonica and vocals, Dick Heckstall-Smith on saxophone, and a guy called Andy Hoogenboom on bass who was quite soon to be replaced by Jack Bruce. I've no idea whatever happened to Andy Hoogenboom; he was actually quite a good stand-up bass player, but Jack Bruce came along to replace him. And, of course, we had Charlie Watts on drums, which was a nice plus—that was before the Stones, of course. And it was a rotating roster of singers, which included Mick Jagger; Paul Jones, who later joined Manfred Mann; me and a couple of other odd people who I've never heard of since; a man called Hogsnort Rupert (maybe it had something to do with his exceptionally large nose), but Hogsnort Rupert; and Art Wood, the older brother of Ronnie Wood. So it was quite a line up, but I guess I was regarded as the permanent singer of the band at that time because I was the only one who ever actually got paid. The rest of them did it just for a pint of beer or the love of it all.

Did the band split off in various directions?

Well, what had happened was I went away to Germany for many months during 1962 after the initial debut of the Korner Blues Incorporated. And then when I came back in January of '63, I discovered that Alexis and Cyril had had the most almighty row and parted company and they had formed two bands: the Alexis Korner Blues Incorporated and Cyril Davies and his All-Stars. And they both wanted me to join their bands and rather than show any kind of support for one above the other, I literally joined the Cyril Davies Band on the toss of a big silver coin (what we called half a crown back in those days, two shillings and six pence). I flipped it up and I think it was tails for Cyril and he won so I started working with Cyril Davies and the All-Stars, which at its initial unveiling had a guy called Bernie Watson on guitar, Ricky Fenson (or Rick Brown sometimes known as) playing bass, Carlo Little on drums, and the guy who used to do all the Stones' piano work (who sadly died very recently actually from cancer with which he'd been living for many, many years), Nicky Hopkins. He was the very first piano player in Cyril's band.

The Hoochie Coochie Men would be your first time then as a bandleader?

What had happened was that Cyril had become increasingly ill through the summer, fall, and winter of '63 and, sadly, he passed on exactly a year from when I came back from Germany and joined his band, that being January 7, 1963. He died on January 7, 1964. And what was I going to do? I didn't really want to call the band the Cyril Davies All-Stars anymore. The name the Rolling Stones had been quite successful for the Rolling Stones so I thought why not Long John Baldry and the Hoochie Coochie Men? And I brought a discovery into the band fairly soon after starting up with the name Long John Baldry and the Hoochie Coochie Men and that, of course, was Rod Stewart. I'd found him in West London when the band actually was the Cyril Davies All-Stars, as it was at the time of Cyril's death that we became the Hoochie Coochie Men.

Another discovery of yours, of course, is Elton John. Is it true that Elton John took the John part of his name because of you?

Yes. His actual family name, his christened name, is Reginald Kenneth Dwight, which is very bland, middle class, English kind of naming—very typical. He had worked with me in the band Bluesology in the years 1966, 1967, and the first quarter of 1968. And then he split the band (but by then we'd already found a replacement for him in Jimmy Horowitz, the keyboard player who was to follow him), he was going to join up with the music publisher Dick James Music. He was going there to pursue a solo career as a piano player/singer in the same vein as Neil Sedaka who was his big hero at that time. And we were sitting on the plane, I think the date would have been like May 12, 1968, I'm sure that's what it was because our last date with him was in Edinburgh, Scotland, and we travelled back to London on a airplane a couple of days before he was due to begin his big new career at Dick James Music. And he said, "You know I can't really be going on a stage and calling myself Reg Dwight, it just doesn't sound right. What can I call myself?" Well, at that particular time in the band, I had a very fine saxophone player by the name of Elton Dean who went on later to form the Soft Machine, which is a fabulous jazz/rock group still in existence as far as I know. Anyway, we combined the name Elton from Elton Dean and John from John Baldry and Elton John was born on that airplane flight on May 12, 1968.

I know you were really close to Willie Dixon, how far back did that go?

Nineteen-fifty nine was the first time I met Willie. Yeah, he came over to Europe to tour with Memphis Slim as a double act and they established a base at Aux Trois Mailletz (The Three Mullets) in Paris where Slim played for many, many years. Of course, Slim moved to Paris. I'd known Slim from a couple of years before when he first came to England. So Willie and I became very good friends. And I saw quite a bit of him from that time on in England because he would organize all the American Folk Blues Festival concert tours for Horst Lippmann and Fritz Rau, his associates in Germany. The Lippmann Rau concerts were some of the best staged blues package tours: they'd have about fifteen artists, all legendary artists on the same bill. It was great to see them in a concert setting with proper amplification and everything. For many of us in England, it was our first opportunity to see people like Sonny Boy Williamson (aka Rice Miller), John Lee Hooker... Muddy, of course, came back on that trip with Otis Spann and Memphis Slim and the list goes on and on and on because those tours went on for ten years, maybe more. And Willie was their booking agent for them in America—he was their man in Chicago—so Willie would always be over for all of these shows in one capacity or another, if not playing, he'd be organizing things. So I saw a lot of Willie in the sixties right through to the seventies. Then, of course, when I moved over here, I would bump into Willie in Vancouver or Chicago. We even went to Jamaica together. That was a treat.

You did a lot of Willie Dixon material and your band The Hoochie Coochie Men, was named after the Willie Dixon song. In the latter years of Willie's life, he put together a band called the Willie Dixon Dream Band that you were part of.

That's right, yes, there were some wonderful people in that band. We had Mose Allison on piano, Carey Bell on harmonica, Al Duncan on drums, and the bass player was Rob Wasserman (who is having a lot of great success with these albums of duets he puts out with other people–an astounding bass player), and Cash McCall on guitar, dear Cash. So it really was a fabulous band.

Sadly when we went to do the Benson & Hedges Blues Festival in Atlanta in '92 (it was shortly after Willie had fallen down steps at his home and he'd been hospitalized), on my return from Atlanta I stopped in Los Angeles at Willie's home in Pasadena. He had bought this fabulous home on a quiet acreage that was, well, like a mansion because he was finally getting the royalties from his songs or whatever. Sadly Willie was wasting away. He had been ill for quite some time and when we were out in his garden, he actually collapsed. Even though he had lost weight and was weak, he was still over 300 pounds that I had to support, I mean, somehow I found the strength to hold him upright until his wife could get the paramedics along and get him off to hospital and, sadly, he never came out of hospital, he later died there. But he had had a long life, a very fruitful life, a very adventurous life, a lot of fun in his life. I don't think I ever saw Willie without a huge smile on his face. I mean, he made everybody's day.

Bill Wyman
(Born 1936)

Since leaving the Rolling Stones in 1993, Bill Wyman has, by far, been the most productive of his former bandmates. After thirty-one years with the Stones, Bill left not to retire, but in fact to have time to follow his many interests.

He's released over a dozen albums both as a solo artist and with his own bands: the Bill Wyman's Rhythm Kings and Willie and the Poor Boys. He has scored, written, and produced for film and television and appeared in several movies. I highly recommend *Bill Wyman's Blues Odyssey: A Journey to Music's Heart and Soul*, which won the Blues Foundation's Keeping the Blues Alive Award for Literature in 2002. It's also available on DVD.

Bill has written seven books, which have sold almost two million copies and been translated into eleven different languages. He's an acclaimed photographer, having staged exhibitions around the world. He's acknowledged as Britain's most celebrated metal detectorist, who has designed and created metal detectors for children and newcomers to the hobby. He's also done countless gigs for charities, including playing cricket for Eric Clapton's XI team. In addition, he been awarded an honorary doctorate, he's an archivist and collector, opened his restaurant–Sticky Fingers–in London, and found time to raise a young family.

As a musician, Bill is one of the great bass players in rock and roll history. He's an innovator who hand made the world's first electric fretless bass in his attempt to reproduce the sound heard on the early

Chess Chicago blues releases. It's that same distinctive bass he used on all the early Stones releases. Bill and Brian Jones were the deepest blues lovers in the early Stones. Because he kept a diary, Bill's recollections of the early days with the band are the most accurate and detailed. His passion for music and commitment to blues, R&B, and rock and roll continue to inspire Bill Wyman's Rhythm Kings, an all-star band that tours and records "for the music."

On a trip that took me through London in January of 2009, I was delighted to have a chance to get together. We met at Bill's Sticky Fingers restaurant before it opened to the lunch crowd. We talked for more then an hour and he apologized several times for not have more time to spend with me that day. The Rhythm Kings were preparing for an annual tour of Europe the following week and there was a new Bill Wyman photo exhibit about to open in Holland that required his attention. It was a true pleasure to spend time with him and to talk about his life, music, and love of the blues.

Bill Wyman, London, UK, 2009. Photo: Holger Petersen.

Bill Wyman's Sticky Fingers, London, UK, 2009. Photo: Holger Petersen.

Bill Wyman's first fretless bass, London, UK, 2009. Photo: Holger Petersen.

The American Folk Blues Festivals had a huge effect on a lot of players in England in the early sixties. Did you go see those festivals when they came through the UK?

I never went to see any of them. No, we were always on the road travelling. If you are talking about '63, '64...I know in '63 we had a week off. We had seven days when we didn't record or play. We played 350-odd gigs that year. We were the hardest working band in those days. And in the following year we had about two or three weeks off. And that was it. Every day you were doing three or four things; you weren't just doing two shows in the evening. You were doing interviews and photo sessions in the morning. You were breaking for a sandwich in Soho somewhere and then you were going off to find some clothes for half an hour, buy a few clothes for the next few gigs and then you would go to the studio and cut two or three tracks in the afternoon in a three-hour session. Then you'd have another bite to eat and then you'd be on the bus and you'd be off to Sheffield to do two shows. And then you'd get home at three in the morning and then you'd have to get up and go to the office at ten in the morning for a meeting about doing a German tour or something. I mean it just never stopped. There was never time to go and see anybody. We missed seeing Little Walter when he came over. I mean people who were less busy than us, like the Yardbirds, did meet those people. And I kind of thought that's not fair really because we were the ones that started all that in England and we didn't have the opportunities to meet these people. So it was just only now and again that we managed to see someone. I saw Jimmy Reed when he came over just by luck because the Herd was supporting him on the show, which was local to me. And in the Herd was Peter Frampton, my mate. I had brought him to the studio at the age of fourteen and from there on in he always regarded me as a kind uncle, sort of thing. I used to give him things to wear: clothes and Beatle boots and stuff. And he just said: "We are doing this gig at Wallington–it's just south London–do you want to come?" I said, "Yeah, but who's on with you?" And he said, "Oh some blues artist." I said, "Who's that?" He said, "He's called Jimmy Reed." I went, "I'm there." And Jimmy just sat on a stool by himself. He had no band, which was perfect, and he did it all by himself.

We missed all that but we bought the albums, obviously. We saw people like Ray Charles at Fairfield Hall in Croydon, just outside London. Me, Keith, and Charlie managed to see that. But it was when you had a day off, and there was something going on, you tried to do it. I mean I saw the first show of Hendrix. But we had already met him in New York. We told the Animals about him, and they were going on tour and Chas Chandler signed him up in New York and brought him over here. The first gig he did was in Bromley, which is right near where I lived. And I was the only known celebrity (if you like) to see him that day. And of course, he came into London a week later and they all saw him. So they always talk about that but never me meeting him in Bromley, setting fire to his guitar and all that when he was sort of practicing all that stuff. But I missed all those festivals because we were such a hard working band. We were never there.

I love the fact that in your book Bill Wyman's Blues Odyssey *there are some old album covers of some of the first albums that you bought and presumably you still have them. It brings to mind the great material the early Stones did and I'm just curious about how some of that material evolved. Did some of that come from your record collection?*

In the very beginning there wasn't a record collection because you couldn't buy blues records. When I joined the Stones in December '62 and Charlie joined in January '63, and that was the band, there were no blues records in shops. Nothing. There was no blues music being played on the radio. There was only a couple of music TV shows at the time and there were only three radio shows about music. I had never heard of blues. If anybody talked about blues it was jazz people, you know. I heard (it first) through friends' records or sometimes on the radio you would hear something. Ray Charles saying now I am going to play a blues and he would sing a soulful thing, which the jazz people call the blues. It's not really like gutsy stuff. I knew nothing about blues.

I went to the first (Stones) rehearsal because my drummer Tony Chapman, who was the drummer who played with them for a while, had told me there was no bass player. When I went there they asked me what music I played and I said, "Mostly rock and roll, Chuck Berry." They went, "Great." "And Fats Domino." "Mmm." "Ray Charles." "Ohhh." And all those kind of people. And then I sort of started to say, "You know, Jerry Lee Lewis?" "Wot? Ooooh! Orrible!" "Eddie Cochrane?" "Nooo!" In later times they all adored those people, but when I went in there they were like *personae non gratae*. They hated them. They got to love them later, but they really killed my love of the rock and roll people at the time. So when we started to do shows in Europe, we'd go to Belgium and Holland and Denmark and you'd go into record shops and they had racks of blues records, which they didn't have in England.

There was one shop in London: Dobell's, a jazz shop, 77 Charing Cross Road, way over by Leicester Square. At Dobell's record shop you could go in there sometimes, and you'd say, "Do you have any old blues records?" And the guy would say, "I have got one under the counter, but it's not cheap." "Who is it?" "Big Bill Broonzy." So you would buy it, you know. But they were all affiliated to jazz because when the blues artists came to England in the late forties—Broonzy in '48, Muddy in '52, and so on—Chris Barber brought them. He had a jazz band. He originally had a skiffle section with Lonnie Donegan and then Lonnie became so famous that he left and Chris replaced him with a blues section, Alexis Korner, and that's who Brian Jones heard. He went to see Chris Barber, saw Alexis and got chatting and decided to have a blues band. And that's how the Stones started really. Brian used to borrow stuff from Long John Baldry, mostly reel-to-reel tapes of a Jimmy Reed album or a Little Walter thing or he'd borrow an EP from Baldry. They used to swap things and pass things around. Paul Jones—Paul Pond, he was called—who was in Manfred Mann later, all those people were borrowing and lending off blues things because they were not available anywhere. As soon as we started getting albums from Europe and then we went to America, we just ran everywhere and got albums and sent them home.

We went to Chess Records and went down to the basement and they gave us, like, twelve albums each. You could choose what you wanted. And I got albums by all these weird people like Ace Cannon, the sax player. You'd go to Chicago or somewhere. Me and Ian Stewart just used to get in a taxi and go to the south side. The guys didn't want to take us. And we would go, "Just take us to a little record store." And we would get out quick, rush to a place on a side street, a little record store. We would run in and get all these singles by Lazy Lester and Lonesome Sundown and all that stuff, Slim Harpo, all those kind of things. We would grab all these singles, a whole batch of them. "How much?" "Thirty dollars." Pay them and just jump back in the taxi and rush back to the safe area. And we would do that kind of stuff and then you would go home with stacks of records and then you would find [songs]. I remember Mick coming up to me after a session once, after we did a gig on the Channel Islands, either Jersey or Guernsey. And he said, "What do you think of this?" We had a little record player and he played the single of Solomon Burke "Everybody Needs Somebody to Love." I said, "Yeah, great. Let's do it." And so that happened. Then we heard "Susie Q" by Dale Hawkins and that's the way it kind of happened.

Then when we went to America, of course, and we heard the beginnings of Otis Redding and we covered stuff of his and so on. But behind it all we were in love with Howlin' Wolf, Muddy, Little Walter. They didn't like John Lee Hooker. They didn't like Lightnin' Hopkins: they didn't like their kind of acousticy [music]...I loved them, but they would never record any of their stuff: it was always the Chicago electric. They weren't interested in the more primitive stuff in those days.

They weren't interested in Robert Johnson's stuff or anybody like that, although they will tell you they were. Keith has got a memory that is very selective. He likes to remember things that just weren't there, never happened. And it becomes part of legend. He tells these stories and they are totally untrue, totally invented, and people take it onboard and it becomes part of the legacy. Like when we went into Chess the first time: Muddy Waters was painting the ceiling. Of course he wasn't. Muddy Waters was one of their two big stars; he and Wolf were like sharing the fame at that time and Muddy helped us carry the gear in. It's in my diary. I kept diaries. Keith didn't. He just invented this story and now it becomes like how it happened. Of course he wasn't painting the bloody ceiling. They were taking turns coming in and hearing us. Muddy came in. Buddy Guy came in. Chuck Berry, Willie Dixon, they all came in during the first two sessions we did those two days. And they were in there, loving what we were doing. Chuck Berry was saying, "You sound mighty fine, guys," because we were doing two of his songs. Of course he liked it. And we were using the engineer, Ron Malo. It was weird. I said, what do I do? Where're the bass amps? He said no, put your lead in that hole in the wall. It was all set up. I just plugged in to a hole in the wall with my lead and the sound was there. That was why we went, because we used to do six Bo Diddley songs in those days and we used to do about six of Jimmy Reed's. You couldn't get the sounds you needed in England at that time. They just didn't know what you were after. The engineers were not experienced in that and so they would always keep it clean and thin and so we had to educate them when we're recording.

Those two days at the Chess Studios were incredibly productive. Some of the songs that you picked to record were originally recorded in that same studio, which must have been, for a lover of that kind of music, absolutely the best experience. To be recreating those same songs, in the same studio with the original engineer.

And [we were] getting a decent sound at last, unlike when we did Bo Diddley songs. We toured with Bo in September/October '63, when we did our first package tour of England with the Everly Brothers, Little Richard, and Bo Diddley. We were fourth on the bill.

Three songs we did. And Bo Diddley said Brian Jones "was the only white cat that ever got my rhythm." And he was totally obsessed by how good Brian was at the time. Because, before the tour, me and Charlie and Brian supported him on the radio, live radio, six songs. He loved us so much he wanted to use us on the tour. The band was on the tour so we couldn't do that. But it was great because Brian just got that tremolo rhythm and he always got it perfect. And so all those Bo Diddley songs we used to do were, like, perfect. They were so hypnotic and Bo heard that and praised Brian for that because he was brilliant.

You mention in your book that Brian was the first electric slide guitar player in England.

He was the only one. I don't think anybody imagined doing that. When you thought of that kind of thing, it was more like country music, slide. It was more like Hawaiian music when you thought of that sliding thing. It wasn't quite blues, but when you heard Elmore James do it (who Brian was totally obsessed by) he [Brian] could do that. To walk into a club, like Mick and Keith and a few of their mates from Dartford, out in the sticks, and hear some white kid doing that, it must have blown their minds. It would have blown mine if I had been there, but I wasn't, of course, and neither was Charlie. And that was how they got so interested, seeing a white cat up there doing Elmore James' "Dust My Broom," which they probably never heard at the time because they were just listening to Chuck Berry and Jimmy Reed and people like that. It must have totally fascinated them and that's probably why they got together. Brian was the leader and they must have been in awe of him.

I loved Brian's playing on "Little Red Rooster" and you playing fretless bass...

I played it on "I'm a King Bee" as well. I made that bass in '61 and in fact, fretless basses weren't invented until '65 or '66. The very first commercially sold fretless bass was made in '65 or '66. I *made* a fretless bass in '61 and it was unheard of. I didn't patent it; that was the trouble. It had frets on it. I just pulled them out because everything rattled. It was horrible. I just pulled them all out and never replaced them. And when we did songs like "I'm a King Bee" by Slim Harpo, I was the first bass player in England who put them slides in and that was in a lot of our records, those kind of slidey things at the end of songs. They used to say, "do something on the bass" at the end of songs and I used to go on "19th Nervous Breakdown" or "Get Off of My Cloud," I was able to do those kind of things and I used that bass for recording all the time. It had a wonderful, wonderful sound. And the cabinet I made at the time had a massive eighteen-inch Goodman speaker in it. No one used those in them days. They used little eight-inch speakers, like the Fenders and the Vox amps and things. I could get that real ballsy blues bass sound, which fattened it right out and it was perfect. But it was so big you couldn't stand my cabinet up. I used to lay it on the floor and sit on it at the back of the stage. It used to take three of us to carry the bloody thing. It was ridiculous. We went on the bus with it once from King's Road, Chelsea, to somewhere over by Ealing. We didn't have any cars or anything and we all got on the bus with the drums, all the amplifiers and equipment and guitars, everything. The bus driver wasn't going to let us on. We had to argue the toss with him. Finally he let us on, but he told us he never wanted to see us again. It was ridiculous going on a bus with drum kits. It's unthinkable that people would even dare to do it nowadays. Would they? They might one guitar. That would be looked strangely on, but to go on with a complete kit on a double-decker bus...

You were very close with Howlin' Wolf and you went to his house and visited with him.

The others didn't want to go. It was disgusting. When we arrived in Chicago I heard from a friend who was a writer, I think he did an interview with me. He said Howlin' Wolf, people had been talking, that he wanted to go to a Stones show and he hasn't got a ticket. People were offering him tickets, but he won't accept them. I said I would sort that out. So I did. I got Buddy Guy to look after him. And he came to the gig and I introduced him to all the band, because I had met him already. They were all like "great," you know? They did love his music, but when we were going on, I said—his wife was there as well—I said, "We're on in ten minutes, you better go and get your seats," and Buddy was there with his brother, Phil. Buddy told me afterwards that as they went out to the auditorium to their seats, people started to recognize them and by the time they had found their seats all the audience was standing up applauding him. And Wolf's wife told me afterwards he was in tears. It was such an emotional moment with forty-odd thousand people there. I'm not saying that every person got up, but a lot of people got up all around him and were applauding and cheering and whistling. And it was a very wonderful moment for him. And after the show they came back and they invited us to dinner at their house the next night, because we had a day off. I asked all the boys, are you going? No, I'm not going to bother. And I was very disappointed that nobody made the effort. I went with my wife and my son, who was about twelve then. And we had a lovely night. I think he [Wolf] was a bit disappointed the others didn't come, but we had a lovely night and stayed up quite late to three or four o'clock in the morning and it was great. We talked about music and everything. He was so gentle and sweet and he was on dialysis. He was in great spirits. I got some nice photos; my son took them, thank God. I said put some of your music on while we're sitting here. I would love to hear "Down in the Bottom" and all that. He said I haven't got any of my music. I said, what do you mean. He said I haven't got any records. Not one? Not one. I said how could that be? He said people, friends, come round you know. And they say, "Can I have that record?" and I let them have that record and I have no records left and no one at Chess would bother to send him stuff. Maybe he was too embarrassed to ask. He didn't have one record. So when he died his wife wrote to me in London and said anything you've got of his, anything like a cassette, album anything you can send so that the family can have something, because all his family were there. And they asked me what kind of food we wanted. "Did we want steak?" I said, "No, just get us some soul food. Get us some pigs trotters and some beans and something." And that's what they did and it was fantastic. I just wanted to get the whole mood of what they would normally eat and normally do. And it was a wonderful night. I'll never forget it. I had done the *London Sessions* album (1971) with him with Eric Clapton and Charlie. The other boys hadn't met him so I kind of knew him a bit, which was great. But I was so disappointed they never made the effort. I really was. It thought it was disgusting actually that they were so into themselves that they couldn't be bothered to go for an hour to see this old guy whose music they adored. And he died the next year.

I loved that London Howlin' Wolf Sessions *album you played on. And also for the fact that Hubert Sumlin, a wonderful character to be around, and Wolf being together must have been amazing?*

I'm here and Eric's [Clapton] next to me on the left, Charlie's [Watts] a way off and Eric's going, "Hubert, turn up because we can't hear you," because he had his amplifier behind him, this tiny little amp. "Can't hear you." Because we were using cans [headsets] on and off, you know, one on and one off, so you can hear what you are doing, because you are not going to have the bass in the room, you can hear a bit of the live drums because you are right on time. But you couldn't really hear Hubert because he was so down in the mix. And Eric's going turn up a bit Hubert, turn up a bit, we can't really hear ya. And he was going, "No, that's how I get my sound. No, I'm not turning up." And Eric says, all right then. Of course when you listen back, it's there, all those great rhythmic things he did. He was lovely. It was a great session actually.

We had two days, because they started out using Ringo and Klaus Voormann and some other bloody people who knew nothing about blues. They didn't play blues. And they spent the whole evening trying to do it with Glyn Johns as the engineer, who was a great friend of the Stones. He was the first person who ever got us into a studio. And they got one song I think, after a whole day with him. Glyn called me—I was in my house in Suffolk, my manor house—and he said, "Do you want to do a session?" I said, "When?" He said, "Tomorrow." I said, "Oh, I just came up to the country with my son." (It was one hundred miles away, Suffolk.) He said, "We need you. I phoned Charlie, Charlie's going to do it." I said, "Who is it?" He said, "Howlin' Wolf." I said, "I'm there."

I got there and he said, "I got Eric as well." That first day we did eight songs. And the next day we did another eight or ten. They didn't use all of them. And then Norman Dayron when he went back to America disappeared with all the masters. For about two months nobody could find him. I think there was a conflict about being paid and so he held on to the tapes until they did a deal or something like that. And then he put horns on some things, which I didn't really like. But generally yeah, it was a nice album.

Wolf was quite unwell the second day. He had heart problems and he couldn't remember the lyrics. Dayron was whispering in his ear, "Tell automatic slim." And if you listen to it he goes out of time on it. He goes on the "on" beat, Wolf, on the lyric, but we kept it because it was genuine and all that. But Norman was whispering the lyric to it because Wolf wasn't well and he didn't remember. But he was all right on the other stuff, he just had a moment or two when he was not well. What a lovely man, though. Frightening. Frighten the life out of you.

We had also met him in '65, when we did that TV show in America...

Shindig?

...Yeah, with James Burton and all them. Leon Russell was there as well. They had a great band. We all sat around and he was great. When he came in there was another little old black man walking with him carrying his bags and all that. And Brian looked and came to me (whispers) he said, "Who's that other guy?" because we knew who Wolf was obviously. I said, "I don't know. He looks familiar. I seem to have seen him before on a record or something." The others didn't give a shit, you know. Me and Brian are trying to work out who this other guy is. And we went over to Wolf and we said to him, "Who's your friend?" You know it was Son House. Me and Brian nearly shit ourselves. It was fantastic. Son House was carrying his bags.

*You recorded with John Hammond and also with Buddy Guy and Junior Wells. [*Drinkin' TNT & Smokin' Dynamite *live from Montreux 1974]*

Oh, yeah, the live thing at Montreux and Muddy at Montreux, too.

That was the same night, yeah. I was in France with Dallas Taylor and Terry Taylor, who is in the Rhythm Kings as my guitarist. And he used to work on my solo albums. And Dallas was there and we were just riffing through some songs in the south of France in preparation for a solo recording in America. And I got a phone call from Claude Nobs, "Can you put a rhythm section together really quickly because I need you?" I said, "What's it for?" He said, "Support Muddy Waters." I said, "Great, yeah, all right." He said, "We got Buddy Guy, Junior Wells, and Pinetop Perkins and we just need a rhythm section." I said, "Well, I've got it here. There's me, Dallas Taylor, and Terry Taylor." Dallas Taylor played with Crosby, Stills, Nash and Young and all those. He was quite a soulful drummer, and Terry could play anything, from classical to blues to whatever. And so we just jumped in the car and went down to Switzerland and we had this very brief rehearsal with Muddy. It was a bit like the Solomon Burke thing I told you earlier. It was a half-a-dozen bars and Muddy said, "Yeah, that's all right. Great," and off he went for dinner or something. And as we went to leave, Buddy and Junior came over and they said, "Can you support us?" because it was in two sections—an hour and a half and then a break, and then an hour and a half with Muddy. But they were going to open on their own. We said, "Why?" They said, "We don't like the band they've given us, the support band. We don't like them. We'd rather you guys do it with us." So we said, "Yeah." So we did the first hour and half with Buddy, Junior and Pinetop and then we all supported Muddy for the second half of the evening. And it was great. It was just off the cuff you know, winged it really. It went really well. Terry Taylor played some lovely slide on a couple of numbers. Muddy gave him solos and Terry was terrified. Muddy would just point and go, "You." It was really enjoyable actually.

Bill, would it be fair to say that after being with the Stones for thirty-one years part of your decision to leave would have been your love of blues and R&B and roots music?

Yeah, I was getting fed up with all that heavy rock stuff and the big stadium shit and all that and the massive travelling all the time. It was non-stop. The main reason was I didn't want to travel any more. I wanted to get my personal life in order and get married again, have a family, settle down, stay in one place, do all the things I hadn't done. The music didn't come into it for the first couple of years. I just wanted to do a lot of things that I hadn't had the chance to do properly. I always fiddled with a few things: photography, solo records, producing other bands. I always did it as hobbies in between Stones stuff. Whenever I did solo albums, I always did them in bits. I would be down at Criteria in Miami for like eight days following Eric Clapton in or something. And I would get phone calls from the Stones saying,

"You've got to meet in Switzerland. We are having meetings on Monday." This was like Friday and I was booked on sessions for another ten days or something. I had the whole band there. I would have to drop it all and get on a plane and go all the way to Switzerland for three days of financial meetings taking about future la, la, la, la, la. Keith, who was living in Switzerland at the time up in the hills two miles away, never attended the meetings. That was what I was having to deal with. Couldn't be bothered to travel two miles to the meeting and I had to come all the way from Miami. There was one instance when Charlie and Ronnie Wood were on safari in Africa and they had to leave the safari and come and do something and then go back. They never considered. Mick and Keith were awful like that. They only did it to their convenience. They would never allow things. I had terrible moments because I was the first one to have a family. My son would say, "Daddy what are we going to do for my fifth birthday?" "I'll take you out and we'll go to the zoo." And I'd suddenly find I would have to do something with the Stones. And I'd say to them, "Can't we just delay it a day?" "The band comes first. Forget family." It was all like that. Aggravation. And it was awful. And all those things build up you know and so I left just to be able to have freedom and do archeology and get into seriously writing books, doing movie scores and doing my own solo recordings and focus on them better and do them properly instead of bits and pieces. Because that's what you ended up doing. Like that Miami thing, then I would have to work with the Stones for two months and then I'd be in LA and do another week on my album and then we would be off to Toronto to do videos or something. I'd have to finish my album again somewhere else. And when I got into the late eighties I did three-quarters of my album and they suddenly decided to tour after seven years. From '82 to '89 we didn't do one gig. In '89 they decided to tour and I had done three-quarters of my album. By the time I went back to my album it was a year and half later. All the keyboard sounds, everything had changed and I had to completely try to rehash it. It never worked and that was the frustration I was dealing with. You never got a chance of writing with the Stones, that was a closed shop, etc, etc. The only way you could collaborate was to suggest doing songs that they might do live. I suggested "2000 Light Years from Home" live, which no one had thought of before, which they ended up doing. I suggested they do Eddie Cochrane's "Twenty Flight Rock." They all loved Eddie Cochrane by then, whom they all hated when I met them. We did things like that live. You could get involved in that kind of thing, but as far as the writing was concerned you didn't have a chance. And they never had any mind for anybody doing anything outside the band as being important. Charlie Watt might want to do jazz or something. So you always had to drop everything for the sake of the Stones because they would do everything for the sake of their convenience and you had to get on with it. And it was frustrating. It was like being at school. You know, you can't have the time off. You can't play with the ball because it was their ball and they wanted to play with it. It was very childish behaviour, but there you are. I'm a bit straighter than the rest of them, so I didn't quite go with it. Charlie just used to go, "All right (moans)." He'd just accept and Woodie was hanging around with them all the time. He was, like, in Keith's pocket all the time. I was the odd one. It was quite hard sometimes.

I'm great mates with them all. I see them all the time and we send each other birthday and Christmas presents all the time. Charlie buys me some wonderful things and I see him sometimes and it's good. It's like family. You don't want to see your uncle and aunt every day of the week, but it is nice three times a year or something. I'm very, very happy with that situation.

You've got a great website. I appreciate your generosity in signing, the CDs, tour programs, and books that are available on your website. That's absolutely great for fans.

I like that idea, you know. They like to have that more personalized, don't they? I've always made that effort for fans, as the Stones always did in the early days. We really focused and made sure the fans were always happy whatever we did. Everything we did was based around the fans: the prices of the tickets for the shows and who was supporting us. We were always conscientious about the fans and all that. I think that has gone out the window in the last ten or fifteen years. They don't think about that anymore, which is a shame because we always swore blind that we would never wear evening dress like penguin suits, and we would never do places like Las Vegas. They've done all that since I left. They've been in penguin suits picking up awards. They've done Vegas on so many occasions. They've done all the wrong things that we swore in the old days, because we saw other people doing it in those days and we said, "We'll never do that. We're never going show bizzy and night clubby," and all that. But they have since I left. I think it's a bit strange sometimes, but it is an awful lot of money that's probably what swings it. Long live blues.

A great story: Muddy Waters, I saw him on this interview, "Mr. Muddy Waters, you've been famous for a long time, so are you a millionaire now?" Muddy said, "No, but all my managers are." And that's it in a nutshell. And Howlin' Wolf in "Going Down Slow," "I ain't no millionaire, but if I had kept all the money I had already spent, I'd have been a millionaire a long time ago." Logic.

I know you're just about to start another tour with Bill Wyman's Rhythm Kings. It seems to me that with the calibre of players, the friendships, and the shared devotion to the blues and R&B, it must be a highlight for you when you to go on tour, especially the camaraderie.

It's fantastic because the band I've put together is principally the same band I started with ten years ago. Now and again I have to change a member who is not available. Georgie Fame can't always do it. Occasionally Albert Lee can't because they are committed months ahead for some other project. But apart from the odd keyboard player or the odd guitarist, the band is the same as it was when we started. And it's such a good band with the two horns and a whole series of vocalists and they all do backup vocals right through the band—everybody—we can do any form of music, so we get picked up as the house band for all these charity projects at the Royal Albert Hall. We just did one last week at Battersea with Robin Gibb and Lulu and the whole host of stars supporting them there. That was really successful. We do the Albert Hall every year for various charities and support people like Eric Clapton, Mark Knopfler, and Peter Green. And they all love the band. We did the Zeppelin thing. We opened the show and did the first half of the Zeppelin concert at the O2, the autumn before last. That was fantastic. We supported all the soul singers after that—Ben E. King, Solomon Burke, Percy Sledge, Sam Moore of Sam & Dave—each of them doing five songs. They all adored the band. We had Paul Rogers. He said "I love this band: I want it." I said, "Get yer own bleedin' band. This is my band." And that's what you get all the time. Everybody just says I love this band. And that's the great thing, we do everything: we do rockabilly, we do boogie-woogie stuff, we do blues, we do soul, gospel, spirituals, early rock and roll, ballads, we can do a Fats Waller song, we can do a Billie Holiday, we can do an Elmore James. It's limitless. We do lots of Ray Charles stuff. Jackie Wilson songs, early Elvis—"Mystery Train," stuff like that. It's a fantastic band and I adore it because I just do it for a few weeks every year. I do five weeks in Europe maybe, and five weeks in the UK and that's it. Musically, it's not like the Stones when you are "hands on" all the year. And the rest of the time I do all the other projects, writing books, doing archeology projects, and the restaurant and my children (I have three little girls), and all the other projects, like photography, I have photo exhibitions, etc., etc. So my life's fantastic now. I've never been as busy or as successful or as happy since I left the Stones. It's been perfect.

Jerry Wexler always said that the best live music he ever heard was Solomon

Burke with a borrowed band. Having done those five songs with Solomon Burke would you agree?

Oh, he's fantastic. He loved the band. When we rehearsed he just did, like, three bars of each song. "How are you going to do it? 'Everybody Needs Somebody'?...boom, boom, boom...Okay that's great." And he was in his chair. But he knows the band because we were on a couple of shows with him in Europe over the years at big band jazz and blues festivals in France. So he had already heard the band and he knew us. But it was lovely to get together with Ben E. King after so many years again. Once again, he adored the band. He said if we come over again, can he use the band? Of course you can. Absolutely. Ben is a lovely guy and he can still do it. He can still sing. Percy's a bit more difficult to get on with. Sam Moore is really good. It's really nice to do those things, but it's great to do our own thing as well, just to go out there and do the two-, three-week things and the odd charities.

Eric Burdon
(Born 1941)

Eric Burdon and the original Animals were part of the British blues and R&B movement in its early days. Formed in Newcastle upon Tyne in 1962, the Animals got their name for their wild stage show. They started as a blues band covering material by Eric's heroes John Lee Hooker, Ray Charles, Jimmy Reed, Brownie McGhee, and Josh White. Their electrified version of the traditional folk song "The House of the Rising Sun" became an international number one record in 1964. The Animals had the grittiest hit singles of any band during the decade of the British Invasion. They briefly rivalled the Beatles and the Rolling Stones in popularity after a string of truly classic singles like "Don't Let Me Be Misunderstood," "We Gotta Get Out of This Place," "It's My Life," "Don't Bring Me Down," and "See See Rider." Eric Burdon's powerful, deep voice is heard on several more hits with him fronting the New Animals and War, including "When I Was Young," "San Franciscan Nights," "Sky Pilot," "Monterey," and "Spill the Wine." For my money Eric Burdon is one of the best white blues singers of his time and his live gigs continue to be an intense, soulful experience. In addition to performing his great body of work through constant touring, Eric Burdon has a deep interest in film. He starred in and did the soundtrack for the semi-autobiographical film *Comeback* and has appeared in Oliver Stone's *The Doors* and *Gibbi–Westgermany*. Eric Burdon and the original Animals were inducted into the Rock and Roll Hall of Fame in 1994. I interview Eric in 2003 after the publication of his second autobiography *Don't Let Me Be Misunderstood.*

Thanks to Eric's co-writer, ex-Edmontonian J. Marshall Craig for providing the introduction. More about Eric can be found online at www.ericburdon.com

Eric Burdon. © Marianna Proestou

Eric Burdon, Genova. © Marianna Proestou

Eric Burdon. © Marianna Proestou

Eric Burdon. © Marianna Proestou

I want to compliment you on your autobiography Don't Let Me Be Misunderstood, *I really enjoyed reading it and especially hearing about your experiences with blues artists and the fact that that was such an important part in your musical development from the very beginning. When did that exposure start?*

Oh, yeah, sure. I mean, exposure to blues just was in the form of records initially. I think the very first record that I ever had was Johnny Ray's "Cry" and on the B-side was "The Little White Cloud That Cried," which was pop then, that was popular music. And he was a white guy, but he had a wail in his voice–he had a moaning voice and I just thought, "Wow, this guy's really different." And then the other record that came in the pack with the Christmas gifts when I got this record player on Christmas was "Don't Roll Those Bloodshot Eyes at Me" by Wynonie Harris. That really impressed me. I mean, I liked Johnny Ray, but I saw an enormous difference between their approaches in the music.

Then there was a movie came out called *Baby Doll* and it starred Caroll Baker. I've seen it just recently and when you look at it now, it's quite funny. I didn't realize it was a humorous movie when I saw it as a kid because I thought it was tolerated. And there was a track in that called "Shame, Shame, Shame" and I think that was by Wynonie Harris. I may be wrong in my assumption that the track was by him, but it was in the soundtrack and it was over titles at the end I think and it put a whole new slant on the movie. It said in a few verses what the total screenplay, in effect, was all about. It was released as a single as well and I was fortunate enough to get it off of somebody's jukebox after it had been worn on the jukebox. So it was a composite of what Hollywood would offer with hours of screen time compacted into two minutes. That had a very great impression on me because I've been equally a fan of the cinema as much as I have been of music, so when I saw film and music come together that way, it really impressed me.

Growing up in Newcastle and starting to become interested in blues, probably in the late fifties or so, you mentioned being able to buy those records. Were blues records readily available in Newcastle during that time period?

No, quite the opposite. I had to make journeys to London and Paris to buy my records and it became a yearly religious march towards Paris to find the record stores, and London. In London, there was a place called Dobell's in the West End of London, they specialized in jazz, but one or two blues artists slipped through the jazz gap and were in the racks. I can't remember where I used to shop in Paris, on the Champs-Élysées somewhere, and I remember getting Clara Ward, a live recording by Clara Ward, the gospel singer, and it just hit me. I already had or was able to get Ray Charles recordings in England, but this was a *find* because nobody had ever heard of her before: nobody knew who she was in England.

Also back then, of course, in London would have been Alexis Korner and Cyril Davies and that whole scene. Did you go see them live?

Well, yeah, a seaman lived downstairs from me and I realized that he could bring the records from his visits to the US, which he did and when I got them, I found they were scratched on one side and perfect on the other. I managed to get a letter to Alexis Korner, I found his address and I wrote to him and I told him about my forays into Paris and why I would like to hook up with him somewhere along the line in London. He, in a letter back, told me that he knew about the phenomenon of records being scratched on one side and pointed out that they were used as packaging material for the Frank Sinatra and Tony Bennett records; that the record companies would use people like Muddy Waters and Bo Diddley as packaging material to protect the pop records in the middle.

And we continued writing to each other and I went down to London one summer and found his club. Actually I first saw him in

London's West End in a pokey little dive that became quite popular and it was so packed on a blues night that Alexis moved out into suburbia and opened up his own club not too far from where the boys, Mick and Keith and Brian, lived out in Ealing way. And I was just blown away to hear Englishmen playing this style, especially Cyril Davies playing electrified harmonica. There were a couple of Americans who had been in the US Air Force and gotten demobbed from the air force and stayed in England because they liked it and one of the guys was Ronnie Jones, a big, tall, good looking black dude. And, of course, Long John Baldry was around on the scene. Rod Stewart. Rod started out singing girl back-up lines for other singers. That's how Rod started out on stage: he would do the girl harmony parts in the Ray Charles songs that we would get into. That's how he started his career—as the high pitch voice became fashionable, it became his thing. Yeah, the joint was jumping, I mean, there was a lot of talent and we all rallied around the blues flag. The interesting thing is that we actually had the impression, each and every division from the various points in England, we all thought that we were the ones who had discovered this phenomenon. It was my mates in Newcastle, we were the only ones that were privy to it. It was a shock to find out that in London the same discovery was being made; that in Liverpool, the same discovery was being made, but that Liverpool also had been transported across the waters to Germany, to Hamburg, where there was a real unique, thriving scene going on of Liverpudlians, including the Beatles and other bands of that ilk, who were entertaining the people in the red light district in Hamburg. So that, actually the red light district, became the birthplace of what became the British invasion.

In your book you describe the Animals as being a raw, straight-ahead blues band and I know the first album certainly had a great selection of blues covers on it. When you started the Animals and started to play around Newcastle did you feel like you were educating an audience about blues?

We were educating not only the audiences, we were educating other musicians in Newcastle. I recorded long before the Animals were ever dreamt of. It was a great collection of jazzmen in my hometown who played in the dancehall circuits, they played in the orchestras, at night in the dance clubs and after hours they would pack up their instruments and head across town to a couple of clubs: one called the New Orleans Club, the other Vieux Carré. And there was a pub on a Monday night, which was their night off. They would get at this pub in Newcastle's west end and I would hang around and wait until I was asked to get up and sing, or make a nuisance of myself enough to the point where they would be, "Okay, let him sing a song." And they were horrified at the terminology "rock and roll"–it was a dirty word to them. Their soul was blues and rhythm and blues. I mean, these guys were jazz heads, totally jazz heads, and were real snobs about it. But along with the help of Ray Charles' recordings, especially *Ray Charles at Newport*, which was recorded in '58 by Atlantic, I could actually demonstrate to them–"Listen to this" and I put this record on and the first cuts were Ray playing alto sax in front of a big jazz band and then he got singing this gospel and blues stuff and even mentioned those words "rock and roll" you know, "it's gone way down into your soul that rock and roll, yes, indeed." And these guys were like, "Wow, man, this is incredible." So then eventually I was allowed to murmur the words "rock and roll" on stage with them and ended up having these guys learn...well, they knew already the head arrangements from Count Basie and Joe Williams' cuts...and I would get up and do the Joe Williams/Joe Turner/Count Basie big band vocal with them and they knew the head arrangement. And there was two brothers, Mike and Ian Carr, who went on to be pretty good jazz stars in England. In fact, Ian Carr, the brother who played horn, went on to write the definitive book on the life of Miles Davis. These guys were educated gentlemen and I got to record with them at a small recording studio. We went straight to disc, no tape and everything had to be done in one take and we came away with lacquered discs and you could play it for a precious, maybe sixteen, twenty times before they turned white.

That's amazing. Do you still have one that's playable?

I wish I did. But I've just recorded an eight-minute piece of music that is, for lack of a better terminology, it's kind of in the rap format with African drums and Rita Coolidge's voice and my piano player from my band and I call it "Black Shellac" because it's about the times when in the backyard, in the summer, that I would get a record that was so hot we would play it on our record players until the black shellac turned white because of the constant play.

The Animals did a tour with Sonny Boy Williamson in 1963 and you did the live recording with Sonny Boy. What are your memories of that tour and what did you think of that recording?

Well, it was the first of many rip-offs. I mean, it was the first recording with a big, well-known, international, original bluesman with a pedigree in history and he loved England. He loved England because he could get real expensive booze reasonably cheap and nobody was standing over his shoulder telling him not to drink. So I watched him in the space of two years actually drink himself to death, unfortunately.

But he was a charming guy and he was really like an Uncle Remus kind of guy, a real Walt Disney type of character and he knew it and he would play that up. He had incredible eyes that he would roll around and he kind of looked like a chameleon. Once he had a suit made in London. He had to have a suit made in the same place that James Bond had his suits made. And this suit had tails on it: the coat had long tails all the way down his lanky legs, halfway down his butt. And he made one leg black and one leg mustard. One arm was black and one arm was mustard coloured and it was a checkerboard suit and these people in London had never been asked to make anything like this. And I went with him to get the initial measurement and watching these wonderful old English gents trying to deal with this crazed guy. And when he got the suit (I wasn't there when he got it) I heard that he went in and tried it on and they said, "Well, Mr. Williamson, what do you think?" and he said, "Well, it's fine but the only thing wrong is you done got the black where the mustard should be and the mustard where the black should be," and they went, "Oh my god!" and he said, "Just joking."

But, yeah, back to his recording, that was the first of many bootleg records which we never saw a dime for. I don't know if he got anything, probably a bottle of Johnnie Walker Black.

I thought it was wonderful in your book that you talked about the history of "House of the Rising Sun," the fact that Texas Alexander recorded it back in 1928 and, of course, Nina Simone did a version. Nina Simone was somebody who had an influence on the Animals. I love your version of "Gin House Blues," that she also did, and "Don't Let Me Be Misunderstood." Were you familiar with her version of "House of the Rising Sun" before you recorded it?

No, I had never heard it until just recently. Well, when I say recently I mean many years after the Animals recorded it. Nina and I sort of locked horns on our first meeting and then we exchanged insults and then she kind of cooled down and we became pretty good friends. I have to say that I'm probably one of the few white friends that she would allow to cross her dressing room door and spend time with her backstage before a performance. And when she came to England, you know, she complained when I first met her about the Animals' cover of "Don't Let Me Be Misunderstood" and I said, "Well, listen, you may not like it, but we've paved the way for you in Britain; the place is ready for you to take" and she kind of, sort of lightened up and I said, "Look, I've got this album here by these guys called the Bee Gees" and she said, "Bee What?" and I said, "The Bee Gees and there are two songs in there, you should check them out." And she went ahead and recorded two Bee Gees songs and had charted hits with both songs: "I Can't See Nobody" and the other one, I can't remember the name of, it escapes me for the moment. But they were charted hits for her in the UK and so she had a great ride in Britain and was an instant hit with the young kids who saw her as this magnificent sort of true, female Black Panther, you know, before the term "Black Panther" had been politically coined, you know, she was it.

And, also, the television people who were having her as a guest on major TV shows, I think they were afraid to deal with her, so I was given the job as her chaperone. I was given the job of looking after her on behalf of the television program. And we were hanging out in London and I said to her, "I'm going to take you to a club tonight to show you your people," and she said "You're gonna show me *my* people?" and I said, "Yeah, yeah, you're gonna like this place, believe me." I took her to the late night session at the Flamingo. The audience was made up of West Indians, Jamaicans, American servicemen...black servicemen...and the place was absolutely packed and there would be regular knifings and riots and, you know, the place was just wild. And we went in and, as we went down the stairs, she just grabbed a hold of my arm and said, "I see what you mean. Hold on tight to me, don't let me go."

But we had a couple of laughs like that. John Lee Hooker came to my hometown and played in the club where we were the house band and it was the place that I helped to build. The only job that I had was a designer when I left college and it was the first and only bona fide job that I had been trained for five years to do, so I kind of look at it as *my* home, *my* place, you know, *our* place—it belonged to the Animals. And when John Lee Hooker came up and played, he was in a state of shock. I mean, there was an interview with him some years later and the interviewer was talking about the heavyocity and the violence that went on in the Chitlin' Circuit in the deep south and John goes, "You ever heard of Newcastle?" and the guy goes, "Newcastle,

Mississippi?" and John goes, "No, Newcastle, England" and the guy said, "Yeah, sure" and John said, "Man, that's the wildest place I seen in my life. I don't want to ever go back to that place... young punks running around, underage and drunk, man, they all had switchblades and everything" he said. "I was shittin' myself." I thought I'd make a T-shirt somewhere along the line that said "Newcastle, Mississippi."

Well, you became very close friends with John Lee Hooker and I believe you actually stayed at his place when he was still living in Detroit.

Yeah, he invited me to his home. I'm not sure if he meant it or not, but I took him up on it anyway. He'd given me his address and I found myself in Detroit with a few days off so I spent three days and nights there in the Hooker household back in 1965 and he took me down Hastings Street. He took me to all the blues joints—I was in heaven. I'd just recorded a track about that experience called "Can't Kill the Boogieman" and we recorded it days before he passed away. It's an homage to him and it's a track that's in his boogie style and I hope it makes it to the final cut CD when we eventually get a release on it.

I wanted to ask you about Jimmy Witherspoon because he was obviously somebody who was a good friend of yours and one of the great blues artists who you had a chance to record with. Did you know Spoon well?

Yeah, I think I did. There was a guy with great razor teeth when need be. But we liked each other from the get-go. In fact, the first night I met him, he was with Joe Turner, the two of them were at a bar that I happened to stumble into after a transatlantic flight and needed some libation and the taxi driver said, "There's a place up here you can get a drink, it's a black joint," and I said, "A what? Get in there." And I went in there and there was a band on stage playing and there's two guys at the bar drinking and I instantly recognized Joe Turner and then a few seconds later I thought, "God, man, that's Jimmy

Witherspoon *and* Joe Turner. I've just been dropped into heaven here." And Spoon knew that I was into managing or trying to get a black band off the starting grid. So he'd heard about that and we got into a conversation and I said "Are you being managed?" He said "No." And I said, "Do you want to work with me? Let's do a project together." And he said "Sure" and that night the big Shure silver microphone was passed to the bar and Joe sang without moving from his seat because he was in bad health at that point in time, so it was propped up against the bar and they brought the microphone to the bar and I got to sing with the two of them. It's a real fond memory.

Then we got into the recording studio. I was supposed to be producing it, but there was no way that I could stay out of the vocal booth and I ended up not producing the album, but just sort of being executive producer and ending up in there with Jimmy Witherspoon on the album.

So that's how that happened? I was curious. I always just assumed that it was a record that the two of you had decided to do together, but it kind of evolved into a duet record.

Yeah, that wasn't the intention from the beginning. But, yeah, Spoon introduced me to the other side of Hollywood, which I knew existed, but I thought it was too dangerous to go there because my arrival in Hollywood would have been around 1965 and there had just been a major riot in 1963/64. I had a book that I would collect my blues experiences in and I wanted to interview the disc jockey who came up with the terminology "Burn, baby, burn." Actually there was a federal suit brought against him for inciting a riot over the radio and I wanted to interview the guy, and I was told quite definitely and up front: we don't speak to white folks. So, I didn't venture into the black neighbourhoods of LA until Witherspoon escorted me there. And he took me to his local club and he introduced me as the guy who'd discovered Jimi Hendrix. [I said], "No, no that's not exactly true." But that was his way of letting these folks know that I wasn't a normal white guy. I don't know, it went from there to unbelievable experiences in the prison systems: we did a lot of prison gigs together. It wasn't good for my career. It didn't do me any good monetarily. It didn't do me any good in the place that I should have been in the music industry at that point in time, but it dropped me into the very heart of soul of revolutionary Black America because I got to work in Soledad where the Jackson brothers had just been gunned down by the guards about a year previous. So the whole state, the whole *country,* was on the brink of revolution and it was amazing to walk down the ramp into the main yard at San Quentin with Jimmy Witherspoon, Muhammad Ali and his wife, and Curtis Mayfield, and I was the only white dude. And we just descended into this field of black men who all had only one thing in their mind, "We want *out*!" and it was pretty bizarre. It was a great experience.

Your book refers to Jimi Hendrix and the close association that you had. Did you talk to him about blues?

No, we didn't talk about blues a lot. We just listened to a lot of blues. And I introduced him to classical music, too. I had a Bang & Olufsen record player and speakers in my house, which was top of the line stuff (and still is) and I listened to classical music on it because the quality of the machinery was so good it loaned itself to classical music, and so Jimi would come over to my pad and we'd play all kinds of music and we'd slip into classical music and he was deep off into it and he loved it. When he wanted to escape from the collective madness that was going on in London, my place was right in the heart of Piccadilly and so we spent a lot of time listening, but we never really talked about it that much. But it was a classic example of a true bluesman who was railroaded into being a pop personality and that's what killed him—that's what ultimately burned him out. I mean, the burning of a guitar at the Monterey Pop Festival. I was just reminded by an interview with

Ravi Shankar on television where he talked about how horrified he was at the burning of an instrument as part of a stage act. You know for Ravi and musicians of his calibre, especially in India, there are only two kinds of music—there's the spiritual kind and there's show business or entertainment. And I've always looked at the blues as not entertainment, it's something else altogether. It's a wellspring of the churches and from religion and I really believe it's got healing powers, but if it's misused, which Jimi did abuse and misuse it, the end result, as we know is what he got—an early death.

Did you jam to blues songs with him on occasion?

Yeah, sure, yeah. That's what I'm saying. When he wasn't in the studio, when he wasn't in the process of being packaged and worked to death by the same management people as I had—left to his own devices, he was a bluesman. That was his natural place; that was where he was coming from. But he took it to another level. He took all those old Muddy Waters songs and Elmo James licks and put them into space.

Mick Fleetwood
(Born 1947)

Mick Fleetwood is the co-founder, drummer, and manager of Fleetwood Mac, one of the most successful bands in the world. After a short stint with John Mayall and the Bluesbreakers, Mick Fleetwood left with Peter Green to form Fleetwood Mac in 1967. After considerable persuasion, bassist John McVie (the Mac in the name) left Mayall and joined Fleetwood and Green shortly after. Jeremy Spencer, an Elmore James specialist, became the fourth member. Fleetwood Mac was initially a hardcore blues band and was one of many that re-introduced American audiences to electric Chicago blues. Their first few albums are regarded as some of the best blues records to have come out of England. Peter Green's ambient instrumental "Albatross" was a British hit for the band in 1969 and featured Mick Fleetwood's tasty tom-tom and cymbal work. Several line-up and direction changes eventually led to incredible success. In 1975 their self-titled album went to #1 in the US. The follow-up *Rumours* become one of the best selling albums of all time with over 40 million sold since its release in 1977.

As Mick mentions in this interview, Fleetwood Mac does a world tour about once every five years. During down time, he put together the Mick Fleetwood Blues Band featuring Rick Vito in 2008 and recorded a live album called *Blue Again* revisiting the great material recorded by the early Mac. I was very grateful to do a rare interview with Mick Fleetwood where we could talk about that band and his love of the blues.

When Fleetwood Mac announced another world tour, they held

a press conference where the international media was "called in" and collectively interviewed the band members over a short period of time. The band's incredible success has made them so high profile that access to them is very controlled. I've found, however, that musicians who have come out of the blues world are very happy to talk about the blues when given a chance.

This telephone interview was done with Mick Fleetwood while Fleetwood Mac was performing in Winnipeg in June of 2009. Thanks to Eric Alper of E1 Entertainment Canada for going to bat for me.

Mick Fleetwood Blues Band, "Boederij" in Zoetermeer, The Netherlands, October 17, 2008. Photo: Kym.Keneko. websites: www.kymdot.com and www.flickr.com/photos/kiyomi-and-the-gang/

Mick Fleetwood, "Boederij" in Zoetermeer, The Netherlands, October 17, 2008. Photo: Kym.Keneko. websites: www.kymdot.com and www.flickr.com/photos/kiyomi-and-the-gang/

Just before we officially start, I'm a bit of a fledgling drummer or was in my early days. We had a band in the early seventies, which was named after the liner notes of your Mr. Wonderful *album. You refer to legendary guitarist* Hot Cottage, *so we called our band* Hot Cottage *and we went on to record an album with Walter "Shakey" Horton.*

Well, so how long ago was that?

That was in 1972.

So a ways back. Do you play at all now?

Not really. I still have set of drums in the basement. Whenever anybody invites me, I'm up there and I'm good for a tune or two, maybe three, and that's about it.

That's a good segue into the Mick Fleetwood Blues Band. I suddenly realized about four years ago that I don't play enough when the Mac is not working. We work now more or less every five years when we go on a big tour. As a musician I was playing, but I wasn't playing enough. So part of the partnership that led to the making of this album came from Rick Vito who had been in Fleetwood Mac in the eighties with me. Our love for blues was a well written situation for us and off we went and did this and we'll continue to do it because when the Mac stops working, I want to be able to go off and do weird, funky, blues tours in Australia...pub tours.

In the liner notes to Blue Again, *you refer to the fact that you've been known as a rock star and a pop star but to quote your liner notes, "in my inner heart, I've always been part bluesman." I'm just wondering where that started for you?*

Well, it started really quite early on, even before I got the opportunity to play some blues, which was pretty much at the beginning of Fleetwood Mac in 1967. But prior to that a dear friend of mine, a keyboard player, Peter Bardens (who is sadly no longer with us), lived next door to me and he literally knocked on my sister's door. He had heard me practising in the garage—when I was about sixteen years old and I went to London with my drum kit, left school and had this pipe dream of being a player and didn't know anybody—and he literally knocked on the door and it was Peter who introduced me to more of a jazzy sense of who was out there, i.e., the Nina Simones, the Mose Allisons. And amongst the other stuff that he used to play for me—the records—was the beginnings of some well-placed blues material that he just happened to have. So that's when I really got my first buzz, which was not really a rock and roll thing in terms of what was going on. It wasn't really a big sort of "Elvis" thing in those terms, but then I realized that Elvis was basically a blues singer in the early days and then you understand where all the rock and roll came from and then all hell broke loose. And I loved that and I still do love the different variant stuff, but my blues roots really started back then and I really owe it to Peter. Often when you hear [about] bands like the Beatles [finding material]—what happened? Well, what happened was a lot of merchant seamen coming in on boats to Liverpool brought all these records that turned all these kids on and Peter was hanging out with a lot of English, colonial, Jamaican, you know, black-as-the-ace-of-spades dudes that also were involved in the military and they had these records because they used to hang out with the black dudes from the United States Forces, so there you go.

You came onto the London scene in the spring of 1967 when you joined John Mayall for a short time before forming Fleetwood Mac. I thought it was interesting that you are on a couple of Mayall tracks—"Double Trouble," the Otis Rush tune, and "It Hurts Me Too." I'm just wondering how the opportunity came about for you to be a part of Mayall's band.

Right. I can honestly say that I'm pretty damn sure that Aynsley Dunbar, who I took over from and who is an incredible drummer and is still very adept, left, I mean, it was sort of ironic, he sort of lost the gig because he was too proficient, I think. He started to expand his incredible technique, which to this day I don't have. I just have a feel for what I do and am happy to fulfil that part of it, so I truly didn't understand how I got the gig to tell you the truth. But what transpired was—Peter Green, who I knew, had played prior to that with Rod Stewart in a band called the Shotgun Express and then when Eric Clapton left John Mayall, Peter joined. Then Eric came back and Peter did some stuff with me and then Eric left again and he went back to John Mayall. So Peter brought me in really and said to John, "I think you should try Mick because he plays really simple, straight-ahead stuff, which is the music that we're playing and we're getting too complicated." And I think John Mayall obviously listened and felt good about trying me out. It didn't last long. The reality was that musically it worked totally fine but the aesthetics of me and John McVie and the brandy bottle was too much. Me and John became instant drinking buddies and one of us had to go and it certainly wasn't going to be John because he'd had a tenure with John Mayall for many, many years with Eric Clapton and Mick Taylor and god knows what so off I went. So you're right, I didn't spend a long time there but it inadvertently led to the forming of Fleetwood Mac, which neither Peter nor I knew anything about or, I might add, had any plans to do when I left.

One thing I've loved about your drumming over the years is your respect for tom-toms. When you hear some of the early Chicago Otis Rush recordings, there's a lot of tom-toms used and I know that Otis Rush was one of the real inspirations for Fleetwood Mac and the material you recorded—did that have something to do with getting you to think more about using tom-toms?

I hadn't thought about it a lot, but I am such a huge fan [of Otis Rush] as was Peter (Peter was probably the hardest pressed not to say that he was his favourite guitar player and singer). Certainly he was devastatingly haunting and just totally unique. I must have worn out a few records listening to him so I am sure that from my love of Otis Rush, the actual delivery of my side of the fence, being a percussionist, would have come from listening like a hawk to what was going on. And you know prior to that my tom-tom thing when I was a very young kid playing the drums, I got into listening to Buddy Holly and, of course, was a huge fan of Sandy Nelson and I found out about a couple of the big band drummers like Louie Bellson, all of whom were very tom-tom friendly, so I think the whole journey probably would have involved no doubt some of them as well.

I was listening to "Albatross" again; that's such a great example of your playing and it's that kind of touch that really makes the record. Do you remember much about recording that song?

Well, certainly the original, I remember, was probably one of my first sort of sonically aware recordings just banging away on the drums and stuff. I used to, of course, tune my drums, but that was the first session that I attempted to actually tune (probably with Peter's help, I'm sure) the toms musically to what was going on with the chords of the song, which are only a couple of chords anyhow. So that would have been, ironically enough, my first time during the recording side of my career that I ever thought of doing something that was actually going to help the recording by being perfectly in tune with the song. And I later on learned a lot about [how to tune] without sacrificing my basic sound. I've always attempted to try and be melodic and I think that's also why I am attracted [to the drums], you know, I don't play any chordal instruments. I wish that I played the piano and I truly believe that before I hang it up and depart this world, even if I'm a bad piano player, I've got to get some lessons and I know I can do it. But having said that, I listen to little melodies as I'm playing and in my own simple way I try to make drum fills become more musical. That's why I get sucked into the whole tom-tom thing: trying to find places around vocals from what I gather or what, of course, I've gathered over the years because half of what I do is very spontaneous. I don't plan too much at all even to this day but what I do is listen to the vocal: that came from my blues playing back in the day. When you listen to guitar lines and vocals like a hawk and if everyone who's playing gets it and listens to the nuances that are there—because the music is really straight-ahead and fundamentally very simple—it then takes it to another height where it then becomes a feel between the players. This is why blues is so infectious and has never gone away. There's a spontaneity that happens if you listen as you're playing. What it demands of you is that you listen intently. That's what I still do to the vocalists in Fleetwood Mac and I put my tom-toms fills around those things. It all came from playing blues and having hopefully that type of dynamic and sensitivity.

That's a really good point about listening and also thinking back to the chemistry of the original Fleetwood Mac between Peter Green and Jeremy Spencer. Obviously listening is exactly what was going on.

Well, it is and if John McVie were on the phone with me, I think he would agree. [Listening] is something that our partnership is about and when people do acknowledge what John and me do as a partnership, musically, that's where it came from. John is so unbelievably creative in a really straight-ahead, simple way and far more of an ultimate musician than myself, I might add. "Less is more" and he never gets away from that. It's the combo of that. He's a lot more able to fit in with my style and is so complementary to what I do, which changes all the time, you know. I hardly play a song the same. It's not that it sounds that different, it's not that I'm messing around, but I don't understand continuous rhythmic patterns because I'm a dyslexic drummer, if you like. I'm always in the moment. For some bass players, it's a nightmare because they're trying to follow the bass drum and it's never really the same. A lot of the time it changes and John is so great because he just catches what I do and now that has become a style that's sort of peculiar to us, too.

You played on some fairly obscure blues records. The Eddie Boyd record that you did and Duster Bennett who then ended up on a Fleetwood Mac record as well. I'm really interested in the experience of the Fleetwood Mac in Chicago *double album set and what it must have been like for Fleetwood Mac to record at the Chess Studios surrounded by people who were your heroes back then.*

Oh, no doubt. That whole Chicago experience. All of us in the band would forever have to thank Mike Vernon and Richard Vernon who headed up Blue Horizon, our record company. Mike was such an incredible blues enthusiast that that journey must have almost been more important to him than it was to us and we were in absolute heaven so god knows where he went when we went there. It was a dream come true: we were playing with a whole bunch of our heroes. The memory was a great one, first of all. I think the tracks that we cut there on that double album to me they really hold up and there's something to be quietly proud of. And it was a real signpost to what was going on, an acid test really for these funny little English boys going back to the source from whence they drew their music and actually not being embarrassed. And I think how that happened almost came out of the whole story of how Peter Green ended up playing the way he did. It came out of the ether. And so when we came to Chicago, we were thrilled. The first session, I remember, (and I forget who was in the studio, obviously a lot of people came in over the few days that we were there) but the general atmosphere was truthfully, "Okay, white boys, what are you going to do now?" It wasn't literally, but you could sort of describe it as that and it was so great to see the session happen very quickly. In truth, someone like J.T. Brown, who played sax with Elmore James, sitting there. And Honeyboy Edwards–this funny little guy who was about 5'1" with a huge guitar on. [The discomfort] very quickly dissipated and it became incredibly comfy. And Willie Dixon was like our father. He took Peter off to places where white boys don't go and Pete blew everyone away in these clubs and we were really accepted. Something transcended from just a bunch of kids copying something. To this day I am so proud of what we did back then and to being able to retranslate it in terms of us getting together and talking about *Blue Again* and the album and revisiting some of the songs and, in truth, revisiting conversations like this. It's sort of important as the years trickle by because in the United States (not in Canada so much because it was a little bit more, in fact, quite a lot more aware back then of what was going on in England) a lot of people are still finding out about that aspect of Fleetwood Mac and, in truth selfishly, it's nice for me to be able to talk about some of that stuff down the road.

I think it's great to draw attention to it and especially with the material that's on Blue Again. *Peter Green is such an amazing songwriter. That's really, at the end of the day, what probably outlasts all of it–the ability of Peter Green as a songwriter..*

No doubt, no doubt. And when I met Rick Vito, I didn't realize that Rick was standing in the front row as a young chap sort of a little younger than me, but standing in the front row in Philadelphia with his whole persona being totally intrigued with Peter's playing and Fleetwood Mac's so there was a great story just underlying all of that. He followed the band and he's really the only person I can feel truly comfortable with doing renditions of Peter's work. He so loved all the stuff that we did then and, of course, became his own person too, very much so, and has made some great little records through the years since his tenure with Fleetwood Mac, but what a perfect sort of way for me to find someone who understands Peter's guitar tone. I mean, there is no one on this planet who came anywhere close or knows the P's and Q's of what Peter did, which is partly, no doubt, style and touch, but it also is a very specific thing that Rick just fell in love with which, I might add, is a little (for sure going back to Peter's side of it) touch of the tone Otis Rush had on his guitar. So when I deliver these songs with Rick, which is just an incredible pleasure for me and we then just get into some of the stuff, of course, that is put together with Rick's writing skills, etc. And we just have so much fun doing what we're doing. We did a tour in England not too long before this present Fleetwood Mac world tour and played some of the town halls that I remember playing way back in the late sixties and it's just a trip. People, of course, in Europe very much so, are just so enthusiastic about hearing these songs again which has been a real eye-opener and we intend to make more music and I will always have fun being able to make selections, as will Rick, from some of the stuff that fits my story as a musician but also to being able to get into doing, in fact, anything we want to do. It won't suddenly become the Mick Fleetwood Country and Western Band that's for sure.

We've been lucky in Western Canada over the years of having Long John Baldry living in Vancouver and John used to spend a lot of time in all of the Western provinces. I know that you're relationship with Long John Baldry went way back and I wondered if you could just say a few words about your remembrances of John Baldry.

Well, first of all, they're all fantastically wonderful memories for me as a young musician when I didn't know him. He was the English icon. You know, Alexis Korner, Long John Baldry, Cyril Davis, John Mayall later, were all the people, these were the guys...if only we could be in their band. So one had this vision of him—and John was nigh on seven foot tall—but the looking up that you would do as a musician was extreme. And he was almost the unlikely blues artist really; he was the gentleman's gentleman, a very classy guy, extremely well dressed to the point that Rod Stewart's tenure...I can tell you Rod's clothes sense came from Long John. And that whole blues ethic, you've got to understand, was a total package where you're trying to live the life and John would come on—and where he got the money from for these Savile Row, impeccable, Ivy League mohair suits—and then he would open up with his voice and the whole package was just so unbelievably powerful and then the fact that he was basically seven feet tall...the whole thing was devastating. So he was a hero to us young guys back in England and ironically enough, Long John later on came out with Savoy Brown and Fleetwood Mac and was the introducer and he did the whole thing with the tour and had a spot on the tour, which he did alone with an acoustic guitar. I had never seen Long John without a band; he always had these huge bands with brass and all sorts of stuff and he came on and just did Lead Belly, you know, and killed them, these kids in college. And Fleetwood Mac and Savoy Brown, we knew we had to pull our socks up because there was this guy alone on the stage commanding. And for the most part they had no idea who he was, I might add, but it didn't matter because his presence transcended, you *had* to listen to him. So he was a major thing in England. And just on this tour when I was last in Canada and—I'm trying to remember where I was—I was out walking and strangely enough a guy outside an Italian restaurant, this is here in Canada, said "Hey, you look like Long John Baldry." This is a maître d' trying to get people to go into his restaurant. And it was such a cool thing and, in truth very unlikely. I walked a few places by and I had a suit on and whatever and I said "Oh my god, no." And he said "I know, but we love Long John." And it was just this odd connection with this guy you'd never think in a million years would know anything about Long John Baldry. It was the coolest thing. So I have great memories and he was a gentle man *period*. And a wonderful sense of humour and sadly missed and had a vast influence on so many of us, way more than anyone will ever really know.

Part 2

Delta and Memphis Blues

Alan Lomax
(1915–2002)

Bob Dylan called him a "missionary."

Lugging around a 300 pound recording machine, Alan Lomax was a teenager travelling with his father, John Lomax, through the American South and West recording the songs of prisoners, plantation workers, and cowboys. He made his first trip to the Mississippi Delta in 1933 to make field recordings of singers and musicians in juke joints, churches, schools, hotel rooms, and on front porches. He was the first to record Muddy Waters, Son House, Honeyboy Edwards, Lead Belly, Mississippi Fred McDowell, and Woody Guthrie. He went on to become not only an archivist, but also a musicologist, author, disc jockey, singer, photographer, talent scout, and television host.

I met Alan Lomax backstage at the Blues Awards (then called the W.C. Handy's) in Memphis in 1995 where he was receiving an award for his historic reissuing of Muddy Waters' *The Complete Plantation Recordings*. He was sitting on the side of the stage. I asked him if we could do an interview and he said "Can we do it right now?" He told me he hated the "modern, derivative blues" being played by a prominent Chicago band and was happy for the diversion. At the age of eighty he was still a music purist.

At the end of the interview, I asked if I could take a few photos. He was sitting in a chair and I was standing over him. He stopped me and said, "You shouldn't take photos of people looking down on them. Take them while you're looking up at them. It honours them that way." Good advice that's stayed with me. I highly recommend his memoir of travelling and recording blues in the deep south, *The Land Where The Blues Began* (1993).

Alan Lomax and Holger in Memphis, 1995. Photo: Rick Fenton.

Mr. Lomax, this is my first time in this incredibly rich musical area of the southern United States. I know that you've been coming here since the nineteen-thirties. I'd be really interested in hearing some observations from your first trip here to the Mississippi Delta and Memphis area.

Well, you know, this show [the W.C. Handy Awards] is a total turn around from what it used to be when I came here first. A blues singer was somebody who lived in the alley and sang in a barrelhouse for pennies, and wasn't considered someone who a polite person could associate with at all, and if you associated with him you were called a nigger lover, and you might get into very serious trouble and so much heat. The blues, as you know, came out of the first experience of the south with industrialization. They were draining all this land, and building railroads and levees along the river to keep the water back, and an enormous amount of labour was needed, so the men left home to join these labour camps because you could do a lot better in those labour camps than you could do at home. You might make fifty dollars a week in the labour camp, and maybe fifty dollars a year on a plantation. So this was the capital. They had a song about it, it went (sings in a strong voice) "I'm going to Memphis when I get my roll/ stand on the levee see the big boats blow/ big boat blow baby/ big boat blow/ Stand on the levee see that big boat blow." They had a thousand songs and rhymes. You see the blues in those days was a lot more informal than it has gotten to be. It went to town and got commercialized, two rhymes two lines, and a punch line. But it was life here in the Delta, it was all sorts of things. It was "Stagger Lee," the bad man "Stagger Lee/ He was a bad man/ and everybody know he carried an old six shooter and a black belt forty-four," and when Stagger Lee went to heaven, "And when I get up in glory/ and sit on that golden stool/ I want old St. Peter to sing me the worried blues."

These were iconoclasts, these blues men, been everywhere and seen everything. They were the outlaws of the black community in a spiritual sense. They didn't believe that you got anywhere by joining the church and praying and being good, and anyway they were in love with guitars and making new music. The music was about all these things that were happening to them, and the feeling was intense. It produced great poetry, like "I've got the blues so bad/ it hurts my feet to walk/ but I've got the blues so bad/ it hurts my teeth to talk." A poet would have been proud to write that couplet, and thousands of these couplets were being tossed off by people looking at the rear end of a mule all day long, and trying to keep a little food in mammie's house when they got home that night. Then of course they'd get home sometimes and there'd be another mule kicking around, and they'd have the blues sure enough. Of course we can laugh about that, but in poverty row, the first thing that goes is the family. Of course there are all these books and articles now about the break up of the family, but that's been going on a long time. Wherever there was poverty, and there was intense poverty here, the relationships between men and women were very fragile. The woman who had had a couple of kids was looking for the man who would bring in more food. If somebody came along with a big roll, she might desert that man and take up with a new one. It was survival of the fittest; it was desperate in those days, when the blues came along. But, there's something about creation that they're just beginning to find out, and that is that new things generally arrive at the edge of chaos. Between the stable condition, where everything is going along just as it's supposed to be, where everybody goes to church and does their job, and so forth, and then complete mad despair on the other hand, like say in the penitentiary world, and the world of crime.

But right on the edge between those two things, you've always had creation. All kinds of great artists have lived at that, and that was the kind of situation you had in those levee camps up and down the river there from 1900 to about 1945. All that pertained. The word was: kill a man, hire another one. Kill a mule and you've got to buy another one. A man wasn't no better than a mule in those places—they knew that, they faced that. We're now facing that in this new very hard-boiled rational, big-time-bottom-line society that's emerging here amidst prosperity. A man's not much better than his qualifications, you know? If you haven't got them, you don't eat, and neither does your family. So we'll begin to sing and feel the blues, you know? It takes a man who has the blues to sing the blues, that was Lead Belly's great phrase about 'em. It takes a man who has the blues to sing the blues. At that point it was the blacks alone in this misery row, here in the Delta. It was a fat land, but it was ruled by Big Daddy—you remember him in the Tennessee Williams play? Big Daddy who was more worried about his bank debts than he was about the people who worked for him? That's the condition out of which this music came. We found buckets of it. We recorded it for the Library of Congress. And going back over our records, I've been playing some of them recently, I'm impressed by the fact that those field recordings are a hell of a lot better than most of the recordings made in studios. We found the people that we thought were the most charming, the most unusual, and then we recorded them wherever they were, wherever it was. They felt relaxed and at home, and they knew that we really did like what they did, because we were steeped in this lore, the way that a collector of paintings is steeped in the art that he knows. They could see our reaction, didn't matter that we were white, because we were turned on to black culture, my father and I, the way that no one else was at that particular time, 'cause people hadn't gotten used to it, interested in it. Those guys gave us wonderful sounds. It wasn't routine. It wasn't just playing the set and going out for a drink. I wasn't just playing a record and pleasing the guy in the control room. They were really singing the songs they loved to sing, the way they wanted to sing them. Those records piled up in the Library of Congress are really something. All the music is great, but that sound we're hearing now...routine. They've done it a million times, and it ceases to mean too much. Anybody can do it, but that wasn't the way it sounded when we were down here. Everything was on fire because the situation demanded that there be a music that could take care of the heartthrobs and be happy enough to carry through the bad situations. Of course the amazing thing about this African tradition is that Africa is a land of dances, so the Afro-American tradition is a dance tradition, always. That's different from yours and my background. We listen to music, sit there, even tapping our feet sometimes, beating time. But a black is always tapping his feet because most black music is a dance music. So they took these lonesome hollers like the one I sang first, and they turned it into dance music. That's the secret of the blues. Is that what you wanted to know? And all of that's in my book, *The Land Where the Blues Began*.

You must have been proud tonight to see the Muddy Waters' Plantation Recordings win a W.C. Handy Award.

I wasn't here, as a matter of fact, but I'm proud whenever something nice comes to that lovely guy who's a fine artist and a lovely, sincere person.

I have this wonderful vision of you lugging this recorder, well it wasn't really a tape recorder, it was 300 pounds?

Well, we were cutting sixteen-inch discs, so the turn-table weighed about one-hundred-and-fifty pounds, and we had a big amplifier and two speakers, and mics and stuff like that. I had really good equipment at that time, it was getting so we could really record fifteen minutes at a stretch on a site, and we got hi-fidelity. Muddy was lucky: when he got to us we had hi-fidelity recording. That next year I picked out all those prized recordings we had made at the library, and published them on shellac. It was the first time that a nation had ever published its own folk music. Muddy had two cuts out of that national series. It was a very extraordinary thing. He deserved it; he was the finest modern singer of the blues that we had found. I sent it back to him in Clarksdale, he put it on the jukebox, and he knew then, of course, that he was as good as anybody alive. And he could show it to his friends–look mama, look baby, that's what I can do, you hear me? He put that right on the jukebox in Clarksdale and pretty soon he was on the train to Chicago. Now I don't regard that as such a wonderful thing, you know, I don't think...this whole blues awards, and this whole industry is based on the great big American word "success," but success and great music don't necessarily go together. What we're all doing is looking for big-time people, and is Joe better than Moe, and who was the originator and all that stuff? That doesn't really matter. In the world that the blues came out of, there were thousands of singers, and a lot of them were better than Muddy Waters, I could tell you that, but they wouldn't get recorded. I mean the people, you could hear them half a mile away, they had voices like bugles, and you couldn't anymore get those people into a recording studio than you could fly. It was only the relatively gentle folks that we ever got recorded. There were a lot of wild birds out in the swamps who never got recorded. But I hate it that this has all been so commercialized. It's all about success, it's all about making money, and that's not what music is about, not what people are about too, is it? I mean the bottom line is ruining our folks, it's ruining our souls, and it certainly is ruining music. Everybody wants to get on the gravy train, so everybody's playing the blues even though they can't hardly pick and they don't have the feeling for the thing. They've forgotten Lead Belly's famous dictum: you've got to have the blues to sing the blues. They like them so they just try, and mess up. We've got more messed up blues than we've got anything else. Acres of them, nations of them, oceans of them. Bewildering universes of messed up baaaad blues. So you come down to the edge where you might hear something good, if you sneak around down there in the delta a little bit with your tape machine.

You and your father discovered Lead Belly. Did you recognize his brilliance the first time that you heard him?

Oh sure, yes. He had a voice; he had one of these trumpet voices. He could sing, and you could hear him half a mile away. Lead Belly was basically not just a blues singer, he was a singer of work songs. He'd sung work songs in his own work on the plantations and farms in Louisiana and Texas where he grew up. Then when he got into the pen, that work music was there. It's what kept the souls of the people alive while they endured working all day at top speed, maybe twelve hours under the hot sun. None of us could even think of doing it. They had the stamina, they had the right skin colour, and they had the spirit. They started singing in the morning and would look up and it would be lunch time. That music of course is the greatest of all music—it's the backbone of music. Lead Belly had all of that. So did a lot of other people, but unlike them, he didn't meet anybody who appreciated that. When he sang it to us, of course, we appreciated his whole repertoire, and we worked with him—well not worked, we enjoyed with him—and talked with him until he finally managed to overcome the inevitable shamefacedness that every person coming from a rural culture feels when he brings his culture to town. People who got there before him had said, oh, that's countrified, boy, don't sing that stuff! They'll throw you out of there! That's what all his new-found friends in the North told him. Things like "Honey I'm all out and down/ Honey I ain't got a dime/ Every good man gets his hard luck sometimes/ Don't it baby..." I mean there's a great song: it's not quite a blues, it's not quite a work song, and that's the kind of things that Lead Belly remembered. We recorded everything he knew, we played it back to him, and we helped him establish his own...a portrait of a really great rural folk singer. He was the only one who has kept to his whole line, and that's what made him different. Lead Belly wasn't great because of his work, unlike my father who was, at that time, the greatest folklorist in the country. He was the man who discovered all the cowboy songs and most of the black songs too. He's the discoverer of "Home on the Range" and "The Boll Weevil,"—I mean you name it, he found them—and he established them as great art before the country. He was the person who lead the banner...1900, man, he was doing it. Lead Belly for him was an example of a great American artist, and he presented him, in the North, as that. Although, Lead Belly was a many time murderer and out of the pen, most people don't understand that at that time this country down here was the last American frontier. It was Deadwood City still in 1930 and '40. Everybody carried guns, and there were shootouts every night, everywhere. If a man got shot at a craps game, then sit on him, and keep right on shooting dice. That was the big folk tale down here, that was the way it was. So that was the background of all these people, and Lead Belly came from the wild frontier out there on the border of Texas and Louisiana, and you had to be a scrapper and a fighter to maintain yourself, and he had some Indian blood in him too, and so you didn't fool around with him. You have to see him in that light, not this namby-pamby oh he has to, because he's a singer, he has to be the Sweetheart of Sigma Chi, no sir, he was a very hard-boiled guy. A wonderful man at the same time, like many Westerners. Anyway, Lead Belly, we met in the penitentiaries, he sang for us, we recorded him, and he begged us to help him, and so my father did help him by taking his recordings to the governor of Louisiana, and he made a musical appeal to the government, and he did get out, maybe for that reason. And he wanted to come and work for my father, and he worked for him. During that trip, he came north, and a newspaper reporter asked him—what are you doing this year John?—talking to my father, and he's like well, I found this amazing fellow here, maybe you'd like to talk to him. So the newspaper reporter went over there and interviewed Lead Belly. He was a very bright guy, and he wrote a great feature story about this amazing fellow who'd had this amazing American experience, which at that time was a very, very unusual kind of story to be in the Herald Tribune, it ran on AP right across the country, and *The March Of Time* [newsreel] took it up and so forth and so forth. We didn't have a darn thing to do with it; it was just publicity guys like you who built up the whole thing. But the thing was that Lead Belly was then able to come through. He was in possession of his whole culture, he knew the game songs and the little ditties that he grew up with, lullabies, and he knew ballads galore, and he became a true representative of the whole culture. Blues were just the one part of his repertoire.

David "Honeyboy" Edwards
(Born 1915)

Honeyboy Edwards' incredible memory for detail and his generosity have been a source for much first-hand information about the life of itinerant Delta blues musicians in the twenties and thirties. He met Tommy Johnson in 1929 and worked with Delta blues greats Charlie Patton, Big Joe Williams, Howlin' Wolf, and Sonny Boy Williamson II (Rice Miller). He was present when Robert Johnson was poisoned and told me that story in great detail. In 1942 Alan Lomax recorded Honeyboy for the Library of Congress on a swing that included historic field recordings with Son House and Muddy Waters. Honeyboy recorded at the Sun Studios in Memphis in 1952 and for Chess Records in Chicago in 1953 and is featured on the *Fleetwood Mac in Chicago* album in 1969. Honeyboy is included on dozens of historical blues anthologies and DVDs, many for the Earwig label.

I've done two extensive interviews with Honeyboy and several short ones at various festivals and award shows. The interview below was recorded backstage at the Edmonton Folk Music Festival in August of 1993. Thanks to Honeyboy's long-time manager and friend Michael Frank and his frequent Canadian guitarist Les Copeland. I highly recommend Honeyboy's autobiography *The World Don't Owe Me Nothing: The Life and Times of Delta Bluesman Honeyboy Edwards.*

Honeyboy Edwards, Edmonton, 2007. Photo: Holger Petersen.

Honeyboy Edwards and Holger, Blues Awards, Memphis, 2005. Photo: Holger Petersen.

You were talking about picking and chopping cotton. When a musician was working in the cotton fields, could you bring your guitar out there and play?

Well, if we was chopping we could go out to the cotton house if we wanted and sit down and play during dinner for a couple of hours. Sit down and drink and play—throw it back in the cotton house, you see? Then go back to the field and work.

Did you pick cotton?

Oh, yeah, when I was about fourteen or fifteen years old, I picked two and three hundred pound of cotton a day and they was paying a dollar a hundred, that's all they was paying. And whiskey and everything was cheap, but I could make three dollars a day. In the summertime, you couldn't pick a dollar, dollar and a half a day. But I get out there and throw me two, three hundred pounds of cotton a day and make me three dollars and I'm all right.

Honeyboy, can you tell me about the first time that you went on the road? I think it was with Big Joe Williams, wasn't it?

Yeah, I was seventeen years old. See, I was born in 1915 and that was 1932 so I was about seventeen and Big Joe came to the country and a lady was giving country dances, they called "juke houses" in the country, and I went over there that night and standing around on the corner, I heard Joe Williams playing and I kept on looking at him. He said, "You're looking at me so hard. Can you play?" I said, "A little bit" like that. He said, "Take my guitar" and I hit a couple licks and he said, "I can learn you how to play." So I stayed with Joe all that night and that Sunday morning he came to my father's house, they fixed breakfast for us and we eat, had a nice time amongst my sisters and brothers playing and he asked my father, he said, "Mr. Henderson, can Honey go with me out to Greenwood? I'll take care of him." And my Daddy said, "It's wintertime, I don't care, Honey can't work on the farm. He can go where he want to go, I don't care, he can't do no work, it's cold and bad." So I went with Joe Williams and I never did come back. I stayed with Joe Williams for eight or nine months, pretty close to a year. And we played around Greenwood, went to Vicksburg, Mississippi, on down to New Orleans, Louisiana, we played a long time together. And what made me left Joe Williams after we got to New Orleans, Joe was starting drinking so much whiskey and wanna fight me, he wanna clown, you know, getting drunk but I had learned pretty good about music out on the road in the past eight or nine months. I had learned a lot of things out there and I could play harp a little bit. I was afraid to get on my own and try to play in the streets because Joe was older and he know'd how to work in the streets for nickels, dimes, quarters and things, pass the hat around and all that, he know how to do that. So I watched how he was doing it so I left Joe, I left out of New Orleans and come down the Route 90 Highway into Gulfport in Biloxi, down the coast and I got on the bridge and they said, "That's a boy with the guitar." They said, "Do you play?" I said, "A little." So I started playing the blues and they started pitching me something so I said, "I'm doing all right. If I keep on doing this, I don't need Joe." And I went on to Gulfport, I picked me up a harp and a harp rack and I started playing harp and guitar, already could play the harp, and I practiced a few days on it with the harp and rack and I got pretty close with my tones and chords on the harp and guitar together, I started playing harp and the guitar. So when I come back to Greenwood, I was playing good, playing good. My sisters and brothers were standing around me and looking and saying, "Honey can play now. Listen, Papa, Honey can play now." So I thought I was something else.

But I left and I come on to Memphis then and I met some of the Memphis Jug bands and a few more guys I know'd (trying to call some guys up), they played all the time in the park (W.C. Handy Park on Beale St. in Memphis); Little Frank Stokes, he was playing in the park;

and Big-Eyed Willie B. was playing guitar. Little Buddy Doyle and Blind Roosevelt Graves was playing in the park—that was just our place there.

With all of these people playing in Handy Park in Memphis, what would make the difference between somebody making more money than somebody else?

The best band; the best blues players had the best sound, they kept the best crowd. See, Handy's Park was four corners to it—on Third and Beale, and then south side of Beale and north side, one corner, one here, one here, and the park was square, just like a square, and it was pretty large. And you could get to playing in one corner, you wouldn't interfere with the other musicians too much because you couldn't hear too much from the other corner to another one, just see a bunch over there. The best blues players you could tell because there'd be a bigger crowd and then you'd follow that crowd.

And I suppose the bigger the band, too, the more volume you had and the better chances of you keeping a crowd, too?

Oh, yeah, you take the Memphis Jug Band—they kept up a lot of noise. Some of the last of the Jug Band weren't like the first of them. Will Shade was around then at the time playing with some of them. Jack Kelly or Son Brimmer or Dewey was an old one in a wheelchair and Sonny was an old one, the last of them at the time. And I come right along and then met Big Walter Horton. I got acquainted with Walter and I went home with Walter and his mother saw me and said, "This boy is near about your age and this who you need to play with." She said, "Them old men is taking your money so y'all play and make your money together and bring it on home and I'll keep it and give it to y'all." So we started playing in the streets and we made two dollars a night, sometimes three dollars a night, from nickels and dimes, but that was a lot of money then because we played the Hotel Peabody. We'd go in the lobby and play.

You could do that: you could go right into the lobby and play?

Yeah, I played there, go right in the lobby and watch them sitting out in chairs and eating, drinking beer and we just started playing in the lobby and they let us play there and they always had money, they'd shuck quarters and dimes to us and when we'd get through playing down on Front Street and at the hotel, we got about three dollars a piece—that was nicer money then. That was money: you'd work all day for a dollar then. Yeah, we'd go home and I'd count with Miss Emma—two dollars here, two dollars there—and we'd have four or five dollars. You could get a hamburger for a nickel or dime then! Yeah, half a pint of whiskey—twenty-five cents, corn whiskey. The sealed whiskey, the higher priced whiskey like Four Roses, that was forty-five cents a half a pint then, cost you about five dollars a half pint now.

When you were playing on the street corners, how did you get a crowd?

See, I talked to some of the black people around them towns and know the liveliest corner and little clubs where people hung out, drank, and had fun and I'd get out on them live corners. Sometime I'd go to the city hall and get permission and they'd tell me the little spots I could sit and play at and when the police come out they wouldn't bother me, they wouldn't run me off the corner, but I didn't sometimes and they'd run me off the corner and you'd block the streets, sometime I used to block the streets and they couldn't get through.

Would you play into the night and have people dancing?

Some of them be out there trying to dance in the street, [they'd be] drinking and come up half high, start hearing the blues and start to dance in the streets and the police had to break them up sometimes. Of course, a lot of times, there wasn't plentiful blues players some of the time. Players would come back and play the blues good and it was some kind of surprise to people, you know? And they enjoyed it, take you home with them and fix meals for you, give you a place to stay, give you whiskey to drink. Sometime I been with people like that: they keep me sometime a couple weeks around. They'd give dances, sell fish and hamburgers and I'd play for the parties and things till I got tired and wanna move up and go somewhere's else for a new place. I got up in my twenties and I recorded for the Library of Congress, Alan Lomax. I made fourteen cuts for him and he give me twenty dollars and that's more money than I'd ever had in my life.

That was 1942 when you recorded for the Library of Congress and those very famous sessions. That was before Muddy recorded for them, wasn't it?

We recorded the same week. Alan Lomax recorded Son House first, coming right out of Memphis. Son House was just out of Memphis into Mississippi and they recorded him first, then they come down to Coahoma—Clarksdale—and recorded me and then went down to Rolling Fork and recorded Muddy in the same two weeks.

I was reading somewhere that Alan Lomax would actually go into somebody's house and he'd look at what records they had. If they had some 78s, what people were reading, everything about the house and the family. I'm sure he did that with your house, too.

Yeah, Alan Lomax was pretty handy, man. His sister give a big anniversary in Washington and I went to that. His sister's still living. But me and Alan are the same age: when he was twenty-seven, I was twenty-seven; me and Muddy Waters the same age; Brownie McGhee, we the same age; Memphis Slim's the same age. Robert Junior Lockwood, we the same age, just different months.

You must have had friends all over the South after you travelled through a town two or three times. Was there a circuit you would travel in?

I used to take turns, like I'd play Greenwood this Saturday, I take turns and go to Keys next Saturday, next Saturday I'd be in Arcola, next Saturday I'd go to Leland, next Saturday I'd be in Greenville, then I go to Shaw to my hometown, next I'd be at Rosedale, so I wouldn't get cold. The last place I left three or four weeks ago and come back and "Boy, where ya been so long?"

So how did you travel? Did you go on trains or buses?

Oh, yeah, I rode a lot of trains, that's the only way I went back then. Of course, when I first started out running around it was not as many cars and not as many transport trucks running like they do today. It wasn't no freeways through the country nowhere then. Through here, there wasn't no freeways. The freeway didn't start until 1962 or '63. All was blacktop up and down, all where it is to this day

And I hitchhiked, buses, for short turns like that. I had some friends had old cars Olds, Fords, something like Chevrolets, a lot of good time people used to make whiskey and everything and them little towns were like four, five, six miles apart. They would carry me. Yeah, and the bus weren't nothing. You'd go like from Memphis to down there in Mississippi for about a dollar and a half, to Shaw. I mean, that's about a hundred and some miles for a dollar, the bus was three cent a mile then–three cent a mile. You take thirty cents and go for forty, fifty miles for thirty cents. Can't do it now.

Would you run into a lot of other blues players along the road? Was it a pretty friendly competition if you were in the same town or would you get together and play the same corners and the same places?

Well, sometimes you'd run up on a little competition. You meet some musicians you don't know, they get off if they find out you better than they is. They'd get kinda hot with you, you know? But I stayed away from that, stayed away and get another corner if something goes that way, you know? And you'd be playing the streets and most of the people in them little towns was bootleggers; they sold whiskey at the houses. If you're a good guitar player, they say, "Come on, go home with me and play that for me, I'll give you two or three dollars and all you want to drink" and all his customers that he had through the week come in buy little half pints and go out on a Saturday, [by] Friday they'd be right at his house shucking nickels and dimes to me.

You must have played some pretty rough places under those circumstances?

I been in a lot of rough places. I got hurt in a rough place, this place right here–no this, this one here.

The scar on your eye?

Yeah, I got hurt in Coahoma, but I wasn't the fault, was the woman's fault. She was dancing with a guy in the middle of the floor and somehow or another she stepped on this man's foot and she told this man to put his damn foot in his pocket, you know? And he went out the door, he said, "I don't take that off of no woman, no whore." And I was playing in my auntie's place and I went to get up and to go get me a cola to drink with my white whiskey and when I got up, he was trying to open the door to the street, open where he could shuck her there, throw her in there and instead of me ducking, I looked back and they said, "Look out, Honey. Look out, Honey" and when I looked back, he hit me right there. Boy, knocked me down. If I hadn't been full of whiskey, I don't know if I'd have made it. And four a.m. that morning–we didn't get a train out of Coahoma till three in the morning coming out of Memphis going to Greenville and I suffered from about twelve to three that night. And I went to Greenville and they operated on me that morning about eight, Dr. Bare operated on me. But I got all right, I come up to my uncle's house, stayed there a week with him and I come on back to Coahoma where I got hurt at, but I never did see this fella no more. I come on board with a piece, a pistol, and he was my man if I ever see'd him again. He was mine. He never come no more. Carter Wheeler, I know his name, but he never showed up no more. Never. But I was waiting for him.

Honeyboy, you're a living historian on the final days of Robert Johnson. You were with Robert Johnson when he was poisoned in 1938. Would you mind telling me exactly what happened that last night and during the last couple of days of his life?

The last couple of days—the Saturday—he was playing on the streets, on Johnson Street. He was playing and this man what run the Three Forks store come up there Saturday evening and I think that was about the first time he'd met Robert. And Tom and them were walking around the street, too, but they were local players and Robert had a few records out at the time, 78s he'd just had recorded and he was popping the "Terraplane Blues," "Kind Hearted Woman Blues," "Hellhound on My Trail," come out right behind him. I mean, he was in Greenwood and the releases wasn't long coming, right behind him. I got it in Texas.

How I got acquainted with him—I know'd of him because he was my cousin's boyfriend, Willie May, and I used to go up there, too, and see Willie May and she said, "Do you know Robert Johnson?" I said, "No, I don't know him, but I heard talk of him." She said, "That's my boyfriend." She said, "That boy sure play a guitar." And after I met him, I met him in Greenwood, so many peoples around him, I couldn't get to him, you know how people try to meet you all night? But I did get a little space to talk to him and I said, "You Robert Johnson?" He said, "Yes, I'm Robert Johnson." I said, "You from Robinsonville?" He said, "Yeah, I'm from Robinsonville." I said, "Do you know Willie May Powell?" He said, "That's my girlfriend." I said, "That's my first cousin." And then we started to get kinda close together and then by me knowing everyone in Greenwood had them old houses and I know'd everybody there so I carried him to all of the juke houses, all the whiskey houses, I carried him around and I started to make the rounds playing with him at the whiskey houses and that's how we got together.

And the Saturday night when he got poisoned, Robert had been there about...before he got poisoned Robert had been in Greenwood about seven or eight months. Of course, he come in the fall of '37 and he didn't get poisoned til in the fall about a year—August. It was August when he got poisoned so that's pretty close to the fall, too, it was August. And I came back after Christmas and Robert was still bumming around Greenwood so I got back with him again. We got all the summer messing around he and I, sometime I'd go out with him. I was younger than Robert. He was twenty-six. I was twenty-two and he was twenty-six, he was four years older than me. So I was with him all the fall and the night that he got poisoned, me and Sonny Boy II was out there. I went out first. I caught an old truck and went out about eleven. Robert was sitting in the corner with the guitar on his arm kinda slumped over like this and by time about near twelve, the people started to pour in because they closed them towns up around twelve. All the people who lived in the country had to go back to the country because they get back to life down there. They had to go home, get out of the city at that time, country time, everybody started to pouring out to where Robert's playing at—old trucks, old cars—when I got out there. They said, "Play me 'Terraplane Blues.' Play me 'Kind Hearted Woman Blues.'" He tried to play once or twice but he said, "I'm sick." He said, "I don't feel good." The people didn't seem to believe that he really was sick, but they said, "You just need another drink, that's all you need." So he kinda said "I need a drink." But Robert didn't really come back too much. He tried but after the people found out that he really was sick, everybody got kinda quiet and walking around drinking. They didn't know what to do, you know? And we didn't want to start to playing when he was sick like that. The cat in the other room laid him out across the bed and about three somebody come in an old car and carried him back to Greenwood, it was about two and half, three miles from Greenwood, carried him back into Baptist Town, he lived in Baptist Town across the southern railroad, and we came back to town. So I didn't go over there Sunday, that was the next morning, I went Monday and Robert was sick, sobbing and crawling around and didn't have no doctors, nothing like that cuz didn't nobody have no money then, nobody had no money. This was during the Depression near about, you know? Weren't no money. And they give him a little home remedy try to make him heave up things like that, but that wasn't no good and Robert died on a Tuesday and if I don't make no mistake, they buried Robert the same day he died—Tuesday. I think they buried him the same day around August seventeenth, something like that he died. And I was young, I was running around over town with most of them girls and everything so when I heard, I came over there, but I didn't go to the funeral. But I don't know what happened cuz they just picked some place, they take him and buried him. Some people says he buried out there by Three Forks, some say he's buried at Quito out there. But I really believe he's buried out there by Three Forks, that church out there. I don't think he buried by Quito cuz Quito was about thirty miles from Greenwood and you don't belong to insurance or nothing, they wouldn't take that much pain to carry you with a hearse that far with no money. So I think he's buried somewhere out there.

I heard he was a pretty well-dressed, elegant kind of man?

Yeah, he liked to dress. Back at the time you could get a suit of clothes for two or three dollars, you know? Yeah, you'd get off the stick, you know, always the people ordered the clothes from Chicago and different places and put them in boxes, nice suits—used suits—and people would get them, have them cleaned, and pressed up and you go. Memphis Slim done the same thing. He always got them second-hand suits, he had them cleaned up, but he'd be dressed up all the time. I remember Slim he be quilted back there. Good front, creased and everything and quilted back there. I know the people back in the Depression, they be playing at Memphis on Beale Street around Third and Beale. Memphis Slim was playing Third and Beale right across from the park. Roosevelt Sykes was playing Second and Beale down there—a dollar a night, one slot a night and all the whiskey to get drank but guitar players, young boys was making more money than them cuz we could go around hustling for nickels and dimes, but piano players had to be in one place because they couldn't carry that piano everywhere. But that dollar was a whole lot of money, dollar and a quarter a night and all the night whiskey? But you would get a whole meal of food for fifteen cent at the One Minute Café—meatball, spaghetti, big hunk of cornbread for fifteen cents.

Did you play most of the night, real late into the night?

We would play like...some nights we would play till about ten-thirty serenading around, then we'd go into the—there was a place on Beale Street called the One Minute Café and right below the One Minute Café, the next door was the Daisy Theatre where the people go to the theatre and on this side of the café there was a big shoeshine place and we'd give this man a dime or a nickel to keep our guitars and he'd put them up for us, the man who ran the shoe parlour, he'd put the guitars up for us and we'd run around and get with the girls and drink our fun most the night until about one the next day and people get awake and start walking and we'd go back and get our guitars and start to serenade again. Hustling with the guitar—that our job. Didn't get no other job, man. A lot of riverboat guys, working on the river called roustabouts. They'd work unloading whiskey and food and stuff off the riverboats, they had a pretty good job.

Did they have the blues players on the riverboats, too?

Yeah, they had a few blues players on the riverboats. I know a couple of guys: Big Walter's mother's old man was a guitar player and he was on the riverboat, he played on the boat—he sure did. A lot of guys would play on the riverboats. Them boats used to go on from Memphis to New Orleans and they would stop at Friars Point there, next stop would be Rosedale and the next stop was Vicksburg and next stop was Baton Rouge right in New Orleans. I know, I know the roads. I walked through there barefooted—no shoes on.

Did you do some gambling on those riverboats as well?

Yeah, I put my guitar by the corner and start shooting them dice with nickels and quarters, man. I could play, too, I could play. I'd shoot anything—six, five, eight, flat five, eight, threes—I could shoot any of them: Top Ts, I could shoot any of them; T Ball combination—that's a three dice combination—yeah, you got the first deck of dice is straight and the third one is the buster, I got two fives, two threes, and two fours on it and the guy playing with the straight dice, you could cut him out, you could come back and cut him out. Bust him out.

I wanted to ask about when you arrived in Chicago the first time—I guess it was about 1945—you came with Little Walter, didn't you? Did you bring him up there?

Yeah, I brought him there. I brought him from Helena, Arkansas, that's the town where Sonny Boy and them were holding a broadcast in the old café station there [radio station KFFA *King Biscuit Time* radio show]. And Little Walter, little boy come in there, all raggedy ass, old shoes wore out; the boy could play a harp. The boy better than

Sonny Boy but Sonny Boy was there recording and he working for the King Biscuit, they had a little thing going on for they self, and he tried to keep his nose to the wall cuz he was too young. But I knowed the boy was a good harp player, I knowed that. They knowed it, too, but they had things going on for they self and they just bad to him like a lot of people do when you're recording. Like Chess done when he recorded with Muddy Waters, he done me the same way, you see? See I was so close to Muddy Waters [in style] and Muddy had made Chess money and Chess didn't want to hurt Muddy, but he didn't care nothing about hurting Muddy, but Muddy had made him money and he didn't wanna do nothing. I was so close to Muddy Water's style that I recorded one number, started out to be a 45, I done "Drop Down Mama." [Chess didn't release it at the time.] If I'd have come out on 45, I'd have made it back up again and I'd have slowed him down. But he wanna keep on doing what he doing, he said, "Keep him out of here." Keep me out, you know?

Little Walter was really nice to me, but he just lived too fast. He was making money that he had never made in his life and started to mess with drugs and lived too fast, that's all the man was doing. All right, I hate to talk about it; he lived too fast. He died at thirty-seven years old. He started going with the man's wife on Fifty-fourth and State, nice looking girl, she had two kids and good looking. She had her husband, they were separated, and at that time the public aid, the relief or public assistance, was giving women a lot of money for their kids then—sixty, seventy, hundred dollars a month and all the food stamps—and every time she get a cheque for feeding her kids, Little Walter would drink it up and get high with it and her husband got on to it. And this was a Saturday morning, her husband come up when she got her cheque, that Saturday and Walter was there dressed up, big Cadillac, sitting at the table smoking and going on. And her husband come in—and I lived about two blocks, three blocks from them—and man came in and said, "I want to speak to you, man." And Walter said, "Okay I got it." He said, "Look, I don't care nothing about you going with my wife, me and my wife is separated," he said. "We ain't no more together, but the only thing I don't like is you taking bread out of my kids' mouths. I don't like that." But he was taking it. The woman was giving it to him and he was taking it, you know? And they got to fighting out there that Saturday morning and, by Walter being high, he lose control and the boy hit him with a blackjack, it had steel or something in it. Walter was high and the man hit him and Walter fell, knocked him out, he went unconscious from being high and he went to Michael Reese Hospital and he never come conscious and he never woke up no more. I knowed all those guys, Snooky Pryor and all of them. I knowed Snooky before he left Lambert, Mississippi.

Could you tell us a little bit about Charlie Patton?

Well, Charlie, I knowed Charlie and I knowed his family, too. Charlie, he wasn't raised in the Delta, Charlie come from the hills of Edwards, Mississippi, out from Jackson in the creeks of Jackson and Vicksburg, a place called Edwards, Mississippi, in the hills. He didn't come from the Delta where I was raised, the Delta just a flat wide country, beautiful. We raised a lot of cotton and corn, a lot of gins and things and Charlie come from where you have a lot of fun. So Charlie died in 1934, he was forty-six years old. I was nineteen I can remember. And his wife, Bertha, me and Bertha was the same age; Bertha was about a year older than me. And Charlie, the last recording he done was in 1934. He recorded in Jackson, Mississippi, and he had about a fight and some guy had cut him on the neck and wasn't plumb well from it. And his last recording, you know it wasn't like his other recordings, he had a stagger in his voice when he sang from that cut and he wasn't really well. He recorded in 1934 it was around January, of course, he died in March, 1934 around the twentieth of March. I remember because I walked to my uncle's house through that little old town he stayed in there, Holly Ridge. I walked through Holly Ridge because I went through there and I went to this little old store and I went in and got a nickel worth of baloney and they give me some baloney in a bag and give me some crackers, give a big thick piece about like that for a nickel. And boy sitting on a stool, he say, "You know Charlie Patton?" I said, "Yeah, I know Charlie." He said, "Well, he died last week. Come on, I show where he's buried." We went down the gravel road right off from the store kinda in a field off to the left and there was some old gumbo dirt and hard mud piled up on a grave with a little old wreath like this, bright little ribbon round the wreath like a cross. He got a big stone there now, great big stone there now. And I went over to Sherman's house, his uncle, Sherman. He was living with Sherman at the time, Charlie was, and Bertha. I knowed Sherman, Charlie Patton was Sherman's sister's kid, that was his uncle, Sherman was, but he lived with his uncle. He didn't farm, Bertha stayed with him. But Sherman was a whiskey maker, Charlie's uncle made whiskey to keep the house going. Charlie was playing music and going and recording and Bertha was with him and he just stayed with his uncle all the time and played for his uncle so his uncle sold a lot of whiskey so that he kept the house going, too.

I guess, Charlie was quite the performer, too, was he?

Oh, he was crazy. Charlie break up his own dances sometime. Get drunk, tear his own guitars up. He was a crazy little fellow, he was crazy. He could play though, he could play.

Sounds like a lot of fun back then.

Well, you had to learn cuz times were so hard. They some good old days back there.

Sam Phillips
(1923–2003)

Few people have made as large an impact on the history of music and culture as Sam Phillips. It can be said that his productions literally broke down racial barriers in America and that his rock and roll records created the rebellious energy that fuelled international political revolution.

The story of Sam Phillips and Sun Records has been told many times. Phillips started as a radio announcer and recording engineer for live big band broadcasts in the late forties. He then parlayed that into being a studio recording engineer, talent scout, record producer, and independent record label owner. Sam opened his Memphis Recording Service on January 3, 1950. With a deep love of blues and gospel music, he understood the artists who passed through the studio. Most were insecure and tentative, making records for the first time. He treated them with huge respect, encouraged them, and intuitively got the best performances out of them.

By the time he formed Sun Records in 1952, Sam had already produced many blues and R&B hits, but had licensed them to various established labels. He was the first to record B.B. King, Ike Turner, Howlin' Wolf, and Rosco Gordon. Sam produced the often-cited "first rock and roll record," "Rocket 88" cut by Jackie Brenston and the Delta Cats. The bandleader and piano player was nineteen-year-old Ike Turner. The first releases on the Sun Records label were by blues and R&B artists Rufus Thomas, Little Junior Parker, Little Milton, James Cotton, and Joe Hill Louis.

By 1954, Sam Phillips was recording more hillbilly and country artists when he hit pay dirt with the discovery of Elvis Presley. Rock and roll exploded and so did the fortunes of Sun Records. Sam was at the forefront, discovering and producing not only Elvis, but Carl Perkins, Jerry Lee Lewis, Johnny Cash, Roy Orbison, and, later in the fifties, Charlie Rich.

Tastes had changed by the early sixties, however, and Sam's biggest acts had left for greener pastures. He sold Sun in 1969 and invested the money in the upstart, Memphis-based Holiday Inn hotel chain and into a string of radio stations. He was making far more money then he had in the record business. Sam Phillips was an inductee into the Rock and Roll, Country Music, and Blues Halls of Fame. He passed away on July 30, 2003, of respiratory failure in Memphis at the age of eighty.

I was honoured to speak with Sam at his home at 79 South Mendenhall Road in Memphis on May 23, 2002, the day after he was inducted into the Blues Hall Of Fame. The Blues Foundation paid tribute to Sam Phillips and Sun Records by inviting B.B. King, Ike Turner, Little Milton, and Rosco Gordon to perform.

Sam's son, Knox, arranged for me to do an interview with his father and Sam kindly welcomed me into his home to talk about the blues artists he had worked with. We also did a short subsequent telephone interview a couple of weeks later to clarify a few further questions I had.

His partner, Sally Wilburn, who had started working with him in the fifties as a secretary in his original studio, poured us a Coke over ice. Sam, ever the prepared professional, had made a list of the blues artists he'd recorded over the years and had that list in front of him. He didn't want to forget any of them.

Sam Phillips at home in Memphis, 2002. Photo: Holger Petersen.

Bottom row: Little Milton, BB King, Sam Phillips, Ike Turner with Maria Muldaur, Charlie Musselwhite, Carla Thomas, and others at the 2002 Blues Awards in Memphis. Photo: Holger Petersen.

I want to acknowledge the hard work that it must have taken to do what you did in the early days of being a recording engineer and announcer at the radio station and then recording so many different artists at your studio. You must have been working long days for so much of your life to be able to accomplish what you did. I think people sometimes forget about the amount of time that you actually have to put into these things, whether you're having a good time or not...the pressure, the obligations, the responsibility.

That's a great observation, Holger, and fifteen to eighteen hours a day was a normal thing for me, and not only that, when I got through deciding whether I could record this act that was unknown, untried, unproven, my work had just begun. But I can tell you that I never went into that studio thinking that I was going to get rich. It was something that I wanted to do, I guess from my birth, to go in and associate myself with somebody who was untried and unproven and get "a phonograph record" that the people wanted out of them. And then I wasn't gonna let it die. I went and promoted it. When I wasn't on the road, I was listening to talent. When I was home, in addition to sessions, I was on the phone. My auditor came in one day and he said "Sam, if I come in this studio—" (and that's the same old studio, Sun Records, same old 6 Union Avenue in Memphis, still there, just like it was when I was operating it) Roy Scott Jr. said, "If I come in here and catch you without a phone in each ear," he says, "I'll probably faint, you know?" And I hadn't thought anything about it. I mean, many times I'd be talking to two distributors, and this sort of thing. So I'm not bragging about myself, but my love, my devotion, my belief for what I was doing...money didn't drive me to do that. It was hoping that I could succeed in what I had dreamed about. I guess I never woke up, because that dream is still with me.

As far as the blues artists who you worked with, what was it that drew you to the blues initially? What made you want to record those artists?

I heard blues, and I heard good black gospel and white gospel music as a child in Florence, Alabama. That's 150 miles due east of where we are right now, Memphis, Tennessee. I heard it as a child, and believe me you hear different ones say, especially country boys like me, say that they were inspired by black people. Well, I was definitely inspired by black people and their spontaneity. They just had something in their soul that they could get out through song. I'm telling you, I can go back as far as four or five years old, and from then on, I was impressed with the things, the sounds...and they would make their own songs up from their experiences, from their desires of things they knew they would never have, but they would dream about...well that was so fascinating to me to hear these things, and do it in such a way, just like, my god this is my life and I'm telling you about it or these are my desires or these are the things that I've been through. It was just an inspiration for me to hear that, and somehow or another, it stuck, and it stuck with me mentally and emotionally. At one time I hoped way before it happened, that maybe I'd have an opportunity to work with black people, whether it be making records (this was before I really had in mind starting a record company), or whether it would just be to be around them, like on Beale Street, that was one of the things that brought me to Memphis, Tennessee, is Beale Street and the big old mighty, muddy Mississippi river. This is some kind of a town. I have to tell you that without Memphis, Tennessee, there would never be a Sam Phillips or an Elvis Presley or a B.B. King. I can tell you that it is a wonderful place.

Sam, when you were producing those blues artists in the early fifties, one comment that I heard you make in an interview was that you were looking to "unlock the key." To let them express themselves. How did you set that process up and encourage that process?

First of all I knew that they were frightened to death that they might fail. Number one, if they had the opportunity to make a record, and

I mean that was so far beyond...well it's hard maybe now to believe that...but these people, like Ike Turner. Ike came from Clarksdale, which is about sixty miles down south in Mississippi, and he knew he'd never have the opportunity to go to Chicago, LA, or New York, it was just one of those impossibilities. So, I really knew how to handle people that were "under-privileged" in their lives, because I was, to an extent, being a child of the great worldwide Depression. So somehow or other I knew that they had to be number one, relaxed, and let them be themselves and feel welcome. I let these wonderful blues artists understand first of all, that we weren't looking for another Count Basie, Nat King Cole, or Duke Ellington, but I let them know that we were looking for the indigenous feel of what they had come up on, and not to try and be something to please a white man. This was so singularly important. Believe me, had I not been able to convey that to them, I don't think I would have had the success that we ultimately did have, and the reception that we got from the people who knew that we were being honest about it and giving the people an opportunity to be themselves, and singing their shoes off so to speak.

When you're in a recording studio, it can go on forever. You can do takes for hours. There's a real fine line of deciding, "this is it." After this point it's going to get worse, or, this solo is not going to get any better. How did you perceive when it was right?

You know, Holger, I was blessed. I think god blesses us all with some talent, whether we ever discover it or not. I was born with an instinctive feel for music, and now you keep in mind, sometimes what you want to hear might not be what the artist could do best, but I don't believe I threw many of the best cuts away. I never let "a little mistake," maybe in a chord or something like that from somebody, or somebody stumbled over a word...that didn't bother me, that became part of the intuitive aspects of that individual making that record. At the same time that was something, it was kind of a challenge, and I think I did, on my score, pretty well on that.

I think so too. You've spoken of the power of music. Music has broken down so many barriers, and the music that you've been involved with has opened so many doors. I know that you had the belief and vision that it would do that in America, but when it started to happen in other parts of the world, was it a surprise to you?

It absolutely was, because even though I was a so-called one man operation, I felt like maybe the music that we put out overseas and even in Canada, our great neighbour to the North, I really was worried as to whether or not people would believe in it, I'm talking about the people who were supposed to promote it and see that it got out to the radio stations. At the same time, I thought that there is a sort of a common denominator between people, even though our religions and our taste and our upbringing and even, to a great extent, our education and everything, is a lot different in many ways, slightly different in others, and hardly different at all in others. But, I truly think there is a thread, one way or the other, that runs through human beings around the world, whether you're black in Africa, or Tunisia, or Canada, or the great Western World...what music can do, as I have preached, when you talk about my attest of the day, it is always what music can do, and nothing else can do it. I guess that music provides a universal soulful thread in communicating. That's the way I feel about it, then and now.

It was wonderful last night to see you receive your lifetime achievement award from the Blues Foundation and to see you and Ike Turner together. "Rocket 88" is such a classic in blues, rock and roll, and R&B. Did you sense how important that record was at the time?

I really do think that I knew I had a different sound. I knew that I had a subject matter—the car Rocket 88 Oldsmobile—that young people [liked] and young people were the ones that I really was interested in. I really felt that, number one, we had a different sound. Number two, I thought the subject matter, because every young person—and old too for that matter—wanted a Rocket 88 Oldsmobile. I mean, it was just the hottest automobile. Anytime you mentioned Rocket back in those days, that meant speed, let's get on with it, and you know how young people are about speed. But I really felt that we had one of the strongest entities of any record on any label that I had heard, and I'd heard some fantastic things on many other record labels, but I really thought we had something great on "Rocket 88."

If you don't mind, I'd like to ask you about a few other specific blues records that you did. Records that I think at the time were probably unusual and maybe had some experimentation involved. Do you remember B.B. King's "She's Dynamite" and the great energy you got on that record?

B.B., well of course everybody knows is an institution now, but also I think knowing what B.B. was doing...see B.B. was one of the most unusual people that you will ever meet, and I never saw anyone have more of a feel for what he was doing. But, if you corrected him in any way, he was one of the very few who might not be, well upset's the wrong word, but maybe not as focused because he was corrected. B.B.'s "She's Dynamite," I just don't think it was hard at all for me to feel that this was a beginning for B.B. I mean a real beginning for him.

You've gone on record saying how much you respected Howlin' Wolf's music and the impact that he had on you. What was he like to work with in the studio on that first session?

Number one, as a physical specimen, he was one of the most unusual looking people...by that I mean he was a big man. I guess to have somebody at six-foot-four back in those days was just unusual, and not an ounce of fat on him. He was a very impressive looking guy, and then, as I got to know Wolf and his silent speech...you had to learn how to talk to the Wolf. I kinda liked that, because he was the best listener you just about would ever run across. He became, I have to say, a real favourite out of all the people I recorded. I was sorry that I lost him to another record label (Chess), and it wasn't the Wolf's fault, he was just tempted by the money that he was offered, and that is why I lost him. But let me tell you, had I had the opportunity to keep the Wolf for three or four years, I honestly think he would be the first gutbucket blues singer who would have absolutely made his imprint on both white and black young people. As much as any of the other white people, maybe not like Elvis Presley, but you would think that with the Wolf's old voice and everything. If you heard one song by the Wolf, if you never heard his voice again, you knew who it was. Same thing with Johnny Cash, I mean, the one-string guitar picking of Luther (Perkins) and Johnny Cash's very distinctive voice, I looked for those things. The Howlin' Wolf is just a classic individual. And I also have to tell you this, Holger, that to see him record, he always wanted to sit down, and he sat down in a chair and he didn't stand up, and you watch him go into his vocal lyric, and boy everything just disappeared around him. I mean he was just right in the soul marks. Just me and you, and here it is for you. It's almost like a...I don't know if you've seen any country preachers or not down south in America, black and white, but they get locked in on the subject matter, and that's the way the Wolf would be on every song that he sang. It was classic to see him. It was difficult for me, actually, and I'm sorry I'm taking so much time, but the Wolf is worth it. It was kind of difficult for me to mix the Wolf because I just had to sit there and look at him through the glass and enjoy the performance.

It sounds like the Wolf would have been somebody easy to record, because he brought it all to the studio. You would probably have to do a lot of coaxing to really get that soulful moment out of other artists. Apart from Wolf, who were some of the other easy people to record?

It's been you know, just about a half century since some of the stuff that I did, but I would say that probably, and this is somebody you probably never heard, but he was a classic that I never did get him accepted like I should. His name is Jimmy DeBerry. This guy was so easy to record; he had a rhythm that was just locked in.

I love the track "Easy" with Jimmy DeBerry and Walter Horton. Walter had that tone like no other harmonica player and the two of them together...that was a great classic.

Thank you so much. I took an old beat up amplifier to amplify Walter's harmonica, and does it ever come together. Thank you for reminding me of that, it is a classic. One of the easiest guys to work with, and I'm sorry, I never did get on him, I really would have liked to have gotten a hit on him. But Little Milton, his name was Little Milton Campbell. He was, and he still is, have you seen a show of Little Milton? This guy is so laid back and yet, he grabs you. And I'll tell you somebody else who was very easy to record: Rosco Gordon. What a pleasant, beautiful soul this man is, right to this day. Rosco is one of my favourite people. Here's a guy I loved, but I have never felt that I did the best that I could on any artist that I ever recorded, because I always felt like there was a little more there, but I wasn't going to let that encumber what we were getting.

A guy I loved to work with is Sleepy John Estes. He was so much of the traditional black great souls. I just love Sleepy John so much. He liked to set up against the wall. All of these little things...we would talk like you and I are talking. A lot of the time we would sit down and talk before we even started anything, just about anything. Hey, that's the way you get acquainted, you know, that's the way you know each other. Here's a guy whose potential people didn't understand. After I started, so many people started grabbing my artists. I was just a one-man operation at Sun Records.

Some people thought of Elvis as a blues singer in his early days. I'm wondering if you saw Elvis as a blues singer when you started recording him?

No, if I said that, what I really meant was that he had a great feel for the blues. There's no question about it. He also had a great feel for southern religious songs, so he was close kin to that and country music, but the odd part about it, Holger, is that he was one that you couldn't really categorize because he could sing some pop songs. If I had wanted to go that route we could have had a record out of him months and months before we did. I didn't mean to say that he was a blues singer, I just meant to say that his leanings were definitely strongly in that direction, as well as the other categories.

Did you encourage him to learn some of those blues tunes you recorded?

No, I really did not. He knew so many of them before I auditioned him, but at the time of the audition I didn't know this until we got a little better acquainted with each other and then I could see that his leanings were potentially in many different areas. But the blues was strongly in his makeup. That just gave me another area to play with and to try and do something that was different with him.

You don't hear the term "record man" anymore. I love that term. You were a record man. Somebody who signs the artist, has the label, puts him in the studio, produces the record, presses it, gets it on the street, gets the distribution together, does the promotion, helps the artist get going, it's all those things...

That's absolutely right. There are people who did that, the independent labels especially, that we just ought to thank, because you and I are enjoying whatever we're doing today and so many others, because of good old record men. I'm glad you defined it for me. As a matter of fact, I can say that Sun Records, an independent label, was one of the most respected labels. And that's not bragging on me, that's bragging on the people and the talent that was on there that we found and recorded. So I just wanted you, and the great show *Saturday Night Blues*, I would love to hear that show, and I promise the only charge I'll make to you is that you've got to tape record a show for me and send me a copy of it. I've got to hear that because I love the blues, and especially if it's *Saturday Night Blues*.

It would be a pleasure. Do you have any final advice, Sam, for potential record men and artists who want to get their music out there?

You know I've always been rather conservative about advising people. Other than don't lose your head about doing it, don't give up too easily. I mean, be willing to make sacrifices. It's very different today, but it was tough back then for different reasons. There is nothing that I can think of that's more rewarding than if you like music and you like to communicate and you can give people opportunities. To share the talents of people, I can't think of any way to do that better than through being a part of some stage of making phonograph records, whether you are a record man or not.

Ike Turner
(1931–2007)

The return of Ike Turner to the music scene in the late nineties was an important occasion for blues fans. Ike was proud of his deep Mississippi blues roots and the role he played as a primary architect of rock and roll. He was on a mission to bring back his style of vintage rhythm and blues. At the age of nineteen, his first recording session took place in March of 1951 at the Sun Studios in Memphis. "Rocket 88" from that session has been hailed as the "first rock and roll song." It was recorded by Ike's band and released under the name "Jackie Brenston and his Delta Cats." It went to number one that summer. Ike went on to discover, produce, arrange and play piano or guitar on countless recordings by many artists including Howlin' Wolf, Sonny Boy Williamson, Elmore James, and Otis Rush.

From 1960 to 1976 the Ike & Tina Turner Revue featuring the Ikettes had several hit records and were one of the most exciting live acts on the international scene. Tina famously escaped from Ike after a violent altercation as documented in her 1987 autobiography *I, Tina* and the subsequent film adaptation *What's Love Got To Do With It?* in 1993. The film focused on her story of breaking free from her abusive husband and left Ike's reputation in ruins.

Ike had ongoing cocaine addiction problems and was arrested eleven times for drugs and weapons offences in the eighties. He was jailed for drunk driving and parole violations in 1991, which caused him to miss his and Tina Turner's induction into the Rock and Roll Hall of Fame that year. His comeback started when Joe Louis Walker persuaded him to be a guest on his 1997 album *Great Guitars* and invited Ike to tour with him. In 2001 Ike released his first solo album in twenty-three years. *Here and Now* was a return to his blues and boogie roots. It was followed by *Rising with the Blues* for which he won the 2007 Grammy for Best Traditional Blues Album. Both releases featured his barrelhouse piano, whammy-bar-stinging guitar licks, and funky horn arrangements. Ike claimed he had been clean and sober for over ten years. His career was back and Ike Turner's Kings of Rhythm, a ten-member band that included many old friends, was in demand.

Ike Turner was found dead in his home near San Diego, California, on December 12, 2007, at the age of seventy-six. The cause of death was reported as "cocaine toxicity with other significant conditions."

I ran into Ike several times during his last few years. We kept in touch and discussed doing a live recording together. This interview was done in his hotel room the afternoon before his performance at Edmonton's Labatt Blues Festival on August 25, 2003. Thanks to the festival producers, Carrol Deen and Cam Hayden, for helping to make it happen.

Ike Turner, Blues Awards, Memphis, 1997. Photo: Holger Petersen.

Ike Turner and Sonny Rhodes, Edmonton, 2002. Photo: Holger Petersen.

Ike and Audrey Turner, Edmonton, 2002. Photo: Holger Petersen.

Ike Turner in Edmonton, 2002. Photo: Holger Petersen.

Ike, I've had the pleasure of seeing you at the W.C. Handy Awards the last two years. I remember the first time we met: you were sitting with Pinetop Perkins. It was great to see the two of you together because Pinetop played a important role in your life, didn't he?

Yeah, he played *the* role in my life as far as music is concerned. Yeah, he taught me everything I know; he was the beginning of my career. When I saw him, the way he fascinated me is the reason that, I guess, I'm in music today and I love it. And today, man, I love him to death; I can't get enough of being around him.

Were you hearing him first on King Biscuit Time *[KFFA Helena, Arkansas, daily radio show] or did you hear him play live?*

No, the first time I heard him I was coming home from school. He and Sonny Boy Williamson and Peck [Curtis] and some more guys from back in those days, they was rehearsing at–Ernest Lane my piano player that I have now–they was rehearsing at his father's house and we were coming home from school (because Lane's mother and father was not living together) and we was passing by his father's house and we heard all this music and this is the first time I ever became aware of a piano. Sure, they had one in church, but I didn't even notice it as a kid. When I saw him play the piano, man, I'd never seen nothing like that in my life. And we was in there one night just peeping in at him and then the next time they rehearsed (I don't remember if it was the next day or the next week) we came from outside and we eased in and got down at the end of the piano and then he starts showing us a little bit. I went home and told my mama I wanted a piano. She told me if I passed to third grade, she would get me one. So I was promoted to third grade, man, and when I got home to show her my report card, she already had the piano sitting there and so that was the beginning of my career.

You're performing again as Ike Turner's Kings of Rhythm. You would have had your first band in the late forties–did you call that band Kings of Rhythm as well?

No, the first band I was with, it was thirty-two of us and we were called the Top Hatters. It was a school band. And then Clayton Love and all these guys (I don't remember all the guys' names), but it was thirty-two and so what they decided is that they was gonna kick the ones out that couldn't read and they kicked all of us out. So they started a band called the Dukes of Swing. That's why I named my group the Kings of Rhythm. We would keep up with whatever was on the jukebox. Whether it was jazz or country or whatever it was, we would play it just like the jukebox and so that was the beginning of the Kings of Rhythm.

People probably don't realize today how successful that band was in the South. You were pretty much the hottest band for a long time during the fifties, weren't you?

Yeah, very much so. Well, our band started playing all around clubs around Mississippi: Marks, Lambert, Greenville, Leland. We was playing in Leland when I ran into B.B. King. I didn't even know who B.B. was. He had stayed at my house some days and I didn't even realize who he was. I didn't realize he was the one drawing all these people to this club in Chambers, Mississippi [now known as Winstonville]. And we would play Greenville, Mississippi, like on a Saturday and we would get off, like one, and so we were driving back from Leland going back to Clarksdale and we passed all of these cars. For two weeks in a row, we saw all of these cars parked down by the highway, and we said, "Man, look at all those cars. I wonder who's playing in there." We knew it was a black club, it was Hezekiah Patton's place–that was his name Hezekiah Patton, called the Harlem Club in Chambers, Mississippi (I don't know if you ever heard of that?)–but I went in there and there was B.B. on stage, man, and I didn't know him as B.B. I'd been seeing signs around saying "B.B. King playing here/playing there," but I didn't know him as B.B. because I knew him as Riley King. I never connected that with B.B., you know? And I walked in there and it was him and his band on stage and I said, "Man, let us play a song." And he let us come up on stage and you know how kids do, he let us come up to play one song and people wanted us to play another one and another one, and then that's when he told us, "Man, you need to record," and I said, "Well, we don't know how to record. What do you do?" And he said he knew Sam Phillips in Memphis and that he would have Sam Phillips to call me and set it up. So he did and that was like a Saturday. Monday Sam Phillips called me and wanted us to record and we said, "Yeah, okay." We was all excited. We didn't think we were going to need nothing original; we hadn't even thought about whether we needed or didn't need an original. So we get in the car on our way up there and that's when we started saying, "Hey, man, what are we going to record? Can we record the stuff that's on the jukebox that we been playing or do we gotta come up with something new?" And that's when we decided to write "Rocket 88." We put that together by the time we got to Memphis. We just about had it complete after going through the thing with the police.

The police stopped you on the way?

Yeah, because I don't know whether we had a flat tire. I don't really remember why we was popped off the road, but we was off the highway—it was only two lanes, one going, one coming—and we had the bass on top, the upright bass was tied up on top of this Chrysler, and we had the drums sitting out of the trunk with a tarpaulin over it and roped in and tied in. That's why the amplifier sounds so funny on "Rocket 88": the tube was cracked. Anyway, when we got to Memphis, we completed it and it took me about fifteen or twenty minutes to put together the music and we just recorded it. They didn't have that three, four-track and all that kind of stuff then; it was basically machine to machine.

And Sam Phillips was the engineer on that one?

Yeah, yeah, that's what he had [the machine to machine]. I'm not sure, but I think in those days Sam Phillips was more used to recording commercials and stuff for radio stations and stuff like that, I don't think he was really into recording bands. Anyway, we recorded "Rocket 88" and you know that's why they say "Rocket 88" was the first rock and roll song (well, they use the language "It's been said about 'Rocket 88'"), but the truth of the matter is, I don't think that "Rocket 88" is rock and roll. I think that "Rocket 88" is really R&B, but I think "Rocket 88" is the *cause* of rock and roll existing. I just came up with this three or four weeks ago. Back in those days, white radio stations didn't play black music: they called it race music. And so what happened is when we recorded "Rocket 88," Sam Phillips was a good friend of Dewey Phillips on *Red, Hot & Blue*. That was a white radio station in Memphis, so after we cut "Rocket 88," Sam Phillips got Dewey Phillips to play "Rocket 88" on his program—and this is like the first black record to be played on a white radio station—and, man, all the white kids broke out to the record shops to buy it. So that's when Sam Phillips got the idea, "Well, man, if I get me a white boy to sound like a black boy, then I got a gold mine," which is the truth. So that's when he got Elvis and he got Jerry Lee Lewis and a bunch of other guys and so they named it rock and roll rather than R&B and so this is the reason I think rock and roll exists—not that "Rocket 88" was the first one, but that was what caused the first one. Now you get my reasoning? So, anyway, that's my interpretation.

And, of course, "Rocket 88" was such a huge hit. Did Oldsmobile ever thank you for that?

No, man. Sam Phillips gave us a twenty dollar fee for cutting that record. People say, "Did they give you an Oldsmobile?" They didn't give us nothing but a hard way to go.

You ended up playing on so many sessions for B.B. and Howlin' Wolf. Were most of those done in Memphis?

Yeah, I used to play on just about everybody's stuff—Rosco Gordon, Little Junior Parker, Willie Nix—I don't know, man, just everybody down there. And then I started being a talent scout for Modern Records and I found a lot of groups down there. Then when I went to Chicago and I played on some stuff for Cobra Records, which turned out to be Otis Rush. I think I also recorded Buddy Guy back in them days, I don't really remember. I wasn't doing anything, you know, I never thought this stuff would mean anything. I was just doing what I do. And so it wasn't no big deal, you know? They make a big deal about what was done with Rosco and Wolf, like "Moanin' at Midnight," "How Many More Years" and all this stuff. Man, we weren't trying to do anything different, we were just doing what we do.

When you worked for Joe Bihari's Modern and RPM Records you were the talent scout, the producer of the records, the songwriter, sometimes the piano player on the session, the band leader, and sometimes you were the artist. As far as discovering and signing other artists for Modern and RPM, was it just a matter of getting in a car and driving to the southern towns?

No, well, about the time I met Joe Bihari I went down to Mississippi and we stopped in Tunica and we stopped in Clarksdale, Jackson, Yazoo City, Brookhaven, but what I would do is I'd just carry Joe Bihari down to Mississippi when I first met him. I went down a couple of times to Mississippi because he asked me was there any more talent. Well, what happened was, they was recording B.B. at Sam Phillips' and they was cutting and recording "You Know I Love You" on B.B.

(either "You Know I Love You" or "You Upset Me Baby" or whatever it was), and so they took a break. I was on a bicycle looking through the window (at Sun) again and when they took the break, I eased in there to the piano (because I see a piano, I want to play on it) and so I started banging on the piano and Joe Bihari said, "*That's* what I want right there!" So I played on B.B.'s thing and when they finished, he said, "Is there any more talent around like you?" I said, "Man, it's all over Mississippi, gobs of talent." So he said, "Will you take me in so I can hear some of them?" And I said, "Sure." So I made ready to go with him the following day to go down to Mississippi. So what I did is, we would go to a place like, for example, we went to Clarksdale and I would go to a pool hall and ask them, "Hey, man, who are some of the singers around here?" And they told me about Robert Nighthawk and different groups and then I let Joe hear Robert. (I'm going way back here, it's a long time ago.) Well, what I would do is, I would go to the pool hall and ask them for whatever name because the people at the pool hall, they the ones who go to dances down in Chambers, Mississippi, and any town I'd go to, the first place I'd go is to the pool hall. Then the next place I would go, I would go and find some church people and ask them who was some good singers around there, and the people from the church would tell me the people who sang good in church. Now, my next problem would be, if they sing in church, could I get them to sing a blues song, you understand? So then I would tell them that I could get them on a record so most of them they wanted to do it. Then I ran into Elmo James in Canton, Mississippi, and I let Joe hear him. That's when he told me, "Hey, man, look, if we give you a car, would you go to these places and write down all of the talent?" And he said, "I'll come down here with some portable recording equipment and we'll go down and we'll record all these people. And in those days the top job in Mississippi–and I don't care if you're the president of the bank–the best job you're gonna get is like twenty-five dollars a week, so here's a guy from California gonna give me–a kid, a teenager–he gonna give me a hundred a week and a car–

that's more than anybody make in Mississippi! And he gave me a '49 Buick and then he would give me one hundred dollars salary a week and then I would send in all of my receipts, which would be one hundred dollars from the gas and stuff running (gas in those days was ten or fifteen cents a gallon), and I would go around and scout talent and I would send the receipts in every week so, man, I had it made. So I would line up the talent and he would come down, him and his brother Jules and we would just go down through Mississippi. We didn't have to rent a studio; we would give somebody a fifth of whiskey and five dollars or something to use their living room, if they had a piano, to let us use their living room to record.

You have always been such a distinctive piano player and then when you switched to guitar, again, you became such a distinctive guitar player with your use of tremolo and the whammy bar.

I never thought about being a guitar player, but in Mississippi it was hard to keep a guitar player. Man, every time you'd get one, he'd run off and go to Chicago. Then Earl Hooker came down. He was real good, but you couldn't keep him down there. I just kept having problems with guitar players. So I started going with this girl, Bonnie, and she played piano so I taught her how to play piano the way I play piano and then I went to Memphis and bought me a guitar and I started learning how to play the guitar. I used to go watch Roy Milton [and his band] and they did a thing called "Junior's Jive" and so I learned to play that on the guitar. Then I heard about Gatemouth Brown and believe me, as of today—I don't care, you can name Clapton or anybody—I think Gatemouth is the baddest guitar player in the world. I'm telling you what, god love him. You know he's playing jazz and all this other stuff, but I don't know anybody that can touch him. Anyway, after I heard about Gatemouth, I went and learned how to do "Okie Dokie Stomp" and it had all the breaks in it and it looked like every time there'd come a break, man, and I'd do a *da, da, da, da, da, da* something would happen and two or three times I'd break a string or something and then, man, I just started doing that *dune, dang* to get through the break and then I started using it as a style because I really didn't know what the whammy bar was for in the first place, the tremolo, so I used it that way and it came to be a unique thing.

Of course, you were in St. Louis at that time and I understand there was a whole bunch of guitar players in St. Louis who all the sudden started playing Ike Turner.

Yeah, a whole lot of them, man. Everybody, oh, yeah, everybody started playing like me. Then I went to Mississippi and brought Little Milton up there. He's another guitar player, but he had a different style from me.

It's amazing to me the scenes you were a part of. You were part of the Memphis scene and developed so many of the people there and then Chicago and then St. Louis. Were you finding great players in the St. Louis area, as well? Were you still doing your A&R [Artist & Repertoire] work?

No, no, I wasn't doing A&R then, I was just playing music. I was more into trying to integrate St. Louis; it was so prejudiced then. We would play all the white clubs and we would play Club Manhattan, which was a black club. My band built that club, I don't know what it was at first but we tore the walls out and made a club out of it, Club Manhattan. And then we'd be working over to another place on Vandeventer in St. Louis, Chapter's place, another place we used to do live broadcasts from. Then we started playing white clubs like the Club Imperial where they had the white kids from eight to sixteen years old. We played there every Tuesday and then we started playing every Friday, also. And so then we would play another place that was a white club way out on Eastern and we got along with the kids. A lot of those people really didn't like that they was associating with the blacks and so what they would do is they would have the police to come down there and back the truck up to the place where we played at and everybody that was associating with us, they would lock them up. They would lock them up in jail and then let them call their parents to come and pick them up and then they'd tell their parents, but it didn't stop nothing. So along during that time I applied for a deputy police badge, a special deputy badge, and I got all my band special deputy badges. When you have a special deputy badge you don't have to pay the toll to come across the bridge, you show your badge and, man, all these white kids would follow us, like fifty cars. They would follow and we'd get to the bridge and I'd show my badge and all of us, wasn't nobody stopped. We did stuff like that and in a way when I think about it now, it was fun. And those same people today, they're the bankers and everything in St. Louis, those kids that was eight years old then, they're the ones that run the town now.

Sounds like you helped change a few opinions there.

Yeah, we did a bit. I wouldn't play at no white club that they wouldn't let blacks in and I wouldn't play no black clubs if they didn't want whites and so we turned that town around. And then you had Chuck Berry and he was just starting (in St. Louis) in those days.

Rosco Gordon
(1928-2002)

Although a Memphis artist, Rosco Gordon has been called the Father of Ska, a Jamaican nineteen-fifties hybrid of calypso and R&B, which pointed the way to reggae music in the late sixties. Sam Phillips, his producer, called the influential, quirky groove "Rosco's Rhythm." Rosco favoured his left hand on the piano and played a slightly off-kilter boogie shuffle.

He had many hits in the fifties including "No More Doggin'," "Just a Little Bit," "Booted," and "Sit Right Here." Rosco toured constantly and appeared in the film *Rock Baby, Rock It* in 1957. He, however, gave up touring by the mid-sixties after moving to New York. As a record collector and fan I'd heard he was living in New York and working at a dry cleaners.

Derek Andrews, President of the Toronto Blues Society, and I were delighted to see a rare performance by Rosco with the legendary Skatalite Horns in Boston at the House of Blues in 1995. I let Rosco know of my interest in recording him and we kept in touch. I loved getting his calls, which usually included playing his latest songs over the phone. I signed Rosco to Stony Plain in 1999 and the album *Memphis, Tennessee*, produced by Duke Robillard, was released the following year. To me, the album is a classic. Rosco was a delight to work with and always seemed to be full of energy and was having fun. He has a presence on that record that has him almost jumping out of the grooves. After some great reviews, Rosco was nominated for a W.C. Handy Award as "Comeback Artist Of The Year." He had a Memphis homecoming in 2002, appearing at the Handy Awards show at the Orpheum Theatre along with B.B. King, Little Milton, and Ike Turner in a tribute to Sam Phillips and Sun Records. A film crew followed him around as part of the Martin Scorsese series called *The Blues*. Rosco said it was all a dream come true. Tragically he passed away only six weeks later at home in Queens, NY, of natural causes.

The interview below is also included as a bonus track on Rosco's CD release *Memphis, Tennessee*.

Rosco Gordon on Beale Street, Memphis 2002. Photo: Holger Petersen.

Rosco Gordon. Peabody Hotel, Memphis 2002. Photo: Holger Petersen.

You first went into the Sun Studios back in 1951. What was it like walking into a recording studio and making records for the first time?

You know it never dawned on me what it was all about because I was having so much fun. It was just some old fun for me, you know, to be able to record. But the good part about it was Sam Phillips, man. He was one of the greatest producers I ever seen in my life; he knew what he was looking for. No matter how long it took you to get what he wanted, he would always get what he wanted. When he say "you got it" more or less you had it. So that was the most exciting part about it as far as me being excited about going into the studio and recording. As a kid I always sang in the cotton field. People, when they'd get off the truck to go to the field, they would flock around me because they knew I was going to entertain them all day. I'd sing in the cotton field, of course, so I was already familiar with the audience. Even before I recorded, I was familiar with the audience because of the people in the cotton fields.

What kind of material would you be singing in the cotton fields when you were a youngster?

I was singing a Nat King Cole song because he excited me and Charles Brown, he excited me and the others...Ivory Joe Hunter. You know I went to his place down in Monroe, Louisiana, and you'd go in his place and, man, he had nothing but songs that he had started and he would play them for you. If you stayed there all day long, you listened to Ivory Joe all day long. Now, I can understand why because he wanted to be Ivory Joe Hunter and no parts of any other act. I don't think he listened to other artists. Because me, I don't listen to other artists, I listen to Country and Western and Gospel and Top Forty, you know, that's what I listen to.

How did you come to Sam Phillips' attention in Memphis back in the early fifties?

Yeah, you see I won first place on the amateur show. This was the Wednesday night amateur show at the Palace Theatre on Beale Street. Rufus Thomas he was the MC. So, at any rate, if you won first prize, that Thursday you on the radio. So this particular night, you know, my friends and I were Mogen David wine drinkers so this particular night we had no money for wine. If you go on the stage, you gonna get X amount of dollars just by appearing there so they boost me up to go on up and do a show to get the wine money. So I go up and I win first prize and that Thursday, I was on WDIA. I was interviewed by Nat D. Williams and everybody sent cards and letters and called and so that Friday, I had to go back. And that Monday, I had my own show like just fifteen or thirty minutes. But anyway I had a show there and B.B. had a show there and, let's see who else, Earl Forrest, he also had a show and Johnny Ace. So anyway we was all on the radio every day. So I don't know how this came about, but the station manager, he set up the meeting with Sam Phillips and me. That's how I went to Sun Records.

So I was interviewed by Sam and he had this song "Booted" and so he asked me if I could do "Booted" so I told him yeah. Well I had the three-piece band: I had an alto player, a drummer and myself, I played the piano and sang. So we put the song together and he liked what we was doing so he said, "Now you've got to have another side." Well, I didn't realize that you had to have a two-sided record when you put out the 45s so, at any rate, I wrote the other side. Bobby Bland, he was my chauffeur, so we was on our way to a gig one night and Bobby started singing "It's early in the morning, I got the early morning blues." So I said, "Hey, man, this thing is messed up," He said, "I'm supposed to be your chauffeur." You know he had this great voice, man, he still does I assume. But anyway that night we got to the gig and I was pretty wild at that time. I was a dice shooter—I believed that I could shoot dice—so anyway Bobby Bland went to the stage that night and I went to the dice table. But now nobody bothered me all night long and Bobby sang all night. I knew he had it once I heard him. So I wrote the song "Love You 'Til The Day I Die" and that was on the other side of "Booted." We thought that was gonna be the song, see Bobby and I did the song together, now we thought that was going to be the song, but instead "Booted" took off.

"Booted" was a big hit. That must have changed your life and everything you were doing.

What changed my life was Shaw Agency. Billy Shaw from Shaw Agency came from New York to Memphis to sign me up. Now that's what changed my life because I had always worked around Memphis. My first job, I'll never forget it, was in Atlanta, Georgia. Would you believe we did three shows? I sang "Booted" twice on the first show, twice on the second show, and twice on the third show and do you know I never sang "Booted" again. No, I don't sing it today because that took all the heart out of me, doing the song that many times back-to-back, it made me hate the song. So, anyway, I said, "I'll write something else." So I wrote "No More Doggin'" next and well, you know "No More Doggin'" is going today. It's in a daytime soap in Hungary—*Romeo and Juliet*. Now what does "No More Doggin'" have to do with *Romeo and Juliet*? [Laughs.] But now that was the first song that I wrote and the song is still popular today like it was recorded yesterday. So I'm proud of you because you gave me the opportunity to re-do "No More Doggin'."

Well, thank you, Rosco. "No More Doggin'" is a great example of "Rosco's Rhythm." What do you think, looking back, are the components that made all this come together for you to invent this new groove?

I wrote "No More Doggin'" and that is what inspired me, but you know back then the guitar, it wasn't a popular instrument. See the horn was the popular instrument. So Willie Sims blew the tenor solo on "No More Doggin'." But, anyway, we knew nothing about guitars so that was out and we also knew very little about the bass. Before then we recorded with no bass, no guitar, just the piano (with lots of left hand) and the horns and the drums.

Rosco, it has been well documented that Rosco's Rhythm *was a big influence on the development of ska music, which, of course, became reggae music in Jamaica in the sixties. Did you know the effect your music was having in Jamaica back then?*

No, see all this was hidden. What was happening here was—Jamaican DJs had to go to New Orleans to get my recordings. So what would happen is they would scratch the name off so nobody would know who the artist was, you know, the buyer or whoever bought the 45, he would take the name off so nobody knew who the artist was. [Note: Jamaican dance DJs scratched the artists names off the 45s so competing DJs couldn't identify and play the same records.] And I didn't find out about this until about seven or eight years ago. I found out that all of this was derived from my *Rosco's Rhythm*.

Have you been to Jamaica? Have you toured over there and worked with some of those players?

I took my own band over there. I went over there several times. But anyway I was a big hit all over there: I played in the Barbados and Victoria and Rio de Janeiro, I worked all over there. I went down there three times. The last time I went down there I had a record I called "The Chicken," so I used to have a chicken as part of my act. Do you remember the dance "The Chicken"? So, anyway, Butch, my chicken, passed away so I got another chicken and I tried to train another, several others, but I was unsuccessful.

I've seen some old photos of you on stage and the chicken is sitting right in front of you on top of the piano.

Yeah, that was the movie called *Rock Baby, Rock It*—he was a moneymaker. Yeah, I liked the clubs because see during the intermission after the show, my valet would put a cup around the chicken's neck and walk him from table to table. They would fill that cup up two or three times a night during these shows, so he was a moneymaker.

"Just A Little Bit" is a classic that's been recorded over and over again. Whenever you see a blues band, chances are they know the song.

Yeah, they're gonna play it. I think about forty different acts recorded "Just A Little Bit." Everybody that recorded it—Jerry Butler, the Beatles, Elvis Presley, and Little Milton and you could just go on, so many different people—Roy Head—everybody got a big hit out of it.

You must have had some wild times playing music in the fifties with some of those rock and roll shows that had a lot of entertainers as part of the package. Did you have a lot of fun back then?

Man, like heaven. The worst about this whole scenario was the segregation thing. You had to change clothes in the car or on the sidewalk or behind a blanket or something, no hotels, you couldn't go in the hotels—that was the baddest part. And I was chased out of Corrigan, Texas. I go to this Dairy Queen, you know you get a hamburger or a cheeseburger? And so I go there and I order a cheeseburger and a milkshake and—would you believe these guys—when I came out of there, they chased me out of there. They chased me out of their town. Man, if I didn't have a good car, boy, I don't know what they would have done to me. But that was the bad part of the whole situation, but other than that, man, working was really fun.

The feeling I get when I see an audience out there clapping their hands and having fun from my music, you could never imagine the feeling you get from that. The best feeling and the strangest feeling I ever got in my life. I worked at a place for retarded kids in Oslo, Norway, and this particular kid, he had his right hand permanently up over his head. Before I finished my show, he was clapping his little hands, you know, dropping his little hands like that. Now that was the weirdest feeling I ever had in my life, especially when the counsellor told me that the kid slept with his hands up like that. He said that he never took his hand down and he asked me what did I do to make him take his little hand down like that. I said, "Man, I just sang from my heart and evidently the feeling I got, it transposed to him. He got the same feeling." So that was one of the strangest, weirdest things.

The worst gig I had I worked with three accordions. Can you imagine "No More Doggin'" and "Booted" with three accordions? No drums, no guitar, no nothing, just three accordions. That was a miserable gig, man. But they had a great big old potbelly stove, red hot. Three accordions—three, not one, three—playing "No More Doggin'" and all the other things. So that was the worst gig I ever been on my life.

But god been good to me, boy, I'll tell ya. I'm god's pet, I know I'm his pet. If anybody's god's pet, I am. You know because look what he did to me: he take care of me. Now he watch over me and I'm able to see all my grandchildren. You know, I gave the music up until my sons became men. I gave the music up for twenty years. I never stopped recording. I continued to record for my own label and I continued to write, but as far as running up and down the highway, I said "I'm gonna stand my sons up." So all my sons are men and I'm back where god wants me to be. He want me to be where I'm happy and I'm happy in the music.

I wanted to ask you about that long time period when you stopped going on the road—was that when you moved to New York?

Yeah, that was when I moved to New York. I came to New York and I went into business with some old guys—a cleaning business. I tried everything. I tried the police force but my wife said she didn't want me to be a policeman. So I tried to be an electrician and so then I wanted to be a presser. So I went to a school over on Chelsea to learn how to press clothes. But, anyway, so I meet these guys and we get together and we opened up a store and the store was already there but the owner, he was selling it to one of the guys that I knew. They asked me if I wanted to be a part of it, so I said yes. I stayed there for seventeen years. And my wife passed away and when she passed away—see my wife passed away in '84, Valentine's Day morning. That was my present. Valentine's Day morning she passed away and I told her on her dying bed, I said, "Don't you worry about the guys," I said. "I'll be there for them." So they're men and I'm proud of them.

Rosco, did you have a good time working with Duke Robillard and his band doing the sessions for your CD Memphis, Tennessee?

Well, I could talk about the whole session forever because it was just that great, man. You know, musicians would just come right in and in ten minutes, they got the song. Ten minutes on each song. The first day we recorded, which was the Monday, we did four songs complete. I don't mean started. Any other time, any other band, any other arranger, it would take two or three days to do one or two songs, but in three days, we completed the whole thirteen songs. I guess that's what made me fall in love with the band; I loved the band. I'm not a beat up old man, but I'm no teenager. They made me feel like a teenager: I was jumping around just singing and playing the piano and having so much fun. I really enjoyed it. I did a thing for you called "You Don't Care About Nothing." I just played the piano and sang, no drum, no bass, no nothing. Now you talking about a feeling, man, that was a joy to me.

Jay McShann
(1916–2006)

Kansas City developed a joyous hybrid of blues, jazz, and swing that never got the acceptance in the blues world compared to that of the Delta, Chicago, or Texas. In the twenties and thirties it was an "open" town controlled by a corrupt mayor. Prohibition passed Kansas City by. The party ran 24/7 in the Vine Street area. The clubs were the perfect setting for musicians to develop "jump blues," which is music for dancers based on playing endless riffs and improvising over them. Count Basie, Big Joe Turner, Charlie Parker, Jimmy Rushing, Pete Johnson, Jay McShann, and so many other great players came out of that scene.

Starting in 1939, Jay McShann led bands that were blues based. Charlie Parker, Ben Webster, Walter Brown, and Jimmy Witherspoon all got their start with "Hootie."

It's hard to imagine that when the Jay McShann Orchestra made their first record in 1941, R&B, rock and roll, soul music, bebop, bluegrass, zydeco, and electric Chicago Blues did not exist. That first record, with the great shouter Walter Brown and twenty-year-old Charlie Parker, made history by pointing the way to both R&B and bebop. Kansas City writer and researcher Chuck Haddix put it best when he said, "'Confessin' The Blues' backed with 'Hootie Blues' was a landmark in recorded sound that inspired the R&B revolution." That record was widely popular for five years. It was a sound that led to R&B, and was the first recording to use a small band within a larger big band. Jay's band came along at the end of the big band era when no other groups were recording that music. Jay also had one of the first modern sounding groups that led to "bebop." When Alan Lomax recorded Muddy Waters in Stovall, Mississippi in 1941, he noted one of the few 78s Muddy's family owned was by Jay McShann. Miles Davis said "Hootie Blues" was one of the first two records he bought while growing up in St. Louis.

Jay McShann's former singer Big Miller moved to Edmonton in 1970 and worked there until his death in 1992. After meeting Jay through Big, I became a fan and in 1997 first recorded him. Duke Robillard and his band were the perfect group to back up Jay. After the release of *Hootie's Jumpin' Blues* I helped Jay get gigs at various festivals. He was well into his eighties so I often accompanied him. What a pleasure it was to spend time with Jay on the road. He was a true blues and jazz legend so many people would seek him out. We had tea with Van Morrison at the North Sea Jazz Festival in Holland where Jay also introduced me to Tony Bennett and Wynton Marsalis. He introduced me to Clint Eastwood when we went to the Monterey Jazz Festival for the premiere of the Eastwood film on piano players that featured Jay. Stony Plain released four CDs by him including the Grammy nominated *Goin' To Kansas City*. I recorded many interviews with Jay which can be heard as "bonus tracks" on those releases. The interview below was recorded in August of 1996 and August of 1998.

Jay McShann and Duke Robillard, Edmonton 1987. Photo: Holger Petersen.

Wynton Marsalis and Jay McShann, The Hague, Holland, 2003. Photo: Holger Petersen.

Did you have blues records in the house when you were growing up?

First blues I ever heard, was it Bessie Smith and James [P. Johnson] who did that "Backwater Blues"? That was the first. You see my dad worked at a furniture store and they sold the old Victrolas and records. When they threw them away, you know, they'd be in the truck so I'd always go out to the truck and look. So I picked one out and brought it in there and played it. It was James P. Johnson and Bessie Smith and, by gosh, man, that knocked me out. I knew right then I liked the blues.

They didn't want me playing the blues records in the house and then if I tried to play the blues in the house, you know, well I had to stop. They wouldn't let me play nothing but church songs. About the only time I got a chance to play anything different is when my grandmother would come over. She'd say "Play me some of that other kind of stuff" and, shit, I'd go and play. I'd do that to defy my parents. You know what I mean? Kids like that, you know? [laughs] They won't let me play it, but grandma told me to play it. Old man would be reading the paper and as a rule he don't do nothing but just lower the paper and look around but he didn't lower the paper, so I'd see that I got by with this. But I knew then that I liked the blues and I was listening to the records, you know, talkin' about—"Trouble in the Lowlands." "When it rained five days, cloud turned dark as night and she was talking about how bad the flood was..." hmm hmm, I can't sing no more...and all that stuff. I could picture that as a kid.

Jay, how did you get your nickname "Hootie"?

Well, I tell you, when I first came to Kansas City, I was going to all the clubs to meet the musicians and these musicians was playing a lot of good swinging blues. So quite naturally that just kept me off balance, seeing all this happening and everything. So the guys took me over to a club one night and they told the bartender, "Bartender, fix this new cat up in town that old special you give us." So bartender—you know they'd always try drinks out on the cats, you know. So the cat he fixed up one of them bombshells, you know, and it tasted so good and he said, "How about another?" and I said, "Yeah, yeah, yeah, good." So I couldn't turn it down and he sent the third one. So I tried the third one. So the guys kept saying, "Are you ready to sit in and play?" and I said "Yeah, yeah, anytime, whenever, let me know when you guys going to start the session." They say, "Okay, we ready, we waiting for you." So I'm way over here trying to get over there to the piano and I tried to get up and I couldn't get to the piano and everybody fell out laughing. That was the laugh of the evening, see, cuz they had that thing put together. They said, "We'll fix him" and they fixed me. So, when they would mention me, they'd say "Man, do you remember the cat that came down to the club the other night. That new cat in town that came down and got hootied?" "Oh, yeah, old Hootie, yeah, that's who I'm talking about." And so they started calling me Hootie from there on and it stayed. "Hey, Hoot, what's happening?" "All right, everything's cool," you know, whatever. "Yeah, man, this cat came on down to the club and got hootied the other night. We was gonna take him by the hootenanny." They were the special spots where the cats hung out.

I can imagine that in Kansas City when you got there in the late thirties there must have been a party going on like nowhere else in the world. I understand there were over two hundred clubs that had live music around the Fourteenth and Vine area. It must have been absolutely wild.

Yes, it was wild and the thing about it is they piped the music right out in the street, right out in front. And people passing by, they'd hear something they liked and turn around and say "Let's go and see who that is." That's the way I heard [Charlie] Yardbird Parker. We was passing by the Barley Duke Club and we was walking and I said, "Man, who is that blowin' in there? Let's go in and see." So we went in and it was Charlie that was blowing. So we talked to him and I said, "Look, man, sure glad I met you. Maybe we get a chance to do something together," and he said, "Yeah, any time. Call me anytime, yeah, I'll be ready." You could hear the music and you could hear it and if it sounded good, you walked in. You hear somebody singing and they'd hit a note that you liked, you know, and it don't have to be but one note, you hear one note that you like, "Let's go check that note out." There were a lot of gigs in Kansas City. I hadn't seen nothing like this. See cats got to work at eight and got off at five in the morning. And there was some bands going to work at six to six in the morning: twelve hours. That's the thing, see, you didn't find that in the little towns down in the southern part of Kansas, see, because, you know what I mean, it would be too disruptive, I guess.

What was that first band that you put together? Was that in Kansas City?

The first band I put together was in Kansas City. That was a small group that I put together, went to work at the Plaza at Martins, Martins 210 was the address. That had to be 1937.

Charlie Parker made his first recordings when he was playing with the Jay McShann Orchestra and went on to rewrite jazz history. Did you know how good he was at the very beginning?

Well, you could tell it, you know? After sitting with a guy working every night, night after night, and listening to the steps that he's doing and the way he's doing it and what he was doing, you know, you can't help but know it. You sit and wonder when will this guy get his dues? When he's gonna get what's due him? You wonder will he ever make it? Wonder will he ever get a chance to get it? But you can stop and say this: if he didn't get it, at least some of the people that he cared for did. They reaped some of the benefit, you know?

I remember one time you said you were surprised at how long it actually took Charlie Parker to get his reputation.

That is true. That's true because you see he had it. I listened to Diz [Dizzy Gillespie] while Diz was talking and Diz told the people all the time he'd said that Charlie Parker had this thing, had more ideas about this thing than anybody around. So, quite naturally, we all clustered around Bird because he had the more advanced thing going. He knew better what to do, what not to do; he had an insight.

I was reading Miles Davis' autobiography and on the very first page he says that one of the first two records that he bought was "Hootie Blues" by the Jay McShann Orchestra in 1942.

Yeah, Miles is quite a guy.

And, of course, Hootie Blues *features the first playing on record of Charlie Parker.*

That's right.

What kind of a man was Charlie Parker?

Well, Charlie was kind of a truthful man in a lot of ways. He'd tell the truth when you wasn't expecting him to tell the truth. He'd give you the straight facts. And a lot of times people don't like straight facts; sometimes they want you to butter it up a little, put a little sugar in there. But he'd give you straight facts. You'd ask him and you'd say, "Why did I ask this guy this? I should have known better," but he was going to shoot it right out to you. Cats would be running around Bird, "Hey, Bird, blow my horn tonight." "No, don't blow his, blow mine." They'd be asking, "Where's your horn, Bird?" So Bird, he'd pick out a horn and say, "I like this horn. Who's horn is this?" He'd say, "Hey, man, can I blow your horn tonight?" "Yeah" "Well, look here I'll have it for you in the morning. See me in the morning, such and such a time, everything will be all right." Bird would take the horn, make the gig that night then the next morning the cat would come by from the gig, you know, come by for his horn. "Hey, Bird, how'd everything go?" "Oh, fine, everything went all right. But look here," Bird would reach into his pocket, feeling around. "But where's my horn?" "Oh, here, here it is....Take this pawn ticket, go to such and such a place down there, a couple blocks down there, they call it so and so's. I had to have a little something. Here's the ticket." He'd say, "I told you I'd take care of your horn." He took care of it.

To the pawn shop?

Yes. But he was truthful about it.

Were you there when he got his nickname "Bird"?

Well, when he actually really got it officially was the time that we were going to Lincoln, Nebraska, to play. They had a football game that day and they'd won the game and they'd have the dance afterward. We went up there to play one of those dances. You know when you drive along the highway going through the country, the chickens run right alongside the highway with the cars sometimes? And so these chickens was way down there close to where the cars was and they hit this chicken so Bird says "Hey, man, you hit one of them chickens back there," he says. "Stop the car, slow down, back up and go get that bird." So the guy did. He stopped the car and backed up, went all the way back and Bird got out and grabbed the chicken and took the chicken into Lincoln. And in those days we had to get rooms at private families, you know, so Bird went over to Miss Joseph's and as soon as he got to Miss Joseph's, he asked, "Miss Joseph, would you fix this bird? We hit this bird, this yardbird, coming down." She said "Yeah,

I'll fix it for you." So she did, she fixed it and he got a room with her at her place. And she fixed it and Bird wouldn't let nobody have none of his chicken. "If I hadn't made y'all stop and pick it up," he said, "wouldn't been no chicken at all." You know, he said, "I'm eat all this bird myself."

Jay, back then with the Jay McShann Orchestra, you were twenty-six years old and you were pretty much the oldest guy in the band. It was a pretty young orchestra in the early forties wasn't it?

Yes, it was.

And I understand that apart from Charlie Parker, there were a lot of other "free spirits" in that band.

You said it when you said "free spirits."

As a band leader, how did you discipline and control them?

Well, you know, a lot of people used to ask me that. And I tell you, the way I found I could control those cats was I found out how to play crazy and let 'em know you playing crazy. They'd say, "Man, look here, this cat is playing crazy on us, man." And so they'd talk that stuff among themselves. And, really, I got me more respect and everything. They got to the point the next thing we did, we looked around and all the cats was playing crazy just letting you know now–now, wait, this ain't going, you know? Everybody wants to draw some [advance] money and I had to work something out because everybody just wants some money. I said, "Listen, I don't have but a dollar, I don't have but a dollar" so then I had to learn how to put the big dollars inside and leave the little dollars on the outside so that I could make no mistakes. So, when I'd say "I only got a dollar," I'd pull it out and there it was and they'd say, "Man, this cat said he only had a dollar."

Did you have a system of fining members of the band?

Oh, yes, we had a system of fining cats whenever they did something wrong or got out of line. We made the cats fine themselves. I mean, they had to put the fine on themselves so that's what we made them do. And so the first guy that got fined, as usual, was Bird. And Bird come up with a fine "Man, I fine myself a dollar because I did so and so" and the cats would jump right on him. "No, you ain't gonna get by with that." And the cats would be standing all around him, "Come on, cut loose with it, what is it?" and he'd say, "Well, I'll pay two dollars." "No, no, you ain't gonna get by with two dollars for that." "Well, man, what do y'all want?" he'd say. "How can I make this fine right?" and they'd say, "Well, how about ten dollars?" "Okay." And they'd say, "Should be more. The next time we're gonna hold out for more." Cats would do that. You know, we had like the judge and the lawyers and all that stuff going on.

And we had a game that the cats played. The game was named "The Bear." Whichever cat had the worst looking babe that night after the gig, when he got to the bandstand the next night, the bear trap was in front of his stand. And, man, those cats would rather for you to beat him up then to put a bear trap in front of his stand. They'd carry on and cry and "Oh, man, I ain't done nothing like that. No, no these cats are wrong, they got the trap out there in front of my stand." And we'd leave the bear trap there. So it was hard to get by that bear in that band, you know. And if you had a bear, you got trapped.

You played the old whorehouses of Kansas City, didn't you? What kind of music would you play?

I used to play every kind of music in the whorehouses. They'd be sitting around, table over there, maybe table over there, somebody upstairs, somebody downstairs and you just reminiscing the blues or whatever you're playing on piano. You'd hear some old guy saying "Hey, hit that blue note again."

I think it's the reason a lot of people like the blues because they assimilate those sevenths that you use with the blues. They assimilate that as a "blue note," you know, telling them that they got the blues. See, because they used to request all kinds of numbers in Kansas City during that time. And when I come into Kansas City, that's when I found out that they used to have tunes, they called "old money tunes." See there's cats that come in there and ask for these funny way out tunes, but he's got probably a hundred dollar bill, fifty dollar bill in his hand. Happened one night some cat come in, "Hey, you guys know 'Old Black Joe'?" "Naw, never heard of it." This guy said, "Man, I been trying to get these guys to play my song all night." He said, "Hot damn, they don't know it." "These guys don't know it?" "No." So somebody must have put him hip cuz the next time he come back he says, "It's too bad you guys didn't know 'Old Black Joe' yet." He had a hundred dollar bill in his hand. One of the cats snatches it out of his hand and he said "Hell, why didn't you say 'Old Black Joe'? I didn't know that was what you was talking about. Shit," and grabbed the hundred and he said, "Hey, man, well, what about the rest of the guys, do they know it?" He say, "Hell, yes, if they don't, we'll get it."

Part 3

Artists Who Helped Build Stony Plain Records

Maria Muldaur

(Born 1943)

Bonnie Raitt

(Born 1949)

Maria Muldaur has rightly been called "America's First Lady of Roots Music." From her early years with John Sebastian, David Grisman, and Stefan Grossman in the Even Dozen Jug Band and Jim Kweskin and his Jug Band in the sixties to her country blues, mountain music, classic jazz and New Orleans R&B releases, her music has been beyond categorizing. Her first solo albums in the mid-seventies were some of the most eclectic in recorded history and included the hit singles "Midnight at the Oasis" and "It Ain't The Meat (It's The Motion)." Now, with over thirty diverse solo albums to her credit, Maria's freestyle spirit has seen her collaborate with Mavis Staples, Taj Mahal, Hoagy Carmichael, Amos Garrett, Dr. John, Doc Watson, Charles Brown, Aaron Neville, Linda Ronstadt, Rory Block, Eric Bibb, Bonnie Raitt, and so many more. All of Maria's work has been from the heart and shows a depth of roots music knowledge and devotion. I've been fortunate to work on many of Maria's releases since Stony Plain put out *Sweet and Slow* in 1983 that featured Dr. John on piano on one side and Kenny Barron on the other, followed by *Jazzabelle* (1993). In 1998 Maria and I were in Memphis at the W.C. Handy Awards. A trip to Memphis Minnie's gravesite in Walls, Mississippi, inspired 2001's *Richland Woman Blues* celebrating the early blues of the 1920s and '30s. Collaborations with fellow "keepers of the flame" resulted in *Sweet Lovin' Ol' Soul* in 2005, *Naughty, Bawdy and Blue* in 2007 and 2009's *Maria Muldaur and her Garden of Joy*, with more to follow. Each project starts with Maria's in-depth search for material from the era and as a "hand's-on" producer selecting the right players and setting the bar high for integrity by serving the music.

Maria calls Bonnie Raitt her "soul sister" and has been inspired by her both as a person and an artist. They've been friends since 1972 and share a dedication and passion for all roots music. Bonnie has done so much to support the original artists who created the music by recording and touring with them. She continues to wave the flag and fight for artists' rights at every opportunity, as a board member of the Rhythm and Blues Foundation. She is also active in many charities. Maria and Bonnie have done many projects together and share a deep love for the blues singers and players they've known and been mentored by like Victoria Spivey, Sippie Wallace, Son House, Mississippi Fred McDowell, Buddy Guy, Junior Wells, Ruth Brown, and Charles Brown. This interview, the first with the two of them together, was done at the Blues Awards in Memphis in May of 2010—the day after Bonnie Raitt received her Blues Hall Of Fame Award. Bonnie's old friend Dick Waterman, writer, photographer and former manager for Son House, Mississippi Fred McDowell, Skip James, Mississippi John Hurt, Buddy Guy and Junior Wells, inducted her.

Bonnie Raitt and Maria Muldaur, 2010 Blues Awards, Memphis.
Photo: Holger Petersen.

Maria Muldaur, Marcia Ball, and Bettye LaVette, Blues Awards, Memphis, 2010.
Photo: Holger Petersen.

Maria Muldaur and BB King, Memphis 2009. Photo: Holger Petersen.

Maria Muldaur and Taj Mahal, Memphis 2009. Photo: Holger Petersen.

First of all, Bonnie, congratulations on your award last night. It was a wonderful occasion to be part of, not only for yourself I'm sure, but just a great feeling for the blues community overall.

BR: Yeah, the tribal gathering feel is just such a wonderful affirmation, especially when the music business is in such turmoil and so many record labels and radio stations are closing down and artists are struggling. This is just a real coming together to reaffirm how much this music has touched everybody and you can't turn it loose. Everybody loves each other and the music.

And a real reminder, I think, of what both you and Maria have done over the years to support the music and turn people on to the music. I really appreciate this opportunity to talk to both of you today. Thank you.

BR: Hey, we never get to do a dual interview: this is great. It takes a special man, Holger. (laughter)

Bonnie, were you aware of Maria's recordings before you actually met?

BR: Oh, yeah, I was a huge fan of the Kweskin Jug Band. I went to college in Cambridge and in '68 I came to see them at the Symphony Hall of Boston. The Symphony Hall was a big highlight of my year in school and Maria was just the Queen of the Hop: I loved her voice, I loved her choice of music...and the Kweskin Jug Band. You guys turned me on to jug band music; I wasn't familiar with it.

MM: Really?

BR: They were legends. You know–Koerner, Ray & Glover, the Kweskin Jug Band, John Hammond, Dave Van Ronk, and Odetta–that was my stuff and the bluesy part of the world.

Last night we heard Dick Waterman say that you and Dick met through Son House. It was actually the first occasion of your first meeting with Son House as well. What a way to start.

BR: You got that right. He was on a radio interview at the Harvard Radio Station and my friend called me up and said, "I know where the manager lives. He's right on Garfield Street" or something, and he said, "Would you like to go meet Son?" and I just dropped whatever deadline I had in school and we went over and met Dick and Son House. I mean, it was like someone saying that Muhammad had showed up—would you like to say hi to Jesus or something.

MM: Really, that's just about it.

BR: He was as charismatic and enigmatic as you might imagine; such a gorgeous man, powerful presence and he just represented so much history. So for me, who grew up with records only, that was my first experience actually meeting someone who really lived the blues.

Maria, do you remember the occasion of meeting Bonnie for the first time?

MM: Very clearly. After living in Cambridge, Massachusetts, for a number of years with the Kweskin Jug Band and my then-husband, Geoff Muldaur, the Kweskin Band broke up in about 1969 and we moved to Woodstock, New York, Geoff and I, and became part of the very, very fertile musical community there. I mean the hills and the woods were literally alive with the sound of music. There were people like, well, Bob Dylan and the Band and Todd Rundgren and the Paul Butterfield Blues Band and just so many wonderful musicians all exchanging musical ideas and cross-pollinating all kinds of wonderful creative projects together...

BR: ...and each other's love lives.

MM: Now, that's a subject for a different interview.

BR: It was a small town.

MM: But, anyway, so that's where I was. I had recently settled there and one day somebody at the Bearsville Studio called me up and said, "You have got to come down right now. There is this young woman here singing the blues. She is doing her second record. She is so hot you're just going to love her, come on down." And I went on down there. This was about the time when the musical and personal partnership between Geoff and I was starting to fray around the edges. People were suggesting to me that maybe I might want to strike out on my own if that [the breakup] were to become an eventuality, but I had no vision of myself. I couldn't imagine how I would be a solo artist. So I go trundle down to the studio and there's this sassy, hot, young, red-headed gal with her guitar in hand telling the guys in the band what to do. I think Freebo was there and who else?

BR: Well, Dennis Whitted, who was playing with Paul Butterfield at the time, he was playing drums...

MM: There were some horns, I think.

BR: Yeah, Marty Grebb and Terry Eaton who where in the [Fabulous] Rhinestones.

MM: Right, right,

BR: There were so many bands. Eric Kaz was around. This was 1972.

MM: Yeah, this was a studio in the woods, literally in the woods.

BR: Which is owned by Albert Grossman and the Band. The Bearsville Studio is legendary: many, many great records have come out of there.

MM: I'm in behind the glass and I'm introduced to her and I just sat there all night and went back several times just in awe and fell in love with her immediately.

BR: Well, you can imagine how thrilled I was. I was so glad that you liked what I did, and that I could tell you that I always thought that you should make a solo record. And I was so happy when you went off and did it.

MM: Well, I did and I...

BR: ...and you had a little success, I might add, right out of the bag.

MM: Just a little bit. But it was really watching you that night and hearing what you did and your command, not only of your instrument (your voice), but of the band and how you wanted it to sound. That you just had the pluck to tell them exactly what you wanted to hear–that was just a revelation to me. It was the first thing that gave me the vision that such a thing might be possible and, so, I thank you all these years later. But she's gone on to just continue to inspire me, record after record, project after project. Not only her voice, which just slays me, I mean, I don't think there's a better ballad singer anywhere, besides all your hot stuff that you do with the blues, but it's always so heartfelt. And, another thing, now that we're here talking together on the air for the first time, another thing I love about your singing, Bonnie, is how you can blend with people. I've had the great pleasure of singing and jamming with you live, but also you've been gracious enough to come and be on several of my different projects. The way you can, as unique as your voice is, find a way of melding with whoever you're singing with and I hear that on, of course, a lot of other duets you do, you've got a really unique gift of that and that means you're listening, which is not something all musicians do.

BR: Well, now that we're having this mutual admiration, I've got to say that I learned so much about sass and subtlety and vulnerability and riding that train of revealing yourself and also just standing up from your attitude. I mean, to me, you were an honest modern blues woman. I fell in love with a lot of old-time music through you. It's hard to divorce our long-time friendship and go back to that time, but over the years, your commitment to creating a wonderful new synthesis of older musical forms and making them your own and your choice of musicians and producers, and your ability to sing and adapt and yet always sound like yourself, has made me feel that it makes us real sisters because everything you just said to me, I could say right back to you. And the fact that you put out these records yearly, sometimes twice a year, and each one of them is so special. I'm lucky to live in the same town as Maria and often I'm around when she calls and says, "Guess what? I just figured out what my next project's going to be and it came like an inspiration from heaven!" Sharing her joy in that because I feel that each one of her records is so much the right record at the right time and yet timeless. And if anyone ever deserved a Lifetime Achievement Award for keeping the blues alive and to be inducted into this Hall of Fame, it's you. So I'm lobbying for that now!

MM: Wow. All right, well, right back at ya. I'm speechless and that's unusual.

BR: We're both verklempt and glad for having waterproof mascara.

Who was it who first discovered Sippie Wallace? I gather that would have been you, Maria, because you recorded with her the first time.

MM: I was in the Kweskin Band, I think it was about 1967 or '68 (I can't remember the exact year), but we had a very ardent teenage fan in Detroit. His name was Ron Harwood and he came to all our gigs and it was back in those days when you used to go to a town and play for a week, remember the luxury of that? You actually got to meet cool people in the town who would then come and take you to the local zoo or to a good Greek restaurant or whatever. So, he was just a staunch fan of ours and we kept in touch with him and one day he calls up Jim Kweskin and says, "Jim, I'm not sure, but I think I found Sippie Wallace playing in a little church down in my neighbourhood," and we went, "You mean 'Up the Country Blues' Sippie Wallace?" He said, "Yeah, I think it's her. That's her name and her voice." So, Jim went on out there and it turned out it was indeed this woman that, to us, like so many of the other artists you were mentioning, they were like these mystical, mythical figures coming out of the misty past on these scratchy old 78s. How lucky we were that we were around to find so many of them alive and well. So, as it was in this case, she was playing a little church in her neighbourhood and at first we were so excited and tried to ask her to come to New York and to bring her out of retirement. First she said, "No, I just like to play the piano in my church. I don't do the blues anymore," but I think with a little coaxing, she warmed up to the idea. We brought her back east, we put her up in concert at Town Hall, then we did a record with her. We brought Otis Spann in from Chicago and backed her up on a record and I sang "Separation Blues" with her on that record and a couple of other little things and that brought her out of retirement and then I guess that's when you first heard her...

BR: Yeah, and in between she had gone to Europe as part of the Lippman + Rau American Folk Blues Festival. Legendary. The most important footage ever historically, the greatest DVDs that anyone who loves music can get: The American Folk Blues '62 to '65. And Sippie Wallace got up and played with Roosevelt Sykes and Little Brother Montgomery and they recorded an album that I found when I was eighteen in London at Dobell's Record Store and I just saw the cover with this kind of faux fur, rhinestone cat's eye glasses. She used to later love to wear a kind of hat that really was like a pimp hat in the seventies...

MM: ...the hat with the big plume...

BR: ...and it was *Sippie Wallace Sings the Blues* and I went, "This is from two years ago; she's alive!" This was before I knew that Maria had met her and I didn't know if she was still alive at that time. I'd cut a couple of her songs on my first album and then we found out from the Ann Arbor Blues and Jazz Festival people or somehow the word got to us when we looked for royalties, that she was actually alive. So we invited her to come out to the historic Ann Arbor Blues and Jazz Festival in '72 and she wasn't going to do blues, she'd come out and take a bow, but she wasn't gonna sing the blues anymore because, like a lot of elderly blues people when they're getting closer to going, she wanted to get in good with god and not sing the devil's music. But she sat in the trailer and we were rehearsing "Women Be Wise" with John Payne on soprano sax. [to Muldaur] (He was on the album that

I met you on.) She just started to go back and forth in this seat in the trailer and said, "Hmm, that sounds pretty good. Well, maybe, I could just do one." And she went out and there were thousands of people that were so floored that this woman, the classic blues singer—lived right in Detroit. It was my first day meeting her and you know how that was, to have your idol right there in front of you! So, how great it was for us, within a few years of each other, to each get to record with Sippie....And then she and I toured together for many, many years, like fifteen years. But Maria, that album you guys made, I hope it gets reissued. Is it out on CD?

MM: Which one?

BR: The Kweskin and Sippie one?

MM: I think it is. That would be something for Stony Plain to reissue, wouldn't it?

BR: But she was just something else.

MM: And I've got to just quickly say—when she was eighty-four, I happened to be in Detroit doing a Broadway show and they decided to have an eighty-fourth birthday party for her. Bonnie came out and Dr. John and James Dapogny and the Chicago Jazz Band that used to back her up when she did her performances because now she was right back in the swing, and we did a wonderful tribute concert to her. And she came out in her gown and her gloves that came up to her elbow that had no fingers, and just put on a show.

BR: Play it, Maestro! That's what she used to say.

MM: Yeah. And at the end of the show, there was birthday cake and so forth and people were saying, "Okay, Sippie, now if you want to go home..." Well, she happened to overhear that Dr. John and I were about to fly back to New York and do a little project, a little duet project together, and she wouldn't leave. She said, "I wanna teach them this song" and here she is at eighty-four, she's been up all night...

BR: Sound checks, everything.

MM: Yeah, sound check, the whole thing and she teaches me a song that she used to do with Louis Armstrong, which is called "Adam and Eve Got the Blues." So here she was about twelve-thirty, one in the morning and she's pitching songs for us to do on the album and I'm so glad she did because it's a classic and I recorded it.

BR: Oh, that great song, you know? "When Adam ate the fruit from the good tree of which the Lord had forbid them not," or something like that.

MM: [sings] Adam said Lord, now don't blame me, cuz every woman's crazy 'bout that good old tree. Adam and Eve they ate the fruit they got confused and Adam and Eve got the blues.

BR: Since that day,

Singing Together: Everybody's had the blues.

MM: I always introduce it by saying it's Sippie's own interpretation of the second book of Genesis.

BR: Exactly. It even trumps R. Crumb. Have you seen that R. Crumb book of Genesis? He's drawn Genesis; it's fantastic. You'd love it. I always thought that Maria should have all of her artwork done by R. Crumb.

MM: Which we kind of did on the new album. [*Maria Muldaur and Her Garden Of Joy*]

BR: That's exactly right.

I'd love to get a few remembrances of Mississippi Fred McDowell from both of you. Bonnie, Fred McDowell is someone you still pay tribute to with the Kokomo Medley in your live act. "It's a Blessing" is such an amazing track that the two of you [Bonnie and Maria] recorded together. Fred McDowell and his family, I believe, first recorded that tune. Bonnie, did you know Fred McDowell before Maria did?

BR: I did. Dick Waterman, who was the man I met Son House through, had managed Mississippi John Hurt and Skip James. I missed John Hurt, who passed away before I met Dick, but I met Fred McDowell through Dick and we immediately loved each other. It was just a soul connection. I mean, I was very lucky to later have a very close friendship with Sippie [Wallace], Charles [Brown], and John Lee [Hooker], but Fred was my first deep relationship and our closeness was one of my greatest gifts. I still miss him. I opened quite a few shows for him. He sadly developed stomach cancer and they didn't want to tell him. I was going to record a duet of his "Kokomo Blues" with him on that *Give It Up* album and he passed away. It was the most difficult thing—at that point I was twenty-two and it was the hardest thing I had ever gone through. First of many losses to come when you get close to those older people, but Fred was just devastating, so I couldn't sing it again on that record. I couldn't do it. I waited for my third album to record it.

MM: Did he teach you a lot about slide guitar? That's what I've always heard.

BR: Not so much physically, but soul-wise from loving his music.

MM: I loved him, too. I didn't know him like you. I was just thrilled to meet him backstage at Newport or various little places. Sometimes it was just so amazing: they [the blues artists] would play these little church basements or coffee houses and we'd be just sitting there at their feet absorbing not only the music, but so much more was coming through them then just the music.

BR: And the joy that these blues people had from being brought out of such different settings into such sudden acclaim. So many of them had been forgotten, gone off to get other jobs and lives. So for them to get re-discovered and have this new, incredible (mostly white) audience the world around, thanks to Europe mostly, but Newport Folk Festival '63/'64 introduced all those people to a wider audience. Can you imagine what a change that was? To sit in the audience and see how much fun they were having, to be treated like royalty; I mean, nobody loved playing better than Fred and it was really hard to believe that he and Muddy Waters were as unhappy as some of those blues were because they were some of the happiest guys I've ever met in my life.

MM: Oh, yeah, they were and they spread that joy, too. Also, for us who lived in the urban North, well, [Bonnie] you lived in California, but so out of the rural South and the birthplace of all this music. The lessons were more than just musical—they were life lessons.

Being around those artists and, in the case with Dick Waterman, it was not just a management/professional situation. I gather that you got to know them really well and took care of them when they needed health benefits and when they needed hospitalization. And [helping them cope with] the cultural shock that they were going through. It was more than just getting them gigs and being around them, it was really becoming part of their families I would imagine.

BR: Yeah, and especially because I grew up idolizing this music and it wasn't something I was planning to do with my life. I was majoring in Social Relations and African Studies at college and always played the guitar as a fan. So, for me, when I found out how little they got paid, that they didn't get royalties, that at some point within a few years my draw would eclipse theirs and it just felt...it was not right. So I just said, I can't control (anymore than I can now) whether Stevie Ray Vaughan made more money than Buddy Guy for a while. And now Stevie Ray's gone and a lot of other blues people like Buddy are up there being able to make money—partly by process of elimination. I made sure, I said—I'm grateful that I'm getting this following, but I'm going to make sure that the people on the bill with me who I idolize, that I pay them better than what their agencies are asking. I mean it's not fair that this sociological upturn of white kids, white people getting paid more than black. I mean, I knew that Pat Boone got the hit and Bill Haley got the hit, but the originators, Big Joe Turner and Little Richard, all those guys didn't get paid. And Ruth Brown. So I didn't want to be a part of that rip-off and Maria was the same.

Yeah, both of you worked with Ruth Brown and that must have been an incredible experience.

MM: I don't remember working with Ruth Brown, but I admired her greatly. When I was a young teenager, I was already checking out her hits on the R&B station. I was listening to R&B before it morphed into rock and roll and loved her voice.

BR: Yeah, you being just a little bit older than me, you got in. And growing up in Greenwich Village, to me, it seems like Mecca to hear you talk about your background. You got to be around for all the beatniks and all the folk music and all those clubs. I would have shredded to be in your place. I just raced to get old enough when I got to Cambridge and it was too late, everybody had moved away, Club 47 was closed.

But, yeah, Ruth Brown was a dear friend of mine and it was because of her royalty plight that the Rhythm and Blues Foundation was formed. At the fortieth anniversary of Atlantic Records, they had a huge Madison Square Garden party with Led Zeppelin and LaVern Baker and Ruth Brown and all these artists that made the label. But the fact that Ruth and LaVern and so many others from the early years had yet to receive record royalties due to the unfairly small percentage of royalties allotted back then, as well has having all the costs of the album charged back to their accounts, was too glaring an injustice not to be addressed. Thankfully, a Washington DC lawyer/music fan, Howell Begle, who represented a lot of those artists, went to bat with Ahmet Ertegun, who agreed to put up an endowment for the R&B Foundation, which could at least start the ball rolling for changing royalty policies and lobbying for funding and health insurance from the other record labels. It took thirteen years for most of them to come around and of course, with downloading and bootlegging, there aren't really any royalties to speak of any more. But the Foundation has had twenty years of magnificent Pioneer Awards shows, honouring and gifting with a cheque, those legends, many of whom have never had their due respect or money. We were able to give out hundreds of thousands in grants to those with financial and medical emergencies. We owe those artists so much. Wouldn't be here without them.

MM: You know, I gotta say, I was so happy to be with you when you got inducted into the Blues Hall of Fame. I just loved when you got up there and what you said and how you, again, started crusading for the rights of these blues artists who have been overlooked and I went to bed thinking: she is the Joan of Arc of the Blues. Everything you do is with such heart and with such purpose and such a sense of justice.

BR: Thank you. Well, that Quaker background my folks had, it was really that....So many of us artists cover songs made famous by our heroes, it's only right that we contribute something to those who weren't from a time or didn't have the lawyers to negotiate a fairer royalty rate. So many of them have sold millions of records and still haven't been paid. Don't get me started!

MM: Don't get her started, she'll tell ya everything she knows!

BR: But wasn't that great what they were talking about last night? How some people actually did keep their royalties?

MM: Like W.C. Handy.

BR: Exactly. But it's so rare because they didn't have the education about the music business. We knew lawyers.

MM: Who knew? You know the joy of making music is something you don't want to sully with all that business-minded stuff but, thank god, some people did it. And something I want to bring up while we're talking about that: another woman artist, who I was blessed to be mentored by when I was not even twenty years old, named Victoria Spivey. She was another one of those classic blues queens, a contemporary of Bessie Smith, who had quite a few hits and was just gorgeous in her day, and was even in a few movies. And then when the classic blues queen era subsided, she moved on up to New York. She's one of the few who survived. And when I first hit the folk scene in the early sixties, she was the presiding queen of that scene and, as far as I know, the first artist I know of to be savvy enough to have started her own record label—Spivey Records—and she was the first person to have recorded Bob Dylan, for instance, and also the first person to sign me on with the Even Dozen Jug Band.

BR: She was an entrepreneur like W.C. Handy. They probably were pals.

MM: And who knows what else?

BR: Exactly.

Thank you so much. I really appreciate you both giving me this opportunity.

BR: And I want to say: Sister Rosetta Tharpe and Memphis Minnie were, of course, pioneers as women who played the guitar. I wasn't as exposed to them until later years and fell in love with Memphis Minnie, knew her story, and Sister Rosetta, but you're the one that really knows so much about that. Maria: I honour your incredibly vast knowledge of so many kinds of old-time and bluegrass music and it's just astonishing to me how much you know about the blues.

MM: Just cuz I been around this long.

BR: And you just get better and better. Your voice and your attitude and your ability to drive the band and produce records. I salute you because you've made, we both have made, Victoria and Sippie proud.

MM: I feel they're smiling down on us.

BR: And Ruth Brown, too.

MM: We're carrying a tradition.

BR: Joan of Arc and Mother Jugs (laughter).

BR: [To Me] Thank you for having us. [To Maria] We should have our own talk show. This is the other view.

Leon Bibb
(Born 1922)
Eric Bibb
(Born 1951)

Leon Bibb arrived on the New York scene in the mid-fifties from Kentucky. As a trained singer, he was able to appear in musical theatre and on Broadway in addition to being part of the folk scene. His role model became Paul Robeson, the brilliant renaissance man. Like Paul Robeson, Leon was blacklisted during the McCarthy era for alleged ties to left-wing groups and causes. During the sixties he was featured on the national television program *Hootenanny*, toured internationally, and recorded extensively for the RCA label. Leon moved to Vancouver in 1969 where he continues to be active as a singer and educator. Leon's son Eric (Paul Robeson is his godfather) grew up in New York surrounded by musicians, writers, and artists, like Pete Seeger, Odetta, and his uncle, John Lewis, who played with the Modern Jazz Quartet. Eric lived in Sweden before beginning his recording career on the Opus 3 label. Eric's reputation grew internationally by the late nineties. His recordings include collaborations with artists like Pops and Mavis Staples, Taj Mahal, Wilson Pickett, Maria Muldaur, Bonnie Raitt, Rory Block, Mamadou Diabaté and Djelimady Tounkara.

Stony Plain released the duet album *Praising Peace* by Eric and Leon Bibb in 2006. The heartfelt recording revisits the music and message of Paul Robeson. They created a historically important and timeless tribute. I spoke with them backstage at the Vancouver Island MusicFest in July of 2009.

L: Leon Bibb, Edmonton, 2007. Photo: Holger Petersen.
R: Eric Bibb, Edmonton, 2007. Photo: Holger Petersen.

Leon and Eric Bibb, Canmore, Alberta, 2003. Photo: Holger Petersen.

Here we are backstage at the Island MusicFest and, Leon, it brings to mind the fact that when you look at folk festivals over the years, it really started with Newport: the blueprint for what we have today in North America and around the world. You were at one of the very first Newport Festivals. That would have been in the late fifties. Is that right?

LB: Yes, I think it was.

EB: '58 or '59

LB: See Eric knows more about these things and remembers these things better than I do.

What do you remember about the early Newport Festival and your performances?

LB: Well, is was a great deal smaller and while it was substantial for those times, it was new. I remember that it was a *new* experience—musical experience—and there were not nearly the number of genres of music played. It was centred on "folk" songs and "folk" music. Pete Seeger was in the Weavers and those kinds of people played. I was an interloper at that time. As a trained singer, I wasn't a folksinger as such, but I loved folk songs. I loved love songs (in English and Irish) and ballads and chain-gang songs—I mixed up with that—so, in that regard, I was different. Earl Rosenthal, my manager, started me. He accepted the fact that there would be a harder road to travel, but he supported me for so many years and by that time I had established a career and I've been very fortunate ever since. When I say trained, I was trained to be on the stage. We had no microphones and I was trained to sing diaphragmatically supported and the whole thing. To that extent, I was totally different sound wise, except I sang chain-gang songs. But the ballads were some of the things that I really most enjoyed.

Eric, I know you were very young when Newport started, but do you remember your first festival?

EB: Yeah, actually I remember vividly—there were others probably that preceded it—but I remember vividly the Newport Folk Festival in 1965. That was the year that Dylan bombed out because he went electric. But it was the year that I went with Barbara Dane and her sons and I remember we were given the job (as fourteen-year-olds) of guarding the Guild Guitar tent and we got to stay up late, late, late with all these beautiful guitars surrounding us that we could play. But that was the year that I met and had a wonderful conversation with the Chambers Brothers, particularly Lester. It was the year that I saw the great Son House perform live. He completely blew my mind singing "Empire State Express." Tim Hardin was there. I went to a party and Dylan was sitting at the top of the steps in a grey top hat. He didn't say anything to anybody, but we clocked him, you know. That's what I remember about that festival. Yeah.

Newport '65 also had a couple of albums that came out that were dedicated to the blues artists of Newport and apart from Son House, I believe, Mississippi John Hurt, Fred McDowell, Sonny Terry, and Brownie McGhee. I know the effect that Mississippi John Hurt has had on your music and to this day there is a certain touch and certain sound that he had that is very unique and that I hear in your playing. Did you meet Mississippi John Hurt back then?

EB: You know, I didn't. He was around that whole coffee house scene that had a wonderful way of giving John Hurt and some of his contemporaries, his generation, a second career. I mean, there was Fred McDowell (as you mentioned), there was Skip James, there was Bukka White (he didn't like to be called Bukka).

What did he want to be called?

EB: Booker. His name was Booker Washington White. There was Mance Lipscomb, at that time. But John Hurt, of all the rediscovered folk/blues artists of the era, was the one that touched me most deeply—and they all did—but John Hurt had a demeanour, something about his whole persona that was so gentle. I call him the Dalai Lama of the country blues because he was so serene. This guy just seemed like he knew something and he wasn't telling, he was just going to let you figure it out. But his gentle manner and he was really also very strong. I remember reading a book about an arm wrestling match that he had with somebody who was really like forty years his junior. He was a farmer so he was quiet, but he had these huge biceps and he just hammered him down. But you'd never know it, he was so gentle—his touch was so gentle. His singing was just totally unforced. There was nothing forced about that man; he was just breathing in time with the music and he's a hero of mine for sure.

I'm so glad that you continue to do his material and honour him in virtually every performance that you do.

EB: Yeah, there are a couple of songs I'd like to add to the repertoire that he put on the map. The one that I'm doing consistently is "Stagger Lee" and his version was really what triggered my arrangement: some kind of a combination of his version and a later version by Taj Mahal that really got me into that tune. But there are so many wonderful songs. He played everything: he played spirituals, he played all kinds of old dance tunes. He was really one of those real, what I call, songster-troubadours who had a very mixed-bag repertoire. He wasn't really a blues player. He had a great way of playing blues-like material, but he was a local musician who played at country dances and played with fiddle players—black and white. He had a real sense of what people liked to hear. He played religious songs on his porch. And then he found out that everybody wanted to hear anything he wanted to play. He did all those great Library of Congress recordings, you know, Smithsonian things, and you could just hear this man was a trove, like Lead Belly, of all kinds of songs.

Leon, when you arrived in New York in the mid-fifties, Lead Belly would have still been around. Did you know Lead Belly at all?

LB: I didn't know him. I heard him one time and I'm trying to remember now where I did hear him. But I remember just *power*, just to walk on a stage, he had that ability to freeze the audience. They just got absolutely dead quiet wherever he played. You know, in those days they played in places where people talked. They listened, intently listened, but they would talk through half, not half but part, of the first song as it was finishing and he would just wait and wait until they were done. He didn't say anything. He didn't say "I'm about ready to perform" or anything like that, he just stood there waiting and everybody began to feel the person next to them get quiet and so they began to get quiet and they began to look at the stage and there he was just standing, waiting. He didn't even start.

Eric, there must have been a lot of music around the house that you would have absorbed...jam sessions, just people dropping by.

EB: When it comes to live music, making live music, here's my memory and it's a great memory. We were really close friends with Millard Lampell one of the Almanac Singers. Woody Guthrie, Millard Lampell, and Pete Seeger, these were the original Almanac Singers, which morphed into the Weavers. And

I remember going over to see the Lampells on Riverside Drive in the Upper West Side of Manhattan and we'd go on little outings. Millard had a red convertible that he was really happy with and he would sing at the top of his lungs. And he's the first one who really introduced me directly to the whole Woody Guthrie collection of songs like "Hard Travelin'," "I been doin' some hard travelin', I thought you knowed." That was something I remembered from Millard singing, "It Takes a Worried Man to Sing a Worried Song," that's a great song. And Millard would just be howling at the wind, you know, and we'd be in the back like osmosis just sopping up these songs because he was a great storyteller. He was a braggart—really—a really eloquent braggart. That's the way I love remembering Millard Lampell.

But otherwise it was records. My dad had an incredible record collection. We'd buy records and people would give us records. I remember hearing people like Mike Settle. I remember hearing an early tape, a reel-to-reel tape, of Leonard Cohen. Leonard was pitching songs to known artists before he got on the map and I remember hearing a reel-to-reel tape of "Suzanne" and falling in love with that song and my dad ended up singing it. I remember listening to everybody from Morgana King singing "Lazy Afternoon" to Big Bill Broonzy to Mahalia Jackson to *Songs Of The Alvern*. Also, my uncle John Lewis with his wonderful music that he'd written with the Modern Jazz Quartet. So it was really a mixed bag.

But then I started on my own going into Greenwich Village on Sundays as an eleven-year-old. My parents just said "you can do it" and I packed up my little guitar and I'd take the subway an hour and a half into Manhattan from Queens and I'd hang out at the hootenannies in Washington Square Park, you know. Amazing.

And that literally was a park, I believe, with a statue and people would hang around.

EB: It was a fountain. There was a fountain right in the middle of the park and there'd be all manner of banjo, dulcimer, harmonica, washtub basses, you know, just everybody was there in little clusters making music. Even bongo players and steel pan players, it was just an amazing thing. Some great music I heard on those Sundays.

Leon, did you go down there as well?

LB: Occasionally I'd go, but there was a period where I wanted Eric to find his own way musically. As he just mentioned, his uncle was John Lewis of the Modern Jazz Quartet and he lived close enough to us where Eric could hear his music. His Mom was the sister of John and we had a lot of music in the house. I kept feeling that he was going to be a guitarist, singer possibly, but not a roots and blues artist. I really, quite frankly, don't remember the exact time he began to know about Robert Johnson.

EB: I do remember. I heard a lot of blues in the mix, you know? The whole folk music umbrella encompassed people like Brother John Sellers, Big Bill Broonzy, Lead Belly for sure, Josh White for sure. I heard all of that music growing up, but I didn't focus on acoustic country blues styles until later. Really the baptism was when I went to Paris when I was eighteen and I met the great Mickey Baker. Mickey Baker from Louisville, my dad's hometown, is a great jazz and blues guitarist who had recorded with people like Ray Charles and then he had that group Mickey & Sylvia that had hits like "Love is Strange." But Mickey was living in Paris and I was introduced to him and he kind of took me under his wing. And I remember he put me in a room, his dining room, and closed the doors with the tape recorder and said, "Just listen to this Eric," and it was Robert Johnson, King of the Delta Blues. This was the early seventies and I listened to it and I was completely mesmerized and I came out and said "Mickey, tell me that was two guitar players," and he said, "No, man, go back and listen one more time to the whole record." And I just couldn't believe that this was coming from one man. It was just mind boggling music and that kind of started a whole period of marinating myself in older country blues, pre-war blues. I then went to Stockholm and met a man with a great record store, Early Bird Records, a guy named Bjorn Hamrin, a great harmonica player, who had an amazing collection of records and that kind of just started a whole life.

The two of you recorded a wonderful CD called Praising Peace *in honour of Eric's godfather and Leon's close friend Paul Robeson. Leon, what effect did Paul Robeson had on you?*

LB : That's hard to talk about actually. Paul taught so many of us, in that period of time, great integrity and belief in one's feelings about peace and honouring the ability to protect your own privacy. He was attacked during the McCarthy period and he, like Pete Seeger, refused to even bend. I have the testimony that was taken during that period when he was before the House of Un-American Activities Committee and when they would ask him "Are you a communist?" he said, "You don't have the right to ask me that question" over and over. And when they took his passport, I along with, oh, you could name the so called supporters–[Harry] Belafonte, [Sidney] Poitier, Maya Angelou, Oss [Davis] and Ruby Dee, I mean, the list was long and lengthy. They would perform with him on stage and supported his efforts to retain his passport. I lived in New York at that time and unfortunately he didn't sing, he couldn't sing. He sang as much as he could, but he couldn't go to Europe and he couldn't go to Canada. And one of the really memorable acts was to stand on the back of a big huge (flatbed) truck with his pianist while it was being driven through the Peace Arch that sits partly in Washington State, partly in Canada, and sing to 53,000 people.

He was a marvellous, marvellous man. I used to tell this story: I heard his version of "Shenandoah" before hardly anybody else sang it and I began to sing it on stage with him. I asked him "I've been singing a song that you sing, could you help me with your interpretation?" And he did. I always think of him every time I sing the song and I sing the song almost every time I sing. It's a standard, if you will, in my whole repertoire and I will always sing it. He was a beautiful human being. You go back and talk to Eric, don't start me on Paul Robeson. Eric knows, I could talk all day for that.

What an honour it must be to go through life with Paul Robeson as your godfather? I'm sure that you remind yourself of that from time to time and have a little smile about that.

EB: I do. It's a tremendous source of empowerment. I remember as a kid, without knowing all of what it really meant, I sensed it and being able to say "Yeah, my godfather is Paul Robeson" was a statement that always left me kind of aglow for awhile. And as I got older and became more aware of who he really was and started reading, really started reading about his very adventurous journey, I was just amazed that this man, this renaissance man, seemed to have the courage of hundreds. He seemed to have the ambition and the stamina and the intelligence and the eloquence of so many, many people before him.

He just seemed like the embodiment of all that was really going to take—not only African-Americans, but a whole community of people bent on true democracy—them forward. He was just one of those people, bigger than life but also down to earth, very much down to earth from what I've read and sensed. He was at my christening, holding me in one big palm and my twin sister in another. He was mostly in exile or had to kind of retreat from the limelight during my childhood, but the photograph of him holding me in one palm and my sister in the other was kind of an icon in my life. It followed me wherever I travelled, when I moved to Europe. And I remember specifically a fan of Paul Robeson who met me somewhere in Europe who said "You know, you should do an album with your dad in tribute to Paul Robeson" and I thought, "What a great idea. Of course. It's a no-brainer." And we talked about it and it came together here in Canada so beautifully with Bill Sample, being our musical director, and the wonderful Paul Baker making his studio available. When I knew that we were going to make it, I decided to write an original song that I felt might have been suitable in Paul Robeson's repertoire. I wanted to compose a song as a writer. I just wanted to contribute a song that was inspired by his kind of music and I wrote a song called "On Our Journey." I think Paul had a song called "On My Journey" so it might have been inspired by that. I remember when I was writing it, I lived in England at the time, but I remember specifically this wonderful, eerie but very comfortable feeling that there was another presence around and I just felt like—yeah, if that's possible then Paul is here helping me write this song.

I really appreciate the Canadian connection and the fact that you recorded that album in Canada. But, Leon, you've had a presence here since the seventies when you moved to Canada.

LB: November 8, 1970. I came into Canada on a Visa permit. I have it still, a little piece of paper that says I could come into Canada. I drove across the country from New York with my furniture in a big van and got to the border and thought that I could just come on in to Canada: here I am. And a nice man at the border said. "Sir, you can't come into Canada just like that. You'll have to have papers that legally allow you to come into the country. I'm going to keep your furniture here; you go into Vancouver. I'll give you two days and you have to work out these papers." And I did. And I took the papers back and he gave me my furniture and I moved into North Vancouver. About three years ago, I was having dinner with some friends and the phone rang and I went to the phone and this man says, "Is this Leon Bibb?" and when people say things like that you always want to know who it is that's calling you that knows your name. I said "Who is calling?" and he said, "This is George Buxter. I let you into Canada." Yes, he did. He said "You came to the border with your furniture and I said no, but you came back a couple of days later and I said yes." It was a very moving experience to get that call.

Eric, you've got a Canadian connection because of your father and you've recorded in Alberta–Canmore and Edmonton. You've worked with Montreal's Michael Jerome Brown.

EB: Yeah, it's a rich connection. It always has been. I was delighted to discover Vancouver through my Dad's moving and then to discover the fabulous festivals that abound in Canada, particularly in Western Canada. I've had amazing experiences, unforgettable experiences having had a chance to be on stage with and record with (in local studios) people like Luis Campana, Taj Mahal, Djelimady Tounkara. This was been an amazing experience for me. Michael Jerome Browne is probably one of the finest musicians who is well versed in so many interrelated genres when it comes to roots, Americana, blues, Cajun, you name it, Michael has got it under his belt in a big way and instruments in his backpack. I first heard him on a Calgary Folk Music Festival stage and he was playing a gourd banjo with such authority and such knowledge of how far it goes back. It really sounded African to me. And I kind of accosted him as I do a lot of musicians I meet on stage in Canada. Ruthie Foster is another example of somebody who I just went right up to after their performance and said "Listen, we have to do something together. I won't let it be. I just won't be able to rest unless we're able to collaborate." And that's what I did with Michael and we ended up recording quite a few things and touring together as well. Any chance I get to hear Michael and then play with him is a chance I'll leap at.

So, yeah, the Canadian connection is deep and strong. I've had a chance to record with legends. Wilson Pickett, I recorded with, and the wonderful Linda Tillery and her wonderful Cultural Heritage Choir at a folk festival in Canada.

I remember that well. It was a gospel stage at the Edmonton Folk Festival and it was Wilson Pickett, yourself, Linda Tillery, and Colin Linden. Eric, any final thoughts about your father that you might like to contribute?

EB: Well, you know, one of the things people express to us pretty often when we have a chance to perform together (as we did at that wonderful workshop this morning), people are just really kind of lit up by the fact that a father and son are performing together and obviously having such a good time in each other's company. We never thought of it as an act or anything like that. We just knew that we would enjoy performing together if we got the chance and every time we do, we kind of leap at it. All I can say is, to be a part of a tradition, to have had music come through my dad to me and then to actually be able to show him the results of what his nutrition—fatherly love and musical inspiration—has come to after four or five decades, it's a gift that I never thought I would receive in such a way, but it's perfect, it's just perfect. It's like a full circle thing and it just tells me how blessed we are and how we do what we can, but the best plans are made probably somewhere else. We're just people who recognize it as the way to go and we go that way and it just turns out great.

Duke Robillard
(Born 1948)

The most productive relationship I've had during the years of Stony Plain has been with Duke Robillard. I was a long-time fan of his playing with Roomful Of Blues, his extensive session work, songwriting, and his solo projects when we first met in 1993 at the Winnipeg Folk Festival. After seeing him perform live with his exceptional band, I asked if he was interested in doing a straight-ahead blues guitar album—something he'd never done as a solo artist. Duke had just signed with Virgin Point Blank Records, a major label, but suggested he might be able to do a special project for Stony Plain as a Canada-only release since Virgin was more interested in recording the "rocking blues" side of his playing. Duke had recently left the Fabulous Thunderbirds (replacing Jimmie Vaughan) and Virgin wanted more of their sound, not straight-ahead blues.

To our surprise, Virgin agreed to let this small Canadian indie do a project which we called *Duke's Blues*. After its initial release in Canada, Virgin realized the worldwide potential and licensed it from Stony Plain. It went on to become one of Duke's best selling releases and started a flood of projects between us. I knew of Duke's love of Kansas City Jump Blues, which led him to produce Jimmy Witherspoon for us. This was the first outside project for Duke as a producer and he took it seriously. He wanted to record Spoon with a Hammond B3 and piano so the first thing he did was help rebuild the studio to accommodate both keyboards. Spoon flew to Rhode Island and finished the sessions ahead of schedule. Aside from producing the sessions, Duke arranged the material, played brilliant guitar, and got his old friend Scott Hamilton to play sax. Duke's also an acclaimed photographer, so he set up lighting and took photos for the packaging. He drove Spoon to the airport and, after arriving back home, told me he couldn't sleep so he wrote the liner notes. That's dedication.

Stony Plain has gone on to release fourteen Duke Robillard albums, two DVDs, and landmark recordings with Duke, Ronnie Earl, and Herb Ellis. In addition to albums with Jimmy Witherspoon, Duke has produced for Stony Plain, including albums for Joe Louis Walker, New Guitar Summit (with Jay Geils and Gerry Beaudoin), Sunny and her Joy Boys, Billy Boy Arnold, Rosco Gordon, the Rockin' Highliners, Doug James, Chris Flory, and Duke and I co-produced Jay McShann's albums together.

There is no end to Duke's creativity and energy. He's won four Blues Awards (formerly W.C. Handy Awards) as Guitarist Of The Year and one as Traditional Blues Artist of the Year. He has been nominated for two Grammy Awards. Outside of the blues world, Duke worked with Bob Dylan on *Time Out of Mind* and has toured as Tom Waits' guitarist. The following combines two interviews I did with Duke in 2001 and 2003.

Duke Robillard, Calgary Blues Festival, 2007. Photo: Holger Petersen.

Duke Robillard and BB King, 2009 Blues Awards, Memphis. Photo: Holger Petersen.

Holger with Duke Robillard, 2010 Grammy Awards, Los Angeles. Photo courtesy of Holger Petersen.

Although you've got a huge reputation and many blues awards as a blues player, I gather you've always been interested in all kinds of music?

I always have been from the start. I grew up in the very beginning listening to early country music, hearing that around my house, and then of course early rock and roll. I got introduced to the blues from the flip sides of Chuck Berry records, but I also got to—living in Rhode Island during the sixties—[go to] the Newport Folk Festival. It was just such an incredible eye-opening experience and to be able to go there and see Mississippi John Hurt and Skip James and Son House and all of these people. The whole—to me, all the music I listen to—the blues has been at the base of all of it, so I just consider it all roots music and all blues-influenced music from jazz to folk music.

You seem to have this great ability to find and write those double entendre songs that I guess were especially popular in R&B music in the forties and in country blues. You've always leaned towards the entertainment side of blues.

Well, there's just not enough of that today, I think. Song writing doesn't have the same flavour generally today as it did in the old days and I really do love that place that people like Louis Jordan came from. There's something—and this is a real strong point to me – there's something really beautiful about the old blues way of expressing sexual things that can imply an awful lot without ever saying it. It can be really funny and really entertaining. I used to back up Helen Humes, a great jazz singer who sang with Count Basie, and she used to have this song "Million Dollar Secret" and when she sang that—it was so bawdy, but it was so classy at the same time—I think that's something that I just really like: that type of sexual innuendo in blues rather than direct. With a lot of today's music, they use straight out profanity, which, I don't know, it's just like movies when they show you too much. In the old days they would make movies that would imply so much; it would make your imagination work. It's much more beautiful artistically, I think.

When you're on the road I know there are other things that occupy your day apart from playing music and driving to the gig, one of those happens to be collecting guitars. You must be familiar with just about every guitar store in every city in North America at this point?

Yeah, it's, I suppose, an addiction of mine. I just love guitars and always have since I was a little kid. When I was young I used to order catalogues from guitar companies and the day that they arrived to my house, I would have some kind of sensory thing where I'd know they were coming and I'd fake being sick and stay home from school and sit there and look at the catalogues all day. I don't know, they're things of beauty sound-wise and visually.

The guys in your band say that it's not unusual for you to go through quite a bit of gear: To go into a store and buy something or trade something. How many guitars do you go through on a regular basis?

Well, it's hard to say. There are periods where I might go for two or three years and pretty much use the same three or four guitars. But I might also purchase some in between along the way that I use at home for recording. But there are times where I weekly trade instruments and change and god knows why. I'm looking for that special certain thing. That one instrument that does everything, which is really impossible because I play so many different styles. It's a fairly harmless addiction.

Another one of your addictions is collecting vinyl, collecting records. How is that going as far as finding gems?

We go to a lot of towns where there are really good vinyl stores. Just recently in Dearborn, Michigan, I made a good score and bought six albums. One of the early Crown B.B. King albums, original cover and everything, great condition. That's something I've never actually owned. I've had the reissues–the United and all the sub-labels–but the original, very first *Singin' the Blues*, B.B. King with the original cover is a real thrill to find.

There must have been some pretty amazing record collections in Rhode Island in the fifties and sixties.

I would imagine there was. I know quite a few people who...one was a record store owner, Big Al Pavlow (who actually wrote a book on rhythm and blues), who has a house that...his house is just all records, you know? And he's still that way. And we had a great music store called Carl's Dig-ins that Carl Henry, who was a DJ and a promoter of the music and always a promoter of black music in Rhode Island. He had a lot to do with the popularity of jazz and rhythm and blues, and blues all throughout the fifties, sixties ,and seventies, and it was a sad day when his store closed, I'll tell ya.

What led you to start Roomful of Blues and have the vision of a horn band? It was going against the grain at the time. I don't think anybody had a jump blues horn band in the late sixties?

No, I don't think anybody did and the very first version of the band, the very first year, I didn't have horns: it was piano, bass, drums, guitar, and sometimes a harmonica player. I was playing B.B. King, Freddie King, Albert King material and Elmore James and Little Walter, Muddy Waters, and all the classic blues material, which, at that time, wasn't that old. I mean, the *Born Under a Bad Sign* album was only a few years old at the time I started the very first version of Roomful of Blues. They were actually fairly new records. *Freddy King Sings* wasn't really an old record at that time–shows you how old I am! But I heard this style and I pursued it and when I moved to Providence from Westerly, Rhode Island, it was a bigger city and there were a lot of antique stores or junk stores basically and I'd go through them to try to find records. I started finding 78s by Amos Milburn and Wynonie Harris and Big Joe Turner. Big Joe was one guy that I didn't know about early who I idolized and always loved that sound, but when I started discovering all of these people—T-Bone Walker and Ruth Brown and Roy Milton—just so many of them, and I just went WOW, this is the greatest thing because it's got the horns. It's got an element of jazz, the riff jazz, Kansas City kind of sound and it's blues and it's just got everything: it's tremendous music. And then when I discovered the Buddy Johnson Orchestra—that just did it. I heard that and I just thought, "Yeah, this is what I need" and I really didn't think about anything else. I was young and I was completely obsessed with what I was doing, and what was going on in the world didn't even faze me. I didn't know what was going on in the world; I was studying this music. What was on the radio, I missed all of that: I was oblivious. I was just a kid who was just into what he was into and oblivious of the world around me and I decided that I had to have that sound. We started off with Rich Lataille and Greg Piccolo both playing tenor (because Rich played tenor before he played alto) and that band lasted a little while. And the drummer was Fran Christina, who was the Thunderbirds' drummer for many years. He had moved to Kentucky with his wife because she had some job that she wanted to go to and at that point we kind of broke up for a short time and then we reformed with the horns. Then we found Doug James who was passing through town and we had heard about him so we auditioned him. That's where the beginning, with the full section with the three saxes started, which is still my favourite sounding Roomful of Blues. Those three guys together—Rich Lataille, Greg Piccolo and Doug [James]—had a really great section sound that was instantly recognizable the way a Basie sax section of the thirties or Ellington, I mean, it really was that recognizable and it really had a lot to do with Rich Lataille's alto playing. He had a very distinct pure tone. No one played with that kind of sound and that way at that time.

As a guitar player, to understand about arranging horns, were you a schooled musician or did you have a lot of help from the players?

Well, I always had an idea what the song should sound like and maybe what riff to play in it. And then Al Copley went to Berklee School of Music and had a good sense of harmony, and we all kind of pitched in together. I would kind of oversee it and very often have the basic riff idea, but, also, it just depends on the song because sometimes someone else would have the idea. But my job would also be to use something or veto it or whatever. I'd have the last say because at that point I was the person who was more knowledgeable about all the sounds because I was just a completely obsessed person. For ten years I listened to records about ten hours a day and that was my studying. It really didn't have anything to do with physically practising. In fact, I don't even know how I learned to play the swing style that I play, I never really practised it, I listened to it so much that it just got into my head and came out my fingers, you know?

Kansas City Jump Blues, you told me once, is your favourite style of music. Having worked with Jay McShann, it must have been a real thrill for you to get to know Jay and to earn his trust and work with him in the studio. It must have been one of your highlights, I would imagine.

Oh, it could be *the* highlight other than maybe opening for Count Basie or playing with Joe Turner and Eddie "Cleanhead" Vinson. It's right up there. But the fact that I got to produce him and play with him, yeah, the whole thing–just to be around Jay is unbelievable, as you know. He's just one of the warmest people and greatest characters. He's just a beautiful, beautiful person and to get to play with him takes you right back to that period. It's a trip into the real heyday of Kansas City just to be able to accompany him because he is just the embodiment of that entire sound.

And to also work with Jimmy Witherspoon, who was Jay McShann's singer for so many years. Even though Spoon wasn't from Kansas City, he really had that sound too, didn't he?

Oh, yeah. What was really special about working with Spoon, for me, is that when I first started listening to blues when I was in high school (I think maybe my last year of high school) I started getting a little more knowledge of other stuff. I still hadn't heard the old R&B records, but I had picked up a couple of Jimmy Witherspoon albums on Prestige and that was my first real taste of a jazz/blues combination, of guys like Kenny Burrell playing with Jimmy Witherspoon and it being blues and jazz at the same time and having that smooth feel, but still being very deep blues rooted music. Jimmy Witherspoon, I spent so many hours in my room when I was in high school listening to him over and over, those two or three albums *Evenin' Blues* and *Baby Baby Baby*, and, oh, I think there might have been one other one, but it really just made the biggest impression on me. It was something that—well, there was just nothing else like it in the world to me and I still feel that way about that music and, in my own way, I try to keep it [Witherspoon's music] alive because it's really one of the most soulful and entertaining but it's still, at the same time, intellectually moving too because you've got that jazz feel and time and improvisation. There are complexities to it that are really deep and beautiful and I'm trying to keep that out there.

I was just thinking back about...I think it would have been Spoon's last actual tour with the Duke Robillard Band that resulted in the live recording that Spoon and your band did in Vancouver. Remember when we were driving in your van with Spoon and he was listening to your big band tapes? I know he totally enjoyed it.

Oh, it was just so great. One minute he'd be sleeping then he'd wake up and say, "That's Ben Webster," who he played with a lot in the fifties and sixies, I guess. It got him really excited and, of course, once you hear that stuff and you know it, it never goes away. Even if he hadn't heard it in ten or twenty years, it instantly got him excited again about the music.

He told me he didn't listen to jazz and blues at home. He listened to what he called "elevator music" and that was about it. I think it was a real treat for him to be surrounded by people like Duke Robillard and your band.

Well, he was very cordial to me. He seemed to really enjoy working with me and working with the band and that was one of the greatest compliments I could have. And you can hear on the live album–you can hear the playfulness–the going back and forth between us, you know, myself or Gordon Beadle answering him and him laughing sometimes or stretching something out. There was a real lot of special interplay between the band on that recording.

You made two records with Herb Ellis. Was that kind of a dream come true for you to play with Herb?

Well, it was more than a dream: I was scared out of my mind, really. The first day, I was so scared I just didn't think I was going to be able to do it because I don't consider myself a jazz player: I'm a jazz influenced blues player. In the old days, blues players–very often early electric guitarists were blues players–could play some jazz. When they soloed they soloed on riff-type progressions that were simple and they were basically known. Even Charlie Parker, a lot of people say he's a blues player (of course, he could play on anything and he was tremendously advanced), but he was a blues player and all the early jazz guitarists were primarily blues players in the sense that it hadn't developed like the later guitarists, like Joe Pass and people like that re-harmonized everything and developed different techniques. The whole technique of soloing was based on the old style of blues playing and the single string early guitar playing by people like Eddie Lang.

The thing about Herb is that he is one of those guys who has a very strong blues influence in his playing and probably started off that way. I just listened to a Jimmy Dorsey recording the other day that he was on (and I didn't even realize before that he played with Jimmy Dorsey) and there was a fantastic guitar solo in there, incredibly technical. He was one of those people who really took jazz guitar to a new level. So for me, I can play some jazz tunes that are simple and I have a jazz feel, a definite jazz feeling and swing in my playing, but I was scared to death. Early on, I think maybe the first song we recorded, I turned the beat around and I was trying to do something and I slipped and I came out in the wrong place so I had the beat backwards and I had to stop the take, and I said, "Oh, Herb, I'm so sorry. I turned the beat around, I'm so embarrassed." And he looked at me and he went, "Shame on you" and he laughed, you know, and it immediately made me comfortable. And then he said, "You know, you can't just put any two guitar players together and have them sound this good. This is something special; we are working very well together." So him saying that gave me confidence to go on and be able to play the rest of the album because I was scared to death, but it really turned out great. As I told you, we initially intended to just record a few songs and we actually did two albums we had so much fun.

So many of the people that you've worked with are characters in a sense and I would put Rosco Gordon pretty close to the top of the list. It must have been a good time working with him.

Oh, Rosco is one of the greatest people. He's just got so much good energy and he's just such a nice guy and full of great stories and he's got just a wonderful personality, you just can't help but love him.

You made a beautiful record with Rosco called Memphis, Tennessee. *It was the first time Rosco had done a record like that in many, many years, but he really had the fire and it seemed like that was a project that went fairly quickly, too.*

Well, it was very similar to recording with Jimmy Witherspoon in a sense. As soon as we started and he heard what the band sounded like and realized that we could actually play his music correctly, he got very excited and just went for it. It was great.

You have a home studio now, Duke, how has that changed your life?

Well, it's a great thing because I've been able to mix a lot of the recordings that I've been doing for Stony Plain right in my house. In fact, three or four albums now I've done the mixing on myself. I've been able to just go down and work until I feel like I might be getting tired or might be losing my perspective and just go upstairs and continue with my normal life and when I'm ready for it again, I just go back down, which is really nice. The technical end of recording, the mixing, is very tedious and I've been known to fall asleep during mixing sessions: I was concentrating so much that after awhile my brain would just give out. I'm looking forward to the future because I think it's going to help me develop some things that I've got in the back of my head. Some different kinds of sound and different kinds of things that may be more experimental that I'll have the freedom to work on. So far I've had so many projects going that I haven't had the freedom [to work on]. I've had specific concepts and things, but it's nice to go into the recording studio with not too much on your mind, not knowing what you're going to do and kind of develop it on the spot where you're not worrying about the clock running (you're paying for this time even though you don't know it) and you don't know really what's going to come out of it. The beauty of a home studio is that you can allow yourself to just kind of have a stream of consciousness to experiment and develop music and maybe get that special thing on tape that's coming out of your head that minute that you might not have had a chance to do if you were in an actual session where you were trying to get a project done within a certain time and budget– restraints that you have when you do recording.

Your dog, Lucy Mae, is starting to become part of the Duke Robillard recording history.

Yeah, so far she's part of one tune on my blues album and I have a tune named after her on my jazz album called "Swinging with Lucy Mae" and we actually got her to bark on someone else's record–growl and bark–so she's a mascot for the studio. She actually sits on my lap and puts her paws up on the console when I mix sometimes; she seems to love it. She loves it when I'm down there. I have a chair that I call the client chair. It's a reclining leather chair with a footstool and she seems to claim that chair most of the time. She'll sit there and listen to me while I'm working on stuff.

And then there's the Doug James tune, "Dog Ate My Reed."

Oh, yeah, we did have a little problem with Lucy finding special affection for the cane reeds that Doug was using on his horns. I kept telling him, "You gotta leave 'em up high. It's not my fault. Don't complain about the dog eating your reed if you don't leave 'em up where she can't get them," because she loves those things.

You have a music book and autobiography that's just come out. Can you tell us about that?

Yeah, I'm excited about it. It's a book that includes a CD and the CD is about ten or twelve songs that are examples of the different styles I play. It's a home recording, but a very good recording and it's with a drummer and I play bass and rhythm guitar and the solo guitar, and the lead guitars on right and the rhythm guitars on left so you can hear exactly what I'm doing and everything is written out in tablature in the book. But it's also an extensive biography with my discography and stories about a lot of people I've played with over the years: Joe Turner, "Cleanhead" Vinson, people like that...Stevie Vaughan...just about everybody in the business who I've had a chance to work with. I've got tips on buying guitars and setting up guitars so it's pretty extensive and there's a lot of reading that I think people will find interesting. I think even if you're not a guitar player you could enjoy the CD because it's not like listening to a Duke Robillard instrumental CD and there's, I think, some pretty interesting reading.

You mentioned Stevie Ray Vaughan. I've never had a chance to ask you about him: you said that you played with him?

Oh, many, many times. I met Stevie the very first time I went to Texas with Roomful of Blues. Stevie was then unknown and pretty much a local guitar player. He was known as Jimmie's little brother; he hadn't really risen to popularity. He was known in Texas but....And he used to come and jam with us and sit in. When his first album came out he came to Rhode Island and we did a concert together at Rhode Island College and we played together on that. And any time that he was off and I played Antone's, he'd come down and sit in with us. Once we did a great show with the T-Birds when Jimmie Vaughan was in, I think Memphis, filming the Jerry Lee Lewis movie that he played a part in, and we did this benefit (it was a Christmas benefit the policemen had for children—toys for children), and the Thunderbirds did this concert. This was before I was in the Thunderbirds, but because of Jimmie's absence, they hired me and Stevie both to play guitar with the band and it was really great. I wish somebody had recorded it. It was a really special evening.

I wanted to ask you about sessions you did with Ronnie Earl. When you left Roomful of Blues, Ronnie Earl was your replacement in the band and I gather at that point he was handpicked by you. Had you kind of groomed him along the way?

Well, in a sense. I mean, I wasn't thinking that way, but when he started playing the blues, he used to always come around to hear us and we became friends and he sat in a lot. We did a lot of jamming back and forth, on stage between the two of us, so when I left, he was the obvious person to come in for guitar. Of course, they hired four people to replace me: Porky Cohen on trombone, Dan Motta on trumpet, Lou Ann Barton on vocals, and Ronnie on guitar so....But, yeah, Ronnie was the perfect guitar player to come in at that point and he had a real good long stint with them and a very fruitful one.

You have a duet CD with Ronnie Earl, The Duke Meets The Earl. *I think it's absolutely great playing all around. You're the producer as well. How did you feel about making a record with Ronnie after all those years of being on stage with him?*

Well, it was definitely an experience very similar to what we used to have in the old days and we don't really see each other very much anymore, so it was a lot of fun in the sense of getting to have a lot of those guitar battles, friendly battles, not trying to outdo each other, but put a lot of feeling into it and respond to each other and be egged on by each other, so it was real fun. I think people are going to love it because it's both very live and very real and us playing very well.

I wanted to ask you about the New Guitar Summit shows that you occasionally do and the albums that you've done. How did this come together?

Well, Jay (Geils) and I have known each other since probably the late sixties. We didn't run across each other's paths very often, once in a while we did a show or two together with The J. Geils Band. But Gerry Beaudoin, a jazz guitarist from the Boston area, was friends with me and friends with Jay, and Gerry occasionally did little jazz gigs with me and with Jay. Jay's been interested in jazz guitar for quite a while now and it has been his main focus, playing jazz guitar. One night when Gerry and I were doing a local gig at a bar where Jay lives, Jay came down to hear us and he sat in. We just kind of got the idea to try to do some shows together. Jay is very into the idea of harmonizing a lot of tunes for three guitars so we worked out some stuff and it sounded good and the response to it has been phenomenal so we've been doing this now for years, but just a couple of times a year. It's a lot of fun, really. It must be the same thing for horn players to play together; they just have so much fun. For guitar players, you're all into the same stuff and into the same instrument, so to play with two other guitar players that all have love for the same styles, it's really just a lot of fun.

I think it's wonderful when you see another side of someone like Jay Geils, who has sold millions of records and is a guitar god in one of the most successful groups, the J. Geils Band. To see him do blues records and now, to do jazz stuff...

Yeah, every time we play, he's got so much more information in his repertoire. He's just really devoted to learning and developing a style of jazz guitar and he's great.

Jeff Healey
(1966–2008)

Jeff Healey was a musicologist and the most serious record collector I've ever met. He had over thirty thousand 78s in his basement and knew where to find every one. Not only that, but he could tell you just about everything you wanted to know about a record. Session players, B-sides, label, and matrix numbers. He was, of course, blind, but he could locate by touch any record from his mostly twenties to forties collection. Once he found it he would run his thumb along the grooves to tell you the condition of the album. By feeling the inside spiral of the run-off groove he could tell you the location of the pressing plant that manufactured the record.

He started playing guitar at the age of four and started collecting old records at the age of eleven, thanks to his father's gift of a pile of 78s from the second-hand store located around the corner. After that, Jeff said "There was no turning back. Any pocket change, birthday contributions, etc., went to 78s." He started as a jazz broadcaster in 1980 at the age of fourteen on CBC Radio's *Fresh Air*. He continued to host *My Kind of Jazz* in Toronto on JAZZ FM till the end of his life in 2008.

Meanwhile Healey became one of Canada's most acclaimed guitarists, singers, and bandleaders, fronting the Jeff Healey Band (with Joe Rockman on bass and Tom Stephen on drums), selling millions of records and touring the world. He worked with George Harrison, Bonnie Raitt, Stevie Ray Vaughan, John Mayall, Ronnie Hawkins, Jerry Lee Lewis, Bo Diddley, Jack Bruce, Ian Gillan, Colin James,

Jimmy Rogers, Mel Brown, Kenny "Blues Boss" Wayne, Randy Bachman, Long John Baldry, Duke Robillard, and dozens more in the rock and blues world. Jeff's passion, however, was the infectious and joyful music from the classic jazz era: the days when Jelly Roll Morton, King Oliver, Louis Armstrong, and Bix Beiderbecke ruled the music world.

In the late nineties Jeff tired of the constant travel and lifestyle of being a rock star. He opened a club in Toronto called Healey's Roadhouse—a reference to the film *Road House*, which featured the Jeff Healey Band. He also started Jeff Healey's Jazz Wizards to play the music that had always been his first love. We started to work together in 2005. Jeff wanted to record nothing but jazz records at that point and I was honoured to work with him. He signed exclusively with Stony Plain Records and we promptly recorded the live album *It's Tight Like That* by the Jazz Wizards with guest Chris Barber. We also reissued his back catalogue of jazz releases and released a DVD with the Jazz Wizards. Jeff eventually did go back to record an electric album called *Mess Of Blues*, which won the Blues Foundation's Rock Blues Album of the Year award.

For his final studio album *Last Call*, Jeff recorded solo, duo, and trio sessions. Jeff is featured on both guitar and trumpet with some of the most relaxed vocals of his career.

This interview was recorded backstage at an Edmonton concert in September of 2005 shortly after recording *It's Tight Like That* with Chris Barber. Also included is material from an interview for CBC's *Saturday Night Blues* when Jeff co-hosted the 2007 Christmas show with me. Jeff passed away March 3, 2008, after a lifelong battle with a rare form of cancer—retinoblastoma—that blinded him from the age of one.

Jeff, Cristie, and Derek at home, 2005. Photo: Holger Petersen.

Jeff Healey at Monster Records in Toronto. Photo: Holger Petersen.

Jeff Healey at home with his record collection, 2005. Photo: Holger Petersen.

Jeff Healey, Holger, and Duke Robillard, Toronto, 2007. Photo courtesy of Holger Petersen.

Jeff, it's a wonderful experience to see you on stage with the Jazz Wizards because there's a real joy that comes off that bandstand. Big smiles all around and there's that musician's sense of humour that comes across. It's obviously a fun kind of music to play.

It's a fun kind of music to play and it helps that we have the personalities in the band and you're right. We improvise as much physically and verbally as we do musically. Nobody knows exactly what's going to happen next, especially with characters like Christopher Plock and Drew Jurecka on violin and Ross Wooldridge on clarinet and just the whole band in general. And bring Terra [Hazelton] into the mix and so forth and it's just a lot of fun. I was sure that Chris Barber was going to walk away from the first set that he worked on with us at Hugh's Room scratching his head wondering what he had gotten into with the whole insane asylum, but he seemed to fit in very nicely and kind of got the hang of it, especially by the final performance that we did. I think he turned out to be as equally off balanced as we were, which worked out very well and he seemed to really have a good time.

It certainly did come across that way. You alluded to your past before stepping out with the Jazz Wizards in the last few years. It's been almost twenty years now since a lot of the music world became aware of who Jeff Healey was...

I was feeling young there for a minute, but now I'm feeling my age and I'm not quite forty yet, which is the frightening thing.

You've had huge success. From being in the film Road House, *having George Harrison play on one of your records, having a million seller with "Angel Eyes" and being basically a rock star.*

A reluctant rock star—I never fit the mould. I wouldn't grow my hair long enough or starve myself to death or do the right kind of drugs. I was the person from South Central Etobicoke, which I still am, and I still live there. I just never fit into the mould and, as I said, it just got to be so much a treadmill. Rock stardom is built for the insecure and those who need this sort of faux reassurance, which is not genuine at all from most people and I chose more to be with people who I enjoyed being with and friends who I enjoyed being with and people that I respected and to do what I wanted to do, which may sound selfish and sort of bratish, but there was no reason not to and I'm proving now that it could have been done. I wanted to get to this place ten years ago. Had I been able to walk away at the end of the second album and all of the rigmarole that went with it—the touring, the ups and downs, and so forth—I would have been much happier and far more positive speaking about the past, I suppose. But I suggested walking away and was met with extreme concern to say the least, if not just plain absolute negativity from my former partners and so I sort of hung in there for what turned out to be a decade of absolute desolation. A lot of garbage ended up getting released—nonetheless, thank you for promoting it—(laughs) but [it was] just a lot of stuff that I otherwise wouldn't have done given my own choices. What's done is done and you sort of walk away learning something from it and now I'm doing what I want to do, so it's all good.

*Another positive side of that experience, I would imagine, was that it opened the door to you guesting on other people's records, for example, the Jimmy Rogers record (*Blues Blues Blues*) and other blues artists that you've played with?*

I suppose, to a degree, yes. But that happened through just a kind of ill-fated association with Atlantic. I would hope that I've walked away with a good rapport with Ahmet Ertegun. You know, we were sort of signed to Atlantic and then never released anything because, frankly, none of it was any good. It was *so* not good that it ended up being put into a package and released here in Canada on the Forte label due to basically Tom Stephen's persistence and stubbornness because he was listed as executive producer and he wasn't going to have all the stuff rejected. But throughout that and during that, yes, there were little bright spots, like the Jimmy Rogers thing and Ahmet and I had a great time. John Koenig was the producer on that. It was quite an experience getting to work with Jimmy and the band overall that day, I mean, what talent? Kim Wilson was, of course, a friend of mine and Johnnie Johnson who has, of course, passed on now, was on piano. Great, great experience.

Could you comment on some of the other Toronto sessions you've done with some of the other blues artists that had been released in Canada?

You probably could more than I could. I'm starting to understand how musicians who were making their livings in the twenties and so forth, who were approached by so many collectors and discographers and researchers (myself included) in the seventies, eighties, and nineties and how we as researchers were frustrated because they couldn't remember certain details. I have problems remembering things that were only seven or eight years ago. Because you get the opportunity, a session comes up and you go and you do it and have a lot of fun and then the next day brings something else, especially when you're self-employed.

The Snooky Pryor session that I did for Electro-Fi Records was really quite an experience in a pleasant way and that was, I think, achieved through my association with Alec Fraser who is a good friend, first and foremost. He's the bass player for me in Healey's House Band and whenever I trot out sort of a Healey Band type of thing into the marketplace. He's my engineer for any of the jazz projects that I've done, by and large. So Alec called me to come down and he and Andrew Galloway thought it might be fun to have me on a session with Snooky and Pinetop Perkins and Willie "Big Eyes" Smith and Bob Stroger and Mel Brown; it was quite a band. And here I am in the middle of all this not quite sure what I'm supposed to be doing, but just sitting back and playing my part and I loved to just be part of the decor. I think this is why I love being associating with and involved with the Jazz Wizards project because I get more entertainment from these guys than probably the audience does at times. I can sit back and maybe call the shots as far as what tunes are going to be played and so forth, and I'm silently conducting the band from behind, but my vocals and my instrumental work are just part of what makes the night what it is. I don't need to be the front person getting all of the applause and all of the attention and that sort of thing. I prefer actually as little as possible. I guess, in a sense, I would be very comfortable in an Eddie Condon circumstance. Eddie Condon, one of the most famous, in a lot of ways, of jazz people. You can call him a jazz guitarist because he was, but he never took a solo; he always played rhythm. But he always organized his bands. He generally called the tunes that they were going to do and then he just sat back and let the band entertain him. I love doing that, and if my name is associated with a project or something through one thing or another, then so be it. And we got way off topic, but I was talking about just being part of the interior or whatever on a session like Snooky Pryor and things like that.

What else have I done? You'd probably remember better than I...I did Kenny "Blues Boss" Wayne's album, an early album with Kenny, who is just a great guy, a marvellous boogie-woogie piano player. [It went] back to my introduction to that kind of music through the records that we had of Pete Johnson and Mary Lou Williams and Freddie Slack. I love boogie-woogie piano. I could sit and listen to it all day and Kenny is able to serve it up probably the best of anybody in this country.

I know you made a move recently. Moving all those 78s must have been a bit of a nightmare.

That will be the last move that I make for some time because that was—

I think I counted—the eighth move maybe the tenth move in that last twenty years and it's just how life works. And, of course, each time that I move, the record collection is bigger. But I've got a nice set-up now and everybody who comes to my new basement quarters just marvels at it. Actually one of the collectors wanted to personally get in touch with the people who helped set up my basement so he could set his up the same way. Yeah, I don't think I'll be moving for a while. Thirty thousand records is a lot to move.

And we're talking 78s here?

Well, we are. They're not quite as light, although LPs aren't all that much lighter, especially when you add all the jackets and the packaging and everything. A box of records is a box of records; it's pretty heavy.

Your interest would be in records from what time period specifically? And what kind of records?

Well, the late teens up to the early forties—that's traditional jazz and, frankly, popular music from that time period as well. I actively pursue and collect dance bands and some entertainment personalities as much as jazz records and they don't cost me nearly as much, too. But I'm just fascinated by that whole time period, the whole era. I've also been, as a sideline, interested in the history of the twentieth century. I usually did very well on history exams and that sort of thing, so it's all kind of part and parcel that's wrapped up for me in the whole research of the era.

What was your entree into that music that started it all for you?

It's hard to say. We always had a lot of old records in the family through various sectors. My grandmother, my dad's mother, had a lot of records and her father-in-law's records, which went back almost to the turn of the century and there was lots of variety in those records from entertainment to dance records to sort of semi-classical to even a couple of very, very early examples of, if not jazz, then sort of hop records. Other aunts and uncles had records that they had bought or had been given or what have you from the twenties and into the thirties. An uncle of mine, who actually passed away in the early fifties, was a piano player and was very interested in jazz, in particular true jazz through the mid to late thirties into the forties. And so he had records of Pete Johnson and Jay McShann and Bob Crosby's Bob-Cats and Andy Kirk and Earl Hines. In fact, he and his wife, my aunt, had Earl Hines over to their house for an all-night party on one occasion. They were all down at the Palais Royale where Hines was playing and somehow Earl was talked into coming back to their house with a big party of people and my cousins have told me that they recall being wakened in the middle of the night and shoved off to my grandparents' place to spend the night. So the guy was very interested in good music and so I guess I have that as a basis. And I was just fascinated by old records and what was in them, what musical content was in them, and I began pursuing. I think truly the illness set in when I discovered that you could buy records at second-hand stores and flea markets and you could get them relatively cheap and so I had my poor father chasing around with me to flea markets and second-hand stores and antique stores all over Southern Ontario throughout my childhood.

I think the first time I realized how deep your love, passion, and interest in this music from the twenties and thirties was was when I saw you at a record fair, maybe fifteen or seventeen years ago, and you had just assembled and released (on the Forte label) the complete recordings of Fletcher Henderson and Louis Armstrong. Nobody in the world had put together those complete recordings and there you were at a booth selling them at a record collectors' show in Toronto.

In one package like that, yeah, exactly. There are so many of these packages that are done over in Europe and the UK and so forth, but there is very little done here in North America. I will refrain, I will stop myself from getting on a rant here because there's just not enough time to get into it, but it's heartbreaking and criminal the neglect the record companies have given or the respect that has not been paid to a lot of this great music. The best transfers of it and issue of it—Bessie Smith is a prime example: CBS did a half-posteriored amount of work on the box sets that they put out in the nineties, but their sound quality was horrible. A company out of England called Frog did an eight CD package (well, you can get them in one package, but eight separate CDs) of all of Bessie Smith's stuff and it sounds ten times better than the Sony stuff. But the Forte set of Armstrong/Henderson was the first reissued package of any of that type of thing to come out of Canada on CD, so we were very proud of that.

When some of these companies do put together compilations and reissues, do they contact you looking for 78s?

I work most closely, I guess, with the Mosaic Company and jazz fans should be familiar with Mosaic out of Connecticut. They are a jazz label, truly. They reissue jazz as far back as the teens and they even put out masters of things that they have recorded for them, contemporarily, and everything in between so, yes, they contact me. I mean, the way that things come together in this respect, especially with the little labels out of UK, is that somebody comes up with a concept for a CD and they become the producer, essentially by default, and they make all the phone calls and gather the records, and the records in one form or another are sent over to a particular engineer who will clean them up and make a master out of them so, yeah, I've been involved in that for some time.

You've recently recorded a live album with Chris Barber. How did you become aware of his music and how did that relationship with Chris Barber start?

Well, to be honest, I'm probably still not fully aware of Chris Barber's music. I would say that Colin Bray, our bassist, is the man most cognisant of Chris' output and so forth right from the beginning. Colin being (among other things) a collector of British trad jazz from the forties, fifties, and sixties. But I certainly was aware of Chris as a musician, a music appreciator (as I am), and one of the moving forces in Britain in the nineteen-fifties. I was aware of what he had done and contributed in traditional jazz and blues and so forth and how he had been instrumental in bringing people over to England, like Big Bill Broonzy and Muddy Waters and Lonnie Johnson and that sort of thing. And so, I was fascinated to meet him. The story kind of goes back and forth as to exactly what happened because, since becoming self-employed, I've actually been extremely busy as opposed to being on this monotonous treadmill of hotels and gigs and alcohol, frankly. You know, I changed lifestyles and so forth years ago and I do what I want to do on my own time and have a much better time doing it. I think that he contacted an agency with which I was working at the time and they contacted me. I was heading off on my delayed honeymoon with my wife to Australia at that time and so I sort of put Colin on the case and said, "You know, can you talk to Chris Barber and explain to him that I'm going to be away for the month, that I do appreciate his interest and will get back to him?" which Colin did. So Chris and I talked on and off throughout 2004 and it came down to just a case of we'd like to play together, but we didn't know exactly how to do it. So we re-touched base earlier this year and it came down to a little hole in his schedule at the end of August and I had a couple of dates for the Wizards anyway in that time period. And then, as fate would have it, Richard Flohil was in England and saw Chris—Richard has been a lifelong fan of Chris and his music—so Richard went to talk to him and Chris said, "You're from Toronto, are you? Well, I'm coming over to Toronto in August." So when Richard got home, he called me immediately and said "What's this about Chris coming to work with you and how can I get involved in anything that you need help with?" So Richard, frankly, came through with a couple of dates at Hugh's Room in Toronto, which was great and kind of rounded out the whole package for me.

Richard also told me that you had kind of met your match as a fellow record collector with Chris Barber in terms of, not only identifying artists and songs and labels and B-sides, but actual catalogue numbers.

Yeah, Chris has been a collector for many, many years and we have a lot of mutual friends not the least of which was John Archie Davis, a very dear friend of mine who passed away last year. John was a musician and collector and musicologist and all around interesting fellow. So Chris and I had that as common ground, with such a good mutual friend.

Dr. Jeff Healey. Feels good to be called Dr. Healey, I'm sure. You've got two honorary doctorates now don't you?

No, just the one so far. Well, this past weekend I was given an honorary licensia from the Conservatory of Music and so that was quite a shock considering my vocation. Yes, I took some years of training, in fact, quite a bit of musical training, but how much of it actually gets put into practice in just strumming a guitar is kind of hard to say.

Ian Tyson
(Born 1933)

Ian Tyson lives in the foothills of the Canadian Rockies on a ranch just east of the town of Longview, Alberta, and the old Cowboy Trail. The prairies are on one side and the front face of shining mountains on the other. It's beautiful country, but it can be brutally tough in the winter. He has a stone cottage about a mile down a gravel road where he walks to most mornings. I've made that walk. It's incredibly scenic, peaceful, and quiet. The cattle on both sides of the gravel road turn their heads and follow your progress. It's a reflective walk that can be spent "thinking of higher things," as Ian puts it. In the old stone house, early in the morning, he's written most of his songs over the last thirty years: songs about the west from his perspective of being a horseman, rancher, historian, environmentalist, and educator.

His work ethic, honesty, and integrity have set a standard for me. Ian has always done things his way and I learned to listen closely to how he wants his business done. I've been incredibly fortunate to have seen many of Ian's songs unfold over the years and to have been present at many sessions, concerts, and a few historical events in his life. Stony Plain Records probably wouldn't exist today if Ian Tyson hadn't given us a chance to release *Cowboyography* back in 1986. I'd been a fan since the Ian and Sylvia days and loved the Great Speckled Bird when their self-titled album came out in 1970. We've gone on to work with not only Ian, but Sylvia Tyson, plus Amos Garrett and David Wilcox who were part of that landmark band. The success of *Cowboyography* came at a critical time for Stony Plain. After ten years of being basically a one-man operation with part-time help from time to time, we became a company that was winning Juno Awards and getting Gold Records. We've released twelve Ian Tyson albums over the years and a tribute album to Ian called *The Gift*.

This interview was conducted in Spruce Grove, Alberta, at the Horizon Stage in January of 2010.

Holger with Ian Tyson, Edmonton,1989. Photo courtesy of Holger Petersen.

Ian Tyson's stone house, Tyson Ranch, 2008. Photo: Holger Petersen.

Ian Tyson at his seventy-fifth birthday party, Tyson Ranch, 2008.
Photo: Holger Petersen.

First of all, congratulations on the award you're receiving in Elko, the Western Horseman Award. What exactly is it for?

Well, it is for a professional horseman, actually. I was very surprised and honoured to receive it because I think I'm the only "non-trainer" horse trainer, who has ever won it. Of course, I have trained as a non-pro for many years, but, yeah, it came right out of the blue and I was blown away by it.

Certainly your accomplishments in the cutting horse world have been huge and sometimes we forget that. We know about you as a musician and songwriter, but you've really reached some high levels of skills in the cutting horse world.

Actually I've never been a very good showman. I never showed cutting horses very successfully, but I could make them. I could build a good foundation on a cutting horse and that was my true love—making a really nice horse at home. I never did showing consistently enough, which you have to do every weekend basically to develop that skill. They're kind of two different things—the training and the showing—and there's only a very select few cowboys that can really do them both at a high level of proficiency. But I always got the enjoyment and the feeling of accomplishment out of making them at home in a relaxed atmosphere.

Your cowboy skills, of course, developed over a very long period of time. I remember you telling me that in the late fifties when you used to be on the cowboy rodeo circuit out in Alberta, you used to listen to jazz records driving around in pick-up trucks. I always thought that was such a fantastic image of cowboys on the rodeo circuit in the fifties listening to jazz.

Well, that might have been just me, I don't know. In art school I heard a lot of jazz. West Coast Jazz, which was popular at the time, that kind of...oh, who were the practitioners? Shorty Rogers and His Giants, Dave Brubeck and those guys, and the music from Seal Beach and those places in California. And we'd been down there and later when I was singing with Sylvia, we went to a lot of those clubs actually down in California, but I don't think cowboys listening to jazz was that prevalent in those days. I don't know, but it was probably more like Lefty Frizzell, I think.

I watched this documentary about Dave Brubeck and Take Five. *The time signature–the 5/4 time. I didn't realize that he's a horseman and he alluded to the fact that 5/4 time was developed from listening to horses hooves while he was riding.*

Yeah, apparently Dave Brubeck was raised on a cattle ranch in California and he'd been a cowboy so, yeah, those cadences are, to horsemen, very deeply embedded in you and I guess it comes out in the music, too. My rhythm is like a fast trot or what we call a high trot, which is a fast tempo trot just before the horse breaks into a lope or a canter, as they say in English. That's a high trot and a lot of my songs, I realized later, were in that cadence.

I know you're also a Miles Davis fan and '59 was a huge year for Miles Davis. Sketches of Spain *came out. There's so much to relate to in* Sketches of Spain *for somebody like your who has that interest in the Spanish cowboys.*

Yes, all of our culture came from Spain, basically. It's strange that more people don't realize that, but it all started in Spain and I think those Spanish composers really influenced that period of Miles' musical statements at the time. That was based on...who's the Spanish composer?

Rodrigo

Rodrigo, right. Yeah, Miles was in New York when we were there. I never met him actually, but I met a lot of the boppers. Coltrane was there a lot and all those guys from that era. They were all playing in the village, the Village Vanguard, so we got to hear quite a bit of it, you know, Cannonball Adderley. Great stuff.

That must have been a musically eclectic time in Greenwich Village, not only with jazz overlapping, but also with the Irish music of Tommy Makem and the Clancy Brothers. You've said before that so much of the Western music really comes from those Celtic themes and those melodies. Were you hanging around with them as well?

Not so much. The Clancys, they hung out a lot over at the White Horse Tavern on the west side, but I guess you can make the case that New York can be a very Irish town on some levels. A lot of the cowboys in the trail drive era, in that immediate post-Civil War period, there were a lot of nationalities, but I think that the Scot and Irish boys dominated it. They came through the Appalachians to Missouri (or Missoura as they called it) and then to Texas and they brought a lot of that Celtic music with them.

You've always brought a real sense of historical significance to many of your songs. They're well researched and in those early Ian and Sylvia days you introduced a lot of folk songs to the world. Back then, researching must have been difficult. How did you find those songs and know about that history?

Well, the Cecil Sharp collection of the Southern Appalachians was, I think, the dominant work on that and it was hard for me because I don't read music, but Sylvia could and back when she was a kid, she did a lot of researching at the little library in Chatham, Ontario. But the Sharp collection—that was the important one. That was before the Lomax collections and others. And really in the fifties, when we started, I guess you could say a lot of that oral tradition was alive still.

You know, TV hadn't completely taken over. In the very early days of the Elko gathering, there was an actual oral tradition that's alive and well in those mountain valleys of northern Nevada because you couldn't get radio reception; there was no television. I remember we went to this first ranch that had it, it was the White Horse, which was a very famous little ranch way out in the desert, and they had some sort of dish or something and when we turned it on there was this awful science fiction movie made in Toronto and there I was: I couldn't get away.

But northern Nevada and southern Idaho and eastern Oregon—and they call that the ION—the poetry tradition was still alive and to a certain extent it still is and I found that to be really fascinating.

Last time Gordon Lightfoot came through, I showed him his first album and got him to sign it. It was the Two-Tones album and there was maybe one original song on there and he pointed to "Dark as a Dungeon" and said "Ian taught me that tune."

Did he? Yeah, that's a great song. Merle Travis wrote that song, I believe. It's a great, great song. Again, if you like the Scots/Irish music tradition, that song springs directly out of that, melodically and lyrically and everything.

Greenwich Village in New York was such a fostering ground for original material. When you got there, was there a songwriting scene or did you see it developing?

It was developing because when we first arrived in New York (and that must have been '61) the folksingers were doing traditional material pretty much. There was some songwriting. Dave Van Ronk, he could have given you chapter and verse on all that stuff because he was the main guy, but a lot of his stuff was traditional black blues and that kind of thing. And Dylan—it's been said over and over again, but it's true—he was the one who really blew it wide open with his own material, you know, writing his own songs. I certainly was influenced by him and that's why I started seriously trying to write good songs. I'd fooled around with it before in BC, but it was just "Yeah, yeah, yeah" in those days, you know, rockabilly and you had to be from Lubbock, Texas, to write those songs, I guess, I don't know. But, yeah, you could see it developing and probably by the time it ended, the folk scare ended when the Beatles stormed America. That was probably the height of the songwriting thing and everybody was doing it. There was a lot of pretty ordinary stuff, but the good stuff rises like cream—Dylan really launched it. But there were guys like Dave Van Ronk and we hung out in a little underground coffee house on MacDougal Street. A really wonderful gentlemen, a old Southern gentleman, ran it with his son...I'm trying to think of their names but I can't...but I know that's where Tom Paxton started writing in that little place and I started writing in there. There was a bar upstairs called Kettle of Fish, I think, and Len Chandler and Johnny Herald [of the Greenbriar Boys], people like that were just beginning to write. But everybody kind of had their eye on Bob Dylan because he was writing five or six songs to our one and they were all great or pretty much all great so it was fairly intimidating.

I can imagine. I hesitate to ask you this question and you can bypass it if you want, but Suze Rotolo, Dylan's girlfriend, wrote the book A Freewheelin' Time. *She claimed that you turned Dylan on to pot. Is that true?*

I don't know. I don't recall it, to be honest, but it's probably true if Suze said it because she is probably as good an observer of that time as anybody. Terrific lady. She was there and she knew exactly what was going on and who it was going on with. Although, I guess, maybe it's true.

Of course, Dylan turned the Beatles on, too. I don't know if you knew that.

Well, no, I didn't. I was running around with a young lady who always had a pretty good supply of weed and she probably supplied it, I think, but it's a long, long time ago. We didn't do it, you know, it wasn't a regular thing, it was kind of a treat because we didn't have any money. Nobody had any money. It was a real scuffle to pay your hotel bill and we stayed at the Earle, which is gone now, it was just a really cool old, old place. Jack Elliott used to stay there and he and I used to hang out and it was right on the square in Greenwich Village.

I thought Jack Elliott did a really good version of Will James. I know how important Will James was to you; I guess to stimulate your imagination as a youngster. You talk about those sketches of horses leaping right off the page. I wonder if they had the same effect on Ramblin' Jack as well?

Oh, yeah, he was a cowboy. It's strange that you would bring that up because right now I'm in that section of my biography which is the Will James section. He was such an important influence in my life, probably more than any one single thing. In the biography I tell about how my father would always give me Will James books for Christmas and for birthdays because there were lots and lots of Will James books; they were all over the place in those days, and it was very convenient for my dad because he didn't have to worry about it, he'd just get me another Will James book and they weren't expensive. They were very affordable and easy to find. My father had no idea who Will James really was because he was an imposter and had invented his whole past and everything: He was a French Canadian from Quebec. Strangely enough I think the real Will James story is probably more interesting than the one he concocted for himself. But he was very influential. I know old cowboys, authentic old cowboys...I know one down in Montana, a great cowboy, he came from Minnesota or someplace because he'd found Will James books when he was a kid. Our generation, we're dying off now, but our generation was really influenced by that. A lot of those guys, a lot of the collectors, refused to believe when Will James was outed by Anthony Amaral. Amaral brought out this book called *The Gilt Edged Cowboy* and it exposed Will James and a lot of those guys wouldn't accept that at all, they just refused to believe, they said, "He said he was born under a covered wagon in Texas." He was born in Montreal, Quebec.

Graphics and visuals have been such an important part of your life, which is obvious from the detail in your lyrics. Apart from Will James, you wrote about Charlie Russell in my all-time favourite Ian Tyson song, "The Gift." Did Charlie Russell have a connection to Alberta and your ranch? Did you mention that once?

He had a strong connection to Alberta because Charlie Russell came to the very first Calgary Stampede in 1912. He was the guest of Guy Weadick. Guy Weadick was a cowboy, a vaudeville performer like a lot of cowboys were in those days, he came out of that Wild West Show Buffalo Bill era. Guy Weadick was the man who talked George Lane and the big four ranchers into putting on the original Calgary Stampede. Guy Weadick bought a ranch just up the valley that is still to this day called the Stampede Ranch and it's just up the valley from where I live. I don't know if Charlie [was there] but Charlie Russell came to Alberta in 1889, I believe. The Blackfeet and the Stoneys were still living pretty traditionally then and he wanted to basically get material for his painting, which he was starting to get serious about. He wanted to see what the Indians looked like, so he stayed for the summer. There were a lot of stories about how he had an Indian girlfriend or lover or whatever and I don't know how true that is, but he did spend the summer in the High River area and there were quite a few paintings in Southern Alberta that were done by Russell and I think now, other than the two or three that are in the Glenbow Museum, they've all been bought by Americans. But he had a strong connection with Rupert's Land, I guess.

I didn't realize until recently that your father actually had come out to Alberta in 1906 on his way from England. He spent some time in Southern Alberta as a rancher or as a cowboy, didn't he?

Yeah, he was a ranch hand, but I think a couple of Alberta winters cured him of that pretty quick and he went on out to Vancouver Island where he applied for a homestead, quarter section, up in the Cowichan Valley out of Duncan. Of course, then the war started and he joined up outside of Victoria, the Willows. I think he joined the Canadian Cavalry, I think it was the cavalry, but fortunately for him, my grandfather back in England bought him a commission, which you could do in those days. He bought him a commission in the English army and I'm sure that saved his life because all those Canadian boys were almost all killed—they were cannon fodder, that's what they were—they were all killed. But he got shot up pretty bad. He was wounded several times and ended up in a German POW camp, hospital actually. He was repatriated back in 1917, back to England. I'm giving you my whole book here.

That's great, thank you. I'm going to jump ahead a few years. I'm really interested in your Alberta roots. Were you coming back here in the Ian and Sylvia days as well? Some of the photos on the albums were taken in Alberta. Were you spending very much time in Alberta in the sixties and seventies?

No, I wasn't. A lot of those photographs were taken in Canada, but probably in Ontario because we were working out of New York and living in Toronto. Well, Sylvia was living in New York; she had a little apartment there and through that intense folk period, which would be '62 to '65, we were pretty much based out of New York City. I didn't get back to Alberta until the early seventies. It was the early- to mid-seventies when I came back because I was trying to set up a situation where I could train horses and still be in music. It was difficult to do that in those days, it still is actually. You can't really be at the top of your game in both or at least I couldn't anyway and it took me a long time to realize that. It's nice if you're not doing your creative stuff really seriously and you can be kind of a dilettante then it's more enjoyable, but if you're taking it very seriously, it's pretty difficult. One will suffer because of the other and that's the way it was.

I think you actually made a decision to leave the music at some point and pursue the cowboy skills and lifestyle in Alberta around that time?

Yeah, the mid-seventies. I was in Nashville for a year and I couldn't find the niche that I had to be in. I'd sung duo for so long that I had to relearn how to sing solo basically. The television work that I was doing through that time was very helpful in that they threw me into the deep end and I had to learn how to sing as a soloist, but it took me quite awhile. When I went to Nashville, we couldn't find the formula or stylistically where I was heading—that happened later. It came organically out of the cowboy thing; it came out of my lifestyle. *Cowboyography* came along and it was just like a gift from the sky. It wasn't intellectual at all. It just came, it just happened, and who knows how that happens.

I think you had wanted to call the previous record Cowboyography, *the one that ended up being called* Ian Tyson. *You were with Columbia at the time and they didn't want to call it* Cowboyography.

Yeah, that second album was kind of forgotten after *Old Corrals and Sagebrush* because they morphed the two albums together, I think, and it bounced around for a while. I think it was on Bear Family over in Europe and it kind of bounced around. And there was some good stuff, I mean, there were a few good things on there, but it didn't have that seamless thing that *Cowboyography* had. *Cowboyography* really was a gift from somewhere else for me. It's too bad that *Cowboyography* came out in the US on a bluegrass label, don't ask me how that happened, but they didn't get it and they were quite out front about it. They just didn't know what to do with it. I think I could have been pretty close to a Grammy at that time had it been with the right label. You guys up here in Canada did very, very well with it. Of course we could get radio play and we did, but it just didn't have a fighting chance in the US. It's gone on and sold, I mean, everybody who likes western music, they've all heard *Cowboyography* now, but that's been twenty-five years.

You said that Lost Herd *was the favourite of the Ian Tyson recordings. What was it about* Lost Herd *that came together for you?*

Again, I don't know. To tell you how it was made, you absolutely wouldn't suspect (it's kind of seamless) that it was done by two entirely separate bands or studio musicians: half of it in Toronto in about two days and the other half with a bunch of cowboys in Nashville in two days. And yet, even today, I'm not sure who's playing on what song because there were two entirely different sessions, two different producers and all the pickers, two groups of pickers, but they all liked the music. I mean jazz guys like Phil Dwyer who are pretty out there jazz pros and the bass player in Nashville was a calf roper, I remember that. You couldn't get more diverse guys playing, but it just happened.

"La Primera" is a great track from Lost Herd. *Apart from the craftsmanship and detail, you obviously spent a lot of time researching the development of the horse in the West.*

Yeah, I think that young man who played flamenco guitar on it really got it and he really brought that song home. He played that live on the track, as I recall. I think we were in RCA Victor's Toronto studios. Jesse Cook really brought a really nice lyrical dimension to that.

I was just really interested in the horse's return to the Americas, as I still am. This seems to be the year that everyone's interested because I've had about three offers to write film scores and assorted things about the horse. And right now is a crucial time because the West in the United States, the big federal pieces of land that are in the West, in Wyoming and Nevada, etc., are being overrun by horses that are just being turned loose because people can't afford them and it's really going to be a major crisis. They're going to have to slaughter horses, which we do in Canada and they do in Mexico, but it has to be done humanely and the shipment of those horses has to be a lot more humane. That's a big, big story and the whole agricultural thing in North America has got to make huge changes, huge changes have to come. And North Americans are going to say "we've had cheap, cheap food for a long, long time" and that's going to end.

You've done so much to help people understand the West along with photographers like Jay Dusard who you've worked with. Are there western authors that you recommend?

Oh, yeah, Cormac McCarthy is, of course, right at the head of that. He's a brilliant, brilliant writer, and Larry McMurtry too, when he wants to be. *Lonesome Dove* is still the greatest Western that's ever been made, and it was made for a movie or television, but still the characters are so beautifully drawn. All his characters in those books, they just live, absolutely live. They're great. There's many, many. I'm now reading the *Westering Man: The Life of Joseph Walker*, who was a great Westering pioneer. Again, another Scots/Irish guy, who came from Kentucky—from Scotland to Kentucky to Missouri—and he was one of the very first who came overland to the Pacific Ocean. But I'd like to write one about David Thompson too because he was just as early as those American guys and, of course, he was a Hudson's Bay employee, like they were, but there's a lot of them. I'm finding it hard to go into those great Western bookstores that they have. I'm finding it hard to go in there and find something I haven't read.

Lucinda Williams
(Born 1953)

A true southern voice, Lucinda Williams was born in Lake Charles, Louisiana, the daughter of acclaimed poet and travelling university professor, Miller Williams. She lived in Jackson, Mississippi, Baton Rouge, New Orleans, Arkansas, and Mexico while growing up. Regarded as one of the most soulful and unconventional songwriters today, Lucinda Williams' music is deeply rooted in blues and folk. Stony Plain proudly released her self-titled 1988 album, *Lucinda Williams*, album in Canada and also the reissues of her two Folkways albums: 1979's *Ramblin'* and 1980's *Happy Woman Blues*. Lucinda has gone on to great success as a multiple Grammy Award winner and Emmylou Harris, Steve Earle, Mary Chapin Carpenter, and Tom Petty have covered her songs. She has inspired countless singer-songwriters and remains one of my favourite artists. This interview about her interest in blues and roots music and early recordings was done on her tour bus after a concert in Edmonton on June 15, 2007. Thanks to Terry Wickham, Producer, Edmonton Folk Music Festival and Lorna Arndt, Project Manager, folkwaysAlive!, University Of Alberta.

Lucinda Williams, Calgary Folk Festival, 2004. Photo: Frank Gasparik.

Lucinda Williams at Winspear, Edmonton, 2011. Photo: Frank Gasparick. Courtesy of the Edmonton Folk Music Festival.

Lucinda, it was great to hear you do so much blues-related material tonight in the set. Is that something that was particular to tonight or have you been doing more blues in your sets?

I've probably been doing more blues-oriented stuff in my sets, but also when we did "Still Long For Your Kiss," when I announced the song, I heard a couple of people yell out and I could tell, based on the way they responded, that they appreciated the sort of bluesier stuff. I always try to base the set around where we're playing and the audience. I try to anticipate what they're going to want to hear more of. It's hard to tell though sometimes.

As you know, the University of Alberta in Edmonton is very closely associated with Folkways Records and the Smithsonian, and has a department called folkwaysAlive! Your very first record, Ramblin', *was recorded for Folkways in 1978 and included country blues and traditional material. Was it representative of the kind of music you were playing at the time?*

Yeah, it was. Some of my earliest influences were artists like Woody Guthrie and Pete Seeger and a lot of the traditional folk music. I had that book, John and Alan Lomax's *Folk Song USA*, and I started out listening to that stuff and then eventually it progressed from that into folk songwriters, people like Gordon Lightfoot and Buffy Sainte-Marie and then, of course, Bob Dylan. Then it went from that into folk rock: the Byrds and all the sixties rock stuff. That was the stuff that I was listening to. In the meantime, my dad was a big country music fan. He loved country music and blues and jazz, so that was all going on at the same time in the household so it's all gotten kind of blended.

But Folkways was always a big, very important part of my life. You know, at the time that I started out, I started playing guitar in 1965 and I was twelve years old. I remember one of the earliest memories I have, as far as listening to an album goes, it was of actually [listening to] a Folkways recording, but it was the old ten-inch Folkways records that were in the real hard cardboard, you know? And there were these two albums called *Songs to Grow On, Volumes I and II* and they were songs for kids—one was all Woody Guthrie and I think the other was Pete Seeger and Peggy Seeger—and I'll never forget that. That was probably when I was eight, nine, and ten years old, before I started playing the guitar so obviously Folkways was very influential really early on. And how it came about was when I first did that Folkways album *Ramblin'*, I had met this songwriter by the name of Jeff Ampolsk and he had recorded an album for Folkways called *God, Guts, and Guns*. We were old friends from New Orleans and, anyway, to make a long story short, we were on the phone talking and he said, "Well, you know, I think you should make a record for Folkways. I told them about you," and everything. And this was when Moe Asch was still alive, and the thing about Folkways was they were so open-minded about recording. I think they were mainly interested in the artistic integrity of music and, obviously, the political leanings of songs rather than the commercial, you know, whether it was going to be a big hit or not. And they weren't really that concerned about whether you recorded in the studio and did all this high-tech stuff. The field recordings that John and Alan Lomax did, that sort of set the precedent for Folkways, as far as the quality of the recordings went. Anyway, this guy indirectly (and I've lost touch with him now) was responsible for me getting my first deal with Folkways Records.

I was living in Arkansas at the time and they sent me this one-page contract and $250 to do this record. My dad, the poet Miller Williams, contacted a friend of the family's, Tom Royals, a civil rights attorney in Jackson, Mississippi. As it turned out, one of his clients was Gerald "Wolf" Stephenson who was an engineer at Malaco Studios at the time, so my dad calls Tom Royals and Tom Royals calls Gerald Stephenson and says, "Hey, can you do me a favour? My best friend's daughter is making this record for Folkways...." So Gerald said, "Yeah, no problem." He took me into the studio with John Grimaudo, a guitar player from Houston who I'd been working with, and the two of us went in and did this record in one afternoon. And I did all covers—traditional folk and blues and country—because I was trying to be very loyal to the whole Folkways name and the tradition and I didn't think they would want to hear my own songs. I had some songs at the time, but I thought, "Well, this is Folkways. I should do all these older traditional kinds of songs." So that's why I ended up putting all those Robert Johnson and Hank Williams songs on there. They were songs I'd been doing in my repertoire at the time. I wasn't a full-fledged songwriter in the way that I am today, so it definitely does represent what I started out doing.

And then, the second Folkways album, I got a little bit more of an advance on that one; I got $500 instead of $250. And the story with that one was that I was living in Houston, Texas, and ended up going to SugarHill Studios and working with this guy, Mickey Moody, who was a partner of Huey Meaux.

I was thinking that because SugarHill was Huey Meaux's studio, wasn't it?

Yeah, yeah. And I was working with these guys, Mickey White and Rex Bell (Mickey White was a guitar player and Rex Bell was a bass player), and they had for years been backing up Lightnin' Hopkins and Townes Van Zandt. They had been working with me around Houston for a couple of years. So I had this opportunity to go in and do this second record for Folkways. We went in and recorded it and we brought in a couple of other people—a slide guitar player. But the funny thing about this is that I was pretty much still a straight folk singer-songwriter; I hadn't really played with a full band with drums and all that up to this point. We were all out of the studio and Mickey Moody decided to put drums on the record, so he brought this session guy in and laid down these drum tracks. I remember coming in the next day and he played it for me and I was really stunned and surprised and felt a little manipulated because he hadn't asked me. That's probably what set the precedent for me being known as a difficult artist or whatever, you know, perfectionist in the studio. But, anyway, you can't tell now, but the drum tracks for *Happy Woman Blues* were actually put on there afterwards, after we recorded everything, so that was kind of an eye-opening experience for me. Then, to top it off, Mickey Moody split town with the money that we had paid him to do the record and the recording studio called up after we were done and said, "Hey, who's paying the bill for these sessions? No one has paid for these sessions." So it turned out that Mickey Moody had split town, he took the money and ran and so that was my introduction to making records.

There was another kind of funny story about that. After I made the *Happy Woman Blues* album, the first Folkways album I made that had my own songs on it, I had to find a publisher for my songs. Well, this was a whole new world for me; I hadn't done anything like this. I didn't have a manager. I didn't have an attorney. I didn't have anyone to advise me. So Folkways apparently had this brother/sister relationship with this company called Alpha Music, which was run by this guy named Mike Nurko, which, apparently, is still active today. So, anyway, I think I got my dad's friend who is an attorney to look at the contract and it was like one page, so I signed the contract. Flash forward a few years and I'm in Los Angeles and I'm on the phone talking to my friend, John T. Davis, who is a music journalist in Austin, and he says, "You know, it's funny. A fan of yours called me at the office and said he could have sworn he heard one of your songs in this film." And I said, "Really? Which song is it?" And he said, "'One Night Stand,' the song 'One Night Stand' off *Happy Woman Blues*." And I said, "Really. Well, what was the name of the film?" And he said, "*All American Girls II: In Heat*." And I said, "Really?" And he said, "Yeah, it's actually an X-rated porno film." And I said, "You gotta be kidding?" So, now I had a manager, David Hirshland, who now works for Bug Music. He went out and rented the film and took it home, watched it, and calls me the next and says, "I hate to tell you this, but your song is in this film." I was dumbfounded, all of us were, because we're talking about Folkways Records–high integrity–all of this and now they're working with this guy who has this publishing company who puts my song in a porno film and it was just really bizarre. And to top it off, I didn't get a cent from it. Not that...whatever...it would be "dirty" money, but that just added to making everything worse. Anyway, it's kind of a joke now that we all laugh about. I totally got ripped off. It was one of those classic–you know how you hear about a lot of the Delta blues artists...they didn't know any better so they signed these deals? Well, that's what happened with me, but what was so weird about it was his connection to Folkways. I never understood that. I'm sure Moe Asch didn't know about it.

Did the fact that you were released on Folkways and probably getting reviews and some attention in different circles, did that make a difference to you in the late seventies?

Well, I remember this really cool review actually by Robert Christgau (this is how far back we go), he reviewed *Happy Woman Blues* for the *Village Voice* and I remember I loved these lines, "as fetching as the dimples on your bed mate's ass." And that was my introduction into the world of music journalism and I thought "Wow, that's really cool. I like that."

At that point, I was building up this cult following more than anything, just from playing around live. And this is something I try to tell kids starting out today, you know, they don't go out there and play enough. They think they can just make a record and then it's just all gonna happen. I know things are a lot different now than they used to be, but I was still fortunate enough to have grown up with kind of that grassroots thinking that said "Go out and play live. Just play, play, play." That's how you build up an audience and that's how you become successful. And that's really how I did it. I just went out there and played every chance I got.

I love your version of "Hard Time Killing Floor Blues," the Skip James song. Does that go way back for you?

Yeah, that was one of the earliest Delta blues albums I heard. There were so many. The fortunate thing was that my dad was into the same kind of music and I guess I was twelve, thirteen, fourteen, you know, in my teens when he started coming home and bringing home albums by Lightnin' Hopkins, Mississippi John Hurt, and, of course, the Robert Johnson stuff. I was just so deeply entrenched in the Delta blues. I mean, once I discovered it, I felt like I found a home. It really just hit me deeply. Memphis Minnie and just all of it. I mean, I listened to everything I could find, you know, and I always enjoyed listening to the really obscure stuff like some of the Yazoo recordings, you know, just people nobody had heard of. The more obscure it was, the better I liked it and so, yeah, the Delta blues stuff—Skip James, Elmore James, just all of them. Muddy Waters.

You mentioned your song "Joy" tonight and the wonderful version Bettye LaVette has recorded. You must have been absolutely delighted when you first heard that.

That was a real thrill and I love it when other people record my songs. I just got turned on to this beautiful version of "Fruits of My Labor" that was recorded by a younger contemporary artist by the name of Ruthie Foster and I was real impressed by that. Yeah, but when Bettye LaVette did it, to me, it was just such an honour because there are so many songs she could choose from. I think it's really important and really great when an older, established blues artists like that seeks out songs from younger, contemporary artists. I felt like that album she did was really important in that regard because she's from that older, more established traditional blues world and yet she branched out and did all these contemporary songs that you wouldn't expect her to do.

Part 4

Bonus Tracks

Mavis Staples
(Born 1939)

After many nominations, Mavis Staples finally won her first Grammy Award in 2011. Her recording career had started over fifty years ago with the Staple Singers hit "Uncloudy Day." In her acceptance speech, Mavis said, "It was a long time coming. Pops, you laid the foundation, and I am still working on the building."

The Staple Singers were rooted in gospel and Delta blues and over time included Southern soul and R&B into their distinctive music. The family was committed to social justice and had a string of hits in the early seventies with impassioned political spirituals, like "Why (Am I Treated So Bad)," "Respect Yourself," and "I'll Take You There." Roebuck "Pops" Staples (1914 –2000) raised his four children well and educated them in the world of gospel music. Mavis started singing as a child and today carries on the family tradition in the spirit of Pops.

Mavis is one of the most soulful people I've had the privilege to meet. I've done two lengthy interviews with her and experienced her kindness and generosity. This interview took place at the Vancouver Island MusicFest. It was recorded on a workshop stage in front of an audience on July 9th, 2008—the day before Mavis' sixty-ninth birthday. The audience sang "Happy Birthday" for her. Thanks to Doug Cox, the Producer of the festival, for providing me with this opportunity.

Mavis Staples, Edmonton, 2005. Photo: Holger Petersen.

Peter Guralnick's recent book on Sam Cooke offers a lot of insight into the gospel music scene of the nineteen-fifties. That was the time when you were growing up and living the life of a child gospel singer. Can you tell us how that developed for you and the Staple Singers?

Early fifties actually. Sam Cooke grew up in Chicago. My older sister and my brother, we were all at a grammar school, Doolittle. They were in the same grades. And we also had Lou Rawls, he was there, and Jerry Butler; these people lived in Chicago. We lived on 33rd Street and we called it the Dirty Thirties because all of these guys were singing then. But Chicago is just a music city: you got good blues, you've got gospel, and R&B. Sam Cooke was just one of the best, Sam and Soul Stirrers. I remember his last gospel concert. Sam had sung a secular song. He had one song "Loveable, My Girl Is So Loveable" and the gospel side was "Wonderful, God Is So Wonderful" and, you know, back in the day, you just don't do that. And we were in Memphis at a concert–The Staple Singers, the Soul Stirrers, Spirit of Memphis, and the Dixie Hummingbirds–and when Sam got up to sing, well, you know them old sisters out in the audience, they just weren't having it. They stayed on him so long that Sam just threw his hands up and that was the last gospel program he did and he was gone from there. But he was a beautiful person.

When we started, our father would take us to the different places and we made a basement record. We were just singing and a lady, Evelyn Gay from the Gay Sisters, heard us and she told Pops, she said, "You know, Staples, you and those children need to be singing on a record" and Pop said, "Well, Evelyn, I don't know nothing about records. I don't know how to do that," and she said, "I know." And she took us in the basement and we made this basement record and they played it around Chicago and Vee-Jay Records heard it and they offered us a contract. By this time Pops had gotten him some more knowledge and we made a gospel record called *Uncloudy Day* back in 1953. And I was actually singing bass; I was a little kid with a heavy voice. And we been going ever since.

You mentioned the controversy about the two-sided song that Sam Cooke sang–which was the gospel side and the popular music side.

Back then you just didn't do that. When we recorded "I'll Take You There" and it went across the board, it had such a beat, you know, and it went across the board and they started playing it on R&B radio and the church wanted to put us out of church. They got started, "Oh, them Staple Singers are singing the devil's music." And I had to do so many interviews, Holger, telling these people that – the devil ain't got no music, you know? All music is god's music! So I would quote (they weren't listening to the lyrics) and we telling you that "I know a place, ain't nobody crying, ain't nobody worried, ain't no smiling faces lying to the races." So where else could I be taking you but to heaven? I said, "I'll take you there." It just happened that it had that beat and the R&B stations jumped on it but now we did so many interviews explaining the song to them, we were invited back to church and guess what the first song that was requested? "I'll Take You There," right up in the pulpit.

So, yes, you just didn't do that back then. I got the worst whipping [from] my grandmother. I happened to be in Mississippi when I was a little kid, you know, they had so many children that Pops couldn't keep us all in shoes so he would send the two youngest down to Mound Bayou, Mississippi, with my grandmother. And the kids in school knew that I could sing so they pushed me out on stage one day. Well, I'm walking down this gravel every morning and on the juke boxes I'm hearing , "You Made Me Leave My Happy Home," by Buddy and Ella Johnson. So when they pushed me on stage, that's the first thing that came out of my mouth. My uncle started walking around, you know, the school was elementary and junior high, and I saw him coming around the wall. Well, I'm thinking he's coming up there to pat me on my head and say, "You're doing a good job." He snatched me off stage and didn't say nothing to me, just pushed me on out the school door, on down the road to my grandmother's house, pushed me in the door and told my grandmother, "This young 'un is up at school singin' the blues." And Grandma say, "Oh, you singin' the blues, huh? You get out there and get me some switches." I had to go find them and I came back in the first time and I say, "Grandma, I can't find no switches." She say, "Young 'un, don't you make me have to go out there." So I sped on back out the door and I got the smallest switches I could, not knowing that these were the ones that hurt the worst, you know? And, boy, she got started on my legs and, "You don't sing no blues in this family, you sing church songs." Well, nobody had ever told me what to sing, you know, I was a kid. And, man, she sent me back to school with little pink slips on my legs 'cuz I was wearing those short dresses, you know, and kids laughed at me, and I started printing letters home to my mother. I said, Mama, I wanna come home. Grandma won't let me sing. So I made it through that and do you know, when I was twenty-one, I recorded that song.

Mavis, I wonder if you wouldn't mind talking about your relationship and Pops' relationship with Dr. Martin Luther King in the sixties. The Staple Singers were involved with many marches and Pops was writing great material for them. How did the format for those marches work? Would you perform and Dr. Martin Luther King would speak before the march?

No, the marches were going on, but in certain cities he would speak and we would sing before he would speak. It just happened that that time in Memphis (when he was assassinated), we weren't there. We were working, so we couldn't be there for that particular speech. But back in the early sixties, we happened to be in Montgomery, Alabama, to work that night, eight o'clock that night, and Pops called us to his room and he said, "Listen, you all, this man Martin is here—Martin Luther King. He has a church here and I wanna go to his eleven o'clock service. Do you all want to go?" And we said, "Yeah, Daddy, we wanna go." We all went to Dr. King's eleven o'clock service at Dexter Avenue Baptist Church in Montgomery, Alabama. Someone let Dr. King know that we were there, so he acknowledged us and said he was glad to have the Staples family in the audience. And when the service was over, Dr. King would stand at the door to greet the worshippers filing out of the church and we all got out and Pops stood there and talked to Dr. King for a while. When we got back to the hotel, he called us to his room again and he said, "Listen, you all, I really like this man's message and I think if he can preach it, we can sing it" and we began writing freedom songs. The first one we wrote was "March Up Freedom's Highway," that was for the march from Selma to Montgomery. Then we wrote "It's A Long Walk to DC But I Got My Walking Shoes On," that was for Washington. Pops wrote a song called "Why (Am I Treated So Bad)." This turned out to be Dr. King's favourite. Every time we would get ready, we'd be down in the parking lot, everyone getting ready to go and Dr. King would tell my father, "Stap, you gonna sing my song, right?" And Pops would say "Oh, yeah, Doctor, we gonna sing your song." And "Why (Am I Treated So Bad)"–he wrote that around Little Rock, Arkansas. There were nine black children–they call themselves the Little Rock Nine now, they all still living–and they were trying to integrate a central high school and these people just would not let those kids board the bus. So one day, eventually, the mayor of Little Rock, the governor of Arkansas, and the President of the United States said, "Let those children go to school, let them board that bus." So we're all watching the news, we wanted to see the kids board the bus and just as they got ready to board that bus there was a policeman standing there. He put his billy club across the door and that's when Pops said, "Why is he doing that? Why he treating them so bad?" and he wrote that song that evening and we're glad he did.

But we marched: we joined the movement when we started writing those songs. We would march and Dr. King wanted us to sing before he spoke and the last time we were right face-to-face with him was in

Chicago and he told Pops, he said, "Stap, I want you and the children to go down to Operation Breadbasket," well, it's Operation PUSH now, [but] he had chose Jesse Jackson to head this up and he said, "Because people in Chicago don't know Jesse Jackson, but they know the Staple Singers and I know you'll draw some people in there." So every Saturday morning we would go down and sing at Operation Breadbasket and now it's grown, like I said, it's grown very big now.

When we heard those songs in Canada, it was great music. It was music that was in some ways pop music that opened many doors for listeners. But I can imagine that in the American South, those songs were in people's hearts. Those songs had such meaning and inspiration and an uplifting effect on people, I'm sure.

That was the key, *uplifting*, that's what we wanted to do. You know Papa'd tell the songwriters, "If you wanna write for the Staples, read the headlines." We wanted to sing about what was happening in the world. We wanted our positive and inspiring message in there, but we wanted it to be about what was happening in the world. If something going on, we wanted to try to sing a song to try to fix it. I tell you, I'm thinking very seriously about singing some of those songs on my next CD because they shouldn't be lost. We should all remember and be there for one another.

You've sung some amazing duets with people. I wonder if you wouldn't mind if I just bounced a few names off of you. Last night, for example, you did a song that you've recorded with Marty Stuart and with The Band–"The Weight"–that is certainly one of your classics. What was that experience like, working with The Band on The Last Waltz*?*

Oh, man, that was fun, that was fun. You know that little [Rick] Danko, he was always doing something funny. We couldn't sing the song down a lot of times because Danko would come make a face in your face; he'd do anything to make you laugh. But Robbie and Levon ... Levon was my father's partner, they were really good friends. And well, we can tell it now. We took a break and Pops went back to say something to Levon and Levon had a cigarette in each hand. And Pops said, "Levon, man, you smokin' two cigarettes at a time?" And Levon he took one, he said, "Awww, Roebuck you gotta try this one." And Pops said, "What is that, man? That's one of them reefas?"—he called them reefas—"Levon, aww man, no." Oh, Pops laughed about that one for a long time. And see he would call Pops "Roebuck." "Awww, Roebuck." Pops would tell that story and he'd sound just like Levon.

You did some work with Ray Charles, too. Could you tell us about that?

Ah, Brother Ray was a really dear friend. Now he would come to the house for dinner when he was in Chicago and last time he came over, he brought some kids with him that they hadn't ever had turnip and mustard greens, you know, and so my mother said, "Brother Ray, these kids they like these greens." He say, "Oh, Sister, they don't know nothing. I brought them just so they could have some of your home-cooked food." And then my mother, after they finished dinner, my mother made the best sweet potato pies in the world and "Brother Ray," she said, "okay, here's your dessert." And he started eating that sweet potato pie and he started rockin'. He started rockin' and he said, "Now, sister, you know we could start a franchise with these sweet potato pies." He loved that sweet potato pie. And Pops was smart, you know. Pops would make sure that, if you had been in Chicago, you'd have gotten some of that sweet potato pie. Because he'd make sure that all the radio announcers got a sweet potato pie. And so the head man at the radio, he came over one day. "Respect Yourself" had come out and the first time he played it, he said, "Oh, man, here come those Staple Singers. Now, I'll tell ya—Staple Singers don't need no payola, they got pie-ola." So I said, "Pops, you are really smart."

Yep, so Brother Ray he'd come to the house. The Five Blind Boys of Alabama, all those guys would come to the house. When Brother Ray came I knew what to expect, but you tell them something one time–if they want the telephone, they want the washroom, they want the kitchen–you tell them one time and they'd go back and sit down in the living room and when they'd get up again they'd know where they were going, they'd find their way. You didn't have to lead them again; you didn't have to show them.

But Brother Ray was, oh, he was a beautiful, beautiful man. We went to his house in California. Now he had a little moped/scooter. So he brought it outside and Pops said, "Man, you gonna ride that thing?" and he said, "You watch me, Pop" and he pointed, he say, "I'm gonna go all the way around that block." Daddy say, "Oh, Ray, don't try that, man." And his wife would say, "Oh, he can do it, Pops. Don't worry about him." And Brother Ray got on that motorcycle or that moped and down the street he went. We watched him all the way. He turned the corner there and all of us are standing there, you know, and we were waiting for him to come back so he was supposed to come from the other way and so we were all faced that way, the whole group, everybody standing and all of the sudden, here he come and I said, "Oh, no, no." I don't know how, but in some kind of way he counted the paces. He figured it out and he went around the block on a moped. Yes, indeed. Yeah, he was a character, Brother Ray. He wasn't gonna let nothing stop him, you know, just because he couldn't see didn't mean he couldn't ride his motorcycle.

I love your version of Bob Dylan's song "Gotta Serve Somebody" and you've also recorded with Bob directly. You discovered his songwriting talents, very early in his career.?

Yes, in fact, we met Bob back in the day. We were in New York, and we were going to do a Westinghouse TV show together and his manager introduced him. He was a little cute kid. Bob said, "Oh, I know the Staple Singers" and Pop said, "How you know us?" He said, "I listen to 'Radio Randy.'" See Randy was on a 50,000-watt station. While we were driving we would play Randy and he'd play our songs. Bob stood there and he said, "Pops, you have a smooth, velvety voice; and Mavis, her voice is heavy and growly and rough." And then he quoted a whole verse of one of our songs, "Sit Down, Servant," and he said, "Mavis says 'Yonder come little David with his rock in a sling, I don't want to meet him he's a dangerous man.'" And, man, we had a fit. So when the concert started, Bob started singing and Pops told us, "Listen. Do y'all hear what that kid is sayin'?" He said, "We can sing that song, that's a song we can sing." And the song was "Blowin' in the Wind." And Pops said, "We gonna record that song." We recorded maybe seven or eight Dylan songs: "A Hard Rain's a-Gonna Fall," "Masters of War," "Blowin' in the Wind." What else did we record? Just a bunch of them.

But Bob he's really, really bashful: he's shy. We're still dear friends and he's just wonderful. I met his son with the Wallflowers, Jakob. He looks like a young Bob Dylan, you know. I have had a wonderful, wonderful life. I can tell you lots and lots and lots of stories.

I don't know how many people recognize the linkage that Pops and the Staples had to the Mississippi Delta and the fact that Pops was from the same plantation as Charlie Patton, the father of Delta blues. Pops learned to play guitar there and was part of that Delta blues tradition.

That's right. He was on Dockery's Farm. Pops' father was a sharecropper and this man, Charlie Patton, he was there and Pops loved his guitar. He would tell us all of these stories about when he was a boy. When he told us that he made ten cents a day working, I said, "Daddy, *ten* cents a day?" He'd say "Mavis, that was big money back then, that was a lot of money." So I said, "Alright." He put him a little guitar in the layaway in a hardware store; that's where they sold the guitars. And when he got that guitar out he started teaching himself how to play. He liked Charlie Patton and Howlin' Wolf was there, too. And he would take us down to Mississippi because he wanted us to know from whence we came because he'd always say, "You gotta know where you come from to know where you're going." So he would take us and he showed us where he proposed to our mother and he showed us where he bought that little guitar. It's not a hardware now. He took us to the cemetery to show us his grandparents' stone: two beautiful stones, two hearts still right there, real beautiful.

You know Pops was a hands-on father: he would read us books, he would make us peanut brittle, and popcorn balls. But the books he would buy us were the magic of thinking positive, the magic of thinking big and he autographed each one of them to all of us. And he wanted us to excel. He wanted us to be better than he was when he was coming up, but I don't think any of us could be better than Pops. My father was, oh, he was the best. And back in the day when we were little kids, you'd hear in the churches the mothers, "Oww, look at that man with his children." Because back then you never knew where the father was; you never saw the children with their father, they were always with the mother. And then we started getting these questions, "Is your mother living?" I say, "Yeah." If we were gonna be with our father, we just didn't have to have our mother there. She saw how he wanted to be a father. He would take us to Sunday school on Sundays, take us to the movies on Saturdays, and if he thought we were getting sick with a cold, he would take us to the drug store. I hated this: he would take us to the drugstore and sit us all up on the stool and have the man behind the fountain make us up a Castor Oil Highball, yeah, with Coca-Cola and they'd stir it and ugh. So I said, "Daddy, I'm not gonna be sick no more. I won't be sick no more." But that was his way of taking care of us, you know, that's my father. On the CD *Have A Little Faith* is a song called "Pops Recipe." Yes, we wrote this song telling you all about Pops, the way he raised us and took care of us, and Dockery's Farm. Now if I had talked about Pops all the way through on that record, that would have been a whole CD, so I couldn't tell it all, but it's a really good song that I'm singing for my father.

Well, you're certainly sharing Pops' message. And I think that over the years, you've probably turned so many people on to your message. Dylan went through his Christianity. You were there when that was happening. I know our mutual friend, Maria Muldaur, is very much influenced by you.

It's part of our life to be there for one another. We sing a song called "Reach Out, Touch a Hand, Make a Friend If You Can." You try to hold on to your old friends, like Maria Muldaur, Bonnie Raitt, all of us come up together, Dylan. I tell you, it's just a beautiful thing because a lot of times new friends, you don't know if they're your friend or not? You don't know if they wanna be your friend because you're on stage or what? So hold on to those old friends–that's a friend. And Maria Muldaur, oh, man, I had to stop Maria one time. She came up on stage with us and she started singing and she was singing the song so long, I said "Maria, Maria, Stop! I'm running out of breath." You know she's a frisky little girl. But she was my father's heart; he loved Maria and she is still, still carrying on...beautiful voice, beautiful voice.

Mavis, I know we're just about out of time. Is there something else you'd like to say to us this morning?

Well, I would like to say that this is my first time to be here on Vancouver Island and I tell you, I think it's just beautiful. I've enjoyed myself immensely, yes. I tell you, I hope it's not the last time. All the people are so beautiful and the greenery that I see. And last night the audience was so receptive, I almost didn't want to stop myself, you know what I'm saying? Yes, I would just like to say that you all have made me one happy golden girl this weekend and I thank you, thank you so much. And you know Monday is my birthday. Yes, I'll make another year, thank the Lord.

["Happy Birthday" chorus]

Thank you. Now I can go back home and let the folks in Chicago know, "Well, hey, the people on Vancouver Island, they sang 'Happy Birthday' to me." Now, I'm really special.

Thank you so much. Thank you, Holger.

Ry Cooder
(Born 1947)

Ry Cooder's body of work, which goes back to the mid-sixties, has probably done more to educate roots music fans and fellow musicians than that of any other artist. Nobody has covered as many musical genres with as much integrity and depth.

Michael Ondaatje wrote in the liner notes of Cooder's 2008 compilation, *The UFO Has Landed*, "Cooder, apart from being a great guitarist, is this wondrous universal and historical fly-catcher plant and musical encyclopedist who lives in Santa Monica.....his albums have been great storybooks of American vernacular music."

Ry got a four-string guitar at the age of three. At eight, he learned to play all the songs on a Josh White album. Over the next few years he studied records by Skip James, Big Joe Williams, Woody Guthrie, Lead Belly, Blind Blake, and Jesse Fuller. In 1963, at the age of sixteen, Ry was already well know at the Ash Grove, the Los Angeles club that booked roots music during the folk revival. He was encouraged to perform a few songs during the open stage nights and formed a short-lived duet with Jackie DeShannon. He loved the Ash Grove scene and in 1964 encouraged fellow blues devotee Taj Mahal to move to LA to become part of it. They formed Rising Sons, soon signing with Columbia. Despite several recording sessions, the label released only one single while the band was together. Ry went on to play on Taj Mahal's debut album in 1966.

Sessions with Captain Beefheart and his Magic Band resulted in Ry becoming a member of that group briefly. His bottleneck playing and arrangements are featured on Beefheart's first release *Safe As Milk* in 1967. With his growing reputation as a unique studio guitarist, the Rolling Stones hired him to play on their 1969 album, *Let It Bleed* and 1971's *Sticky Fingers* albums. He also contributed to the soundtrack of the 1970 film *Performance* starring Mick Jagger and appears with various Stones on the 1969 *Jamming with Edward!* sessions. During that time he played on Randy Newman's early sides as well as performing with him. He also co-produced three tracks on Neil Young's 1969 first solo album.

Ry Cooder's first, self-titled solo album came out on Reprise (via Warner Bros. Records) in 1970 showcasing Ry's unique approach to blues, gospel, and hillbilly music. A series of brilliant albums followed, including 1972's *Into the Purple Valley* and *Boomer's Story*, *Paradise and Lunch* in 1974, *Chicken Skin Music* in 1976, *Jazz* in 1977, 1982's *The Slide Area* and *Get Rhythm* in 1987. Albums that included his personal eclectic take on everything from folk, blues, country, Tex-Mex, Hawaiian, calypso, R&B, rock and roll, and classic jazz material.

His innovative *Bop Till You Drop* released in 1979 was advertised as "the first commercially available all-digital recording." With the exception of that release, Ry never sold many records for Reprise and was a reluctant touring artist. Movie soundtracks, however, kept him creative, at home, and paying the bills. Walter Hill opened the door to movie soundtracks with films like *The Long Riders*, *Southern Comfort*, *Johnny Handsome*, and five others. That led to Wim Wenders (*Paris, Texas*; *Buena Vista Social Club*), Louis Malle (*Alamo Bay*), and Mike Nichols (*Primary Colors*) asking him to soundtrack their films. Cooder also contributed music for *Crossroads*, *The Border*, *Last Man Standing*, *Brewster's Millions*, and *Geronimo: An American Legend*.

Contributing to the notes of the 1995 compilation CD *Music by Ry Cooder*, Walter Hill wrote, "As to Ry's film music, suffice to say that it doesn't work in the traditional manner; doesn't underscore, as much as it envelops; doesn't heighten the moment as much as it adds to the atmosphere–surrounds the story–supplies missing information—champions the mood rather than the event."

In addition to the film soundtracks, Ry has worked extensively as a producer and session player finding common ground with artists as diverse as Johnny Cash, Ali Farka Touré, the Chieftains, John Lee Hooker, Pops and Mavis Staples, Jim Dickinson, Little Feat, Little Village, Gabby Pahinui, Flaco Jimenez, Van Morrison, John Hiatt, Nick Lowe, Maria Muldaur, V.M. Bhatt, Eric Clapton, and Gordon Lightfoot.

In 1997 he helped open the door to the appreciation of traditional Cuban music with the successful *Buena Vista Social Club* CD release, film documentary in 1999, and subsequent recordings and concerts. In 2005, his *Chávez Ravine* release was the first of the ambitious "California Trilogy," along with 2007's *My Name is Buddy* and 2008's *I, Flathead.* The press release describes the series as "the singer and guitarist journeys through the real and imagined history of mid-twentieth century, multi-ethnic California, sampling the sounds of its barrios and byways, its nightclubs and honkytonks." The Deluxe Edition of *I, Flathead* includes a hard cover, 104 page, Ry-Cooder-written novella to accompany the disc.

Ry Cooder rarely does interviews. The good timing of a trip to LA the same week as the release of *I, Flathead*, plus the support of Colin Nairne of Macklam Feldman Management made it possible—an opportunity I'll be forever grateful for.

Taking the LA freeways into consideration, I arrived at the Santa Monica Airport for the interview (June 30, 2008) about an hour early. I found the hangar where I was instructed to go and found I was the lone car in the parking lot. I decided to go for a walk and check out the hanger, which I was told was also where Jay Leno kept part of his collection of cars.

I took my camera, crossed the street, and got one shot. I walked inside the hanger, saw nothing, and went back to the car to continue reading Ry Cooder's novella, *I, Flathead.* I then noticed in the rearview mirror that someone from the hanger was watching me and a few minutes later a car pulled up. "What are you doing? Why are you here? What's your name and are you paparazzi?" I passed the test. Ry told me later that it was "The best security in the country," because the location is part of a federal airport.

The studio turned out to be two rooms absolutely filled with gear. He moved a few things around, made some space and we sat down. The interview timed out at fifty-two minutes on the mini disc. Many more things to talk about, but as far as radio interviews go, it was a long one and Ry was very generous with his time. He signed several albums for me, but when he got to the Rising Sons reissue (1964 with Taj Mahal) he put it aside and said "You don't want to waste your time listening to this."

As I was packing up, I asked Ry if he would be doing any live gigs. He told me that back in 1988 he decided to stop gigging and has only done the odd one since. He said he was never satisfied with his shows and in the early days drove the promoters crazy because he wanted to give everyone their money back. "I never felt happy about a single show I ever did. Even when my heart was into it, my stomach and other parts of my body told me otherwise. I decided my heart was outvoted by the other parts."

Ry Cooder, 1992. Photo: Frank Gasparik.
Courtesy of the Edmonton Folk Music Festival.

Ry Cooder, 1995. Photo: Frank Gasparik. Courtesy of the Edmonton Folk Music Festival.

Ry Cooder, 1992. Photo: Brent Kirby. Courtesy of the Edmonton Folk Music Festival.

First, I want to thank you for inviting me here. It's nice to be able to interview you on your own turf.

South Santa Monica is where I grew up, right across the street, and this is the old Santa Monica Airport and the scene of the aircraft factory that built the C-47s and the DC-3s all during the war. Long gone now, like everything.

You've been paying tribute to Johnny Cash for many years. Back in 1954, do you remember hearing Johnny Cash for the first time and the effect that that had on you?

Well sure, of course. They gave me a radio, a little Sears sort of a brown anodized little job (AM only, didn't have a lot of FM in those days). I was cruising through the dial, I mean there weren't a lot of stations in those days, just a handful. And I came across the hillbilly station, the station that existed primarily for the people that worked in this aircraft factory and elsewhere in the defence plants during the war effort. These people were mostly southerners that had come out, country people, to work in these plants. There was a huge explosion of work...they were either fleeing the dustbowl or poverty in general, or lack of work at home. They came here and they wanted to hear their music and they liked to hear it, so this radio station appeared for that purpose. So I found that station and it was honky-tonk music twenty-four hours a day, and I'd never heard it before. I was eight years old...and that did it for me. I thought "That's what I like; this is the stuff I like." These little story songs and the guitars and the simple honky-tonk rhythms and that.

Johnny Cash appeared on the scene right around that time. "Hey, Porter" was the first one—it was a B-side—and they played this and people liked it. The image of the south, you know the guy in the train...the train is bringing him back home and he's seeing the cotton fields and smelling the frost and he can't wait to get off the train. I thought,

"Well, that's fantastic, I see everything he's saying."

You could visualize it. And the rhythm was good, and the voice had this spooky quality that was unusual in those days. Most country singers were tenors or baritones and it was more polite, more of a measured thing, like Hank Snow for instance. Rich and measured. But Johnny Cash wasn't measured; there was something almost perilous about him, and really gripping. So of course the first time I heard "Hey, Porter" I was sitting at home. I used to tell my parents "I can't go to school, I'm sick." And they go, "What's the matter?" And I say "Oh, I've got a sore throat." So they'd go off to work and I'd sit at home in bed and listen to the radio. I had my soap operas until noon then we hit KXLA and on we went.

So I sat there listening to this thing, and I memorized it because I had a good memory and I could memorize a song if I heard it one time. And I thought, that's the guy. I wonder what he's going to do. And they released records, well singles, pretty regularly at that time, so that was followed by "I Walk the Line" and that was followed by "Big River," "Folsom Prison Blues," and then Jerry Lee Lewis was soon after "Great Balls of Fire" and what was the other one?

Anyway, so Sun Records coming right out of the south, at the same time you had Capitol Records in Hollywood who had just discovered this market, and they said we can do that. So they hired Cliffie Stone, who was an upright bass player, to become the talent scout and he brought Merle Travis, Speedy West, Jimmy Bryant, and all of these hotshots who were imported here and had come out here for work.

And all these bars sprang up, and all these nightclubs where you could go see this music, it was all over the place in Los Angeles. But I didn't know this; I didn't know where these people came from or who they possibly could be. I had no idea except that it was jumping out of the radio at me, I'll tell ya. And I remember all of those songs like it was yesterday; I could sing you some of the jingles. Cliffie Stone was actually hired by KXLA to record the local advertising for car dealers, and he had Merle Travis and Speedy West playing on them. Songs like the Stanley Chevrolet song, that you never could forget once you'd heard it. Good as any record. This really fascinated me, and I thought well, they're out here in town somewhere, they're not in Santa Monica, I could see that. It was a very dull place, Santa Monica. But out there...just a short drive away.

When you think of regional American music, Texas, Louisiana, Mississippi, and Tennessee would probably first come to mind. But California has an equally rich culture that's very different.

Of course the mix is the key, you know? LA is a mix of people who came here from somewhere else, and you know that everything flourished here. Rhythm and Blues was strong, bebop was strong, Mexican music, and Chicanos evolved in the generational sense as the immigrant population took hold...the hillbillies, the country people....

But the thing that happens to everyone in LA is that they begin to absorb the sounds and styles and tendencies from one another. For the first time black people were living right next door to Mexican people. That never had happened before. As far as I know, in these little neighbourhoods where there weren't restricted covenants and people could actually live there, from these poor neighbourhoods downtown you'd get all kinds of music. Pacheco music, and Richard Berry doing "Louie Louie," which is essentially a salsa bag song. He went to Latin music shows and picked up that chord progression.

The thing about LA is that it changes people. Plus the recording industry was here, and the technology was here. First there's technology and then people make things out of the technology. It was certainly true—I mean look at Les Paul, working on his multitrack out in Burbank, because what happens during any war is that you get this explosion of technology, which then is translated in peace time to cheaper technological advances that the average Joe can get his hands on, like speed equipment for his flathead or louder guitars such as Leo Fender was involved in.

He took his inspiration from Paul Bigsby who was a guy who made cast aluminium for fighter planes in the war. [Fender] learned casting, then he went and designed pedal steel guitars with the same stuff. I have one made out of the air force surplus stuff from Lockheed. He also made motorcycles from scratch and went racing on the dry lake with Merle Travis.

So all that was going on, and then the music takes a cue there and starts to speed up. Jimmy Bryant and Speedy West played faster and better than they did back there once they got here. And it was all aided and abetted by the superior technology that was in place here already because of the film business.

Therefore there's going to be better microphones than in Texas, better equipment than there's going to be anywhere else. So the records sound better. Capitol Records is a good example of this. High tech for the day. HiFi, beautiful studios, echo chambers...do you think they have any of that in Bristol, Tennessee? No way!

So these same guys come out here and find out what they have available to them...Oh and players! You look at those Speedy West records....And the sidemen are usually jazz musicians—very sophisticated—who really could lay a groove down. Because, they were already doing modern jazz. So you take these guys and have them come down for a country western session. So then you have that jazz thing blending in, and the sophistication going up. And they sold these things because they had a huge audience. If you don't have an audience and you can't sell the records then you can't record.

But LA was growing up, I mean the population after the war had tripled or something, and everyone was coming from somewhere else and homesick. LA is a city of the homesick. Everybody's homesick, so they want to hear their thing. But then it doesn't stay the same: it's not conserved, it's given this injection of high octane fuel and pumped up! Pretty interesting.

I've really appreciated getting to know the characters in I, Flathead. *They all seem to have a dream.*

That's true, you've got to have it. You've got to have some kind of aspirations or whatever it may be.

I love the references to vintage Hi/Lo shag carpeting.

Well there used to be a guy on TV, Ben Hunter, and he had the *Ben Hunter Movie Matinee*, and he sat in a movie set that was made to look like a lanai with potted plants and a tweed couch, and he had a collie dog which slept the whole time, and he had a toupee, and he'd sit there and say, "Hi, I'm Ben Hunter and today we're going to watch...whatever, some old movie"...and I loved these things.

I loved old movies shot in Los Angeles before the war. And it was junk—B, C quality, but it was my kind of thing. But his advertising was a custom craft carpet company that would install luxurious nylon pile continuous filament Hi/Lo shag carpet—$9.99 a square yard.

And if you were among the first one hundred to call, they would come out and install these aluminium frame glass louver windows, which had never been seen before, you know, luxury item. And of course they let the air in, they let the dust in, they were terrible, but people loved them! Look it goes up and down—brand new idea. But of course with the Hi/Lo shag, with continuous filament, if one strand breaks like the guy says in the store, the whole thing goes. If your dog or cat scratches the thing once, it's cut and it's separated, the whole thing's gone. And that was the trouble with Hi/Lo shag.

I liked all that, I thought at the time. And he had all these little theme songs... "Sincerely Ben Hunter"...you know it was cool. And I'd sit there in my aunt's house out in Reseda, out where Sunny Clover lives, and it was hot and the house was dark and we'd sit there and watch Ben Hunter on the TV and I thought it was great.

And your references to steel guitar players and to watching Spade Cooley on TV. I gather he was a pretty rough character. Didn't he murder his wife?

He did. He killed his wife and went to prison, and the sheriffs, who loved him, took him out to play a benefit, and he died on stage. He appears on Elroy here and there. He had the most successful West Coast thing going. He had the ballroom out here at the beach that he played in. Was it the Aragon ballroom? I forget. And he had the TV show, and that's amazing, to have a country-swing guy, fiddle player in a cowboy suit on television. They discovered that all these people had TV sets and they wanted to see themselves essentially; their own thing on television.

It was the same way people wanted to see Frank Sinatra on television. So once they began to work these demographics out, then they had a town hall party, which was fantastic. All of these swingin' cats, hi dee hi everybody...oh hey, here comes Hank Snow, whatcha going to do for us, Hank? "I'm Moving On." Oh my god, I'm sitting there watching this, and Hank Snow was good every time. Tough as a boot. But Spade Cooley was worse, by all accounts.

And they died a sad death. I mean many steel players appeared as I grew older and learned more, to be preferential. You know alcohol, addicted...you know... unsung and unpraised. [Steel guitar players are] like this weird sub fraternity honoured by their own. And it's now true that they've become a cause. Now they have steel guitar conventions and everyone's remembered...but not then. That was a tough life.

I wanted to be in Ray Price's band in those days. I thought, "That's it." When I heard "My Shoes Keep Walking Back To You" I thought, "That's it. That's what life is all about." So let's go do that. How do you do that? My dad says "No, you don't want to do that. That's a bunch of hillbillies...a bunch of rednecks. You don't want to do that." He used to say, "Well don't go up on Ocean Park Boulevard," where all the bars were for all the aircraft workers. They were open twenty-four hours because the shifts were twenty-four hours, so they got a variance in the law. They had jukeboxes in there, pumping this stuff day and night, and my dad says, "Never go up there." So I went up there to see what the hell was going on, and I heard this music coming out of there, and I said "That's it...that's all I want to do."

Of course it was impossible in Santa Monica to know how to get into that world: it was impenetrable. I thought "How do you do that?" I ended up recording, it's true, but I never did make it to Ray Price. I would have liked to have, but it's also true that it's a terribly hard life... you end up face down on the Hi/Lo shag like Vance Terry or somebody...not a good way to go.

Don Helms is still at it and he's 91. [Hank Williams' steel guitar player, who unfortunately died a few weeks after this interview.]

Ray Price is still on the road...two hundred dates a year. How do they do it? My god. Tough cats. The last of the best, too. The last of that generation. The honky-tonk now is themed out. It's no longer the way of life that it was. My generation, we can say we grew up listening to it and it was just the stuff. You know it wasn't like celebrity-driven or transactional so much; it was just what you heard on the radio while you did your little mechanics job.

I wanted to ask you about the Ash Grove scene. It must have been a great time to catch folk music and country blues. What impact did that have on you and who were some of your favourite people who played the Ash Grove?

It's amazing to think back now–I actually sat there–like within a few feet like we're doing now. There was Jesse Fuller, Bukka White, Mississippi John Hurt, the original Stanley Brothers: the list went on and on. It was incredible. And [the owner] Ed Pearl just kept bringing in these people, as they were made available, and this folk festival thing had taken hold, and that's how they found that audience. You know Joan Baez inspired, Bob Dylan inspired, you know, whatever got them there.

And then Ed Pearl got the core people out to Los Angeles to play in his club. There wasn't a series of venues like there is now...it wasn't organized in those days. Maybe San Francisco. But if you came all the way to Los Angeles just to play in this kinda dumpy little club, you know it was amazing. There was no scrim, like invisible shield, in those days. And I used to say, like for instance to Jesse Fuller, "Can you just show me how this tune goes? Where do I put my fingers?" "Well sure," he'd go. And most of them did, and he'd go well here, here, and here.

Reverend Gary Davis, who was vaguely aware of the world, he'd just sit there and crank this stuff out. And he'd go, "Well, you just go home and practice."

But, what I began to realize at that time was that it was something to do with the people. It wasn't just where you put your hands, it was these people, and they were really coming from somewhere else. That's what interested me, because in Santa Monica we don't have people like that. It was pretty straightlaced, but these cats were coming from Mississippi and the Appalachians and this and that, and they had another way of life in their heads.

They were wired differently, they were very different people, and they saw music as a way out of working in various different factories or mills or what have you. It had to do with survival. It gave it a kind of immediacy, a kind of reality that wasn't dressed up. So I thought, "This is something, this has got power." I thought, "Now, how do you do this?" The tremendous luck of it all was that I could play good enough so that I could learn how to do it. It wasn't so hard for me, you know?

I also realized that I wasn't one of them and I wasn't going to sound like them. I was never going to sound like Jessie Fuller. At first I didn't understand why: "I'm playing the notes, what's the matter here?" So I kept trying to break through for about a ten-year period. You got to see up close and talk to and touch these cats who were still alive, who had been found either working in a post office or fixing fenders somewhere...and god knows what they thought. Out here in

LA, they were transplanted into an intellectual milieu of left wing.

You know Pete Seeger created this. Popular music is a bridge, and we have to have unity in the classes. Class warfare is the enemy, so let's bridge to the proletariat, the country people, the city intellectuals. And all that was a powerful notion. It certainly worked for Pete. But these folks that they brought in, they didn't know anything about that. They just sat there and did their thing.

And the records began to appear, LPs made, you know Folkways and all that. They became more and more available. I met record collectors older than me, who gathered these precious old 78s and you could actually listen to this stuff. Now it's all available on CD so it's nothing, but back then it was hard to get a hold of this stuff. I used to get my Starday records, and Jimmy Martin...Jimmy Martin affected me rather like Johnny Cash did, it killed me. And I kept thinking, what do you do? How do you work towards these sounds? But I realized, it's the records. You'd go to a show and it was good, but it was nothing like the records. Why? What's the difference? Why is it not as exciting as the records? It took years to figure that out.

But then I got through all this and I got into the position where I was able to be part of recording and then I began to figure it out. I had a chance to record with some of these people too, to a certain extent, at least. I could be in the studio on the other end of a microphone and be able to hear back over the earphones what's going on. And, oh my god, the transformation that happens electronically, listening back, because you weren't allowed in the control room in those days if you were a session musician...never walked in the control room.

I could hear in the earphones what was happening...a kind of compression, a kind of enhancement, because if records weren't great to listen to, they would have been thrown out. But because of tube compression or tape compression or just compression of the grooves, when the needle goes down, it's as Jim Keltner the drummer says, "The call of the playback." You want to hear it played back, and hear what happened when you all played, because it sounds nothing like what you're doing.

We're just sitting in a soundproof room, very dry, and you hear the playback and it's big and it's huge and it's fat and it's been affected by all these tricky things they have like Pultec equalizers and compressors and I don't know what...I mean in those days tube equipment, oh my god. Once you hear that you can never go back to real life. Or high school in my case...I had to go to school the next day, which I hated. It was a stupid waste of time. I resented it then, I resent it now. It was a waste of twelve years I'll never get back.

There are some specific sessions I wanted to ask you about. You did a couple of sessions with Earl Hines. You must have been very honoured to work with him. How did that come about?

How do you even describe it? Here I have my Earl Hines records and I think to myself, "This is the ultimate music state." To take a great big piece of furniture like the piano and just...it's like as fluid and subtle a thing that ever could be. And this guy was doing it in the twenties, and now I find out that this particular week he was in LA, in the seventies, doing some jazz solo. And I call the club and I said, "Where's Earl?" "Oh, he's over at the such and such motel in midtown." So I called the motel, I said "Connect me with Earl Hines" and he says, "Hello!" and that's all there was to it. I thought, do it..."Hello, Earl! You don't know me, but I know you...blah blah blah... I'm recording and I'm playing guitar, and I've got a little thing that I'd like you to try, if you've got time." "Well sure, I ain't doing nothing," he says, so we go down, pick him up, take him to the studio. And I figured that "Ditty Wah Ditty" would work, sort of a stride thing, you know it was sort of a primitive little thing, and I didn't play very well. I was so overcome I didn't know what to do with myself. I wished I'd have...well, you can't look back now. I wish I could have done it now, I'd have been in much better shape, but there he was.

And a friendly and nice guy and just happy to be there and telling stories, and we had a ball, and it amazed me, and amazes me now looking back, how unlikely that was. How absolutely freakish a day that really was. We have photographs, you know, Suzie took pictures as she always does, and I can go, there he is, and I'm sitting there and that's it.

And I'd make these records and put them out...and they would bring them to me at Warner and go, "OK. Here's your record." And I'd hold it and say, well, something got disconnected, I don't know what. There was always this tremendous let down; it didn't do what I wanted it to do. Well, put it aside and try some more, keep trying. That's all I ever do. I'd think to myself, "Don't give up, just keep trying," and that's what I'd do. But along the way there were some of these episodes like that there, of course.

On those early Warner releases, were you disappointed with your performance or the production?

Well both, it disappointed me because it didn't do what my favourite records did. I wondered why and at first I thought, well it's me. I'm not playing good and I'm not singing good, you know, good ideas, bad execution. So I thought I've got to get better, keep trying harder. Work on this thing of arranging and trying to make these tunes work, and try to assemble something.

Much later I realized it was the lack of context. The thing had no context, so it was just sort of free floating, so it didn't take hold. It wasn't part of a thing. It wasn't honky-tonk really, it wasn't jazz, I wasn't shoulder to shoulder with somebody like Ray Price like I would have liked to have been. And that's a hard lesson to learn, I mean, you're just not there...I mean come on. These people are fantastic geniuses in their way, whoever they may be, whether it's Ray Price or Louis Armstrong or Jimmy Martin or Earl Hines: you're not of that calibre. You've just got to work harder and tighten up. But it kept disappointing me and it's something you have to live with, I guess. Because they also weren't hits; it created a problem bureaucratically because the record company kept saying, when are you gonna get your hit? Why don't you just play your guitar and do that thing you do with the glass? Now the Stones, you go do that. Now be like that.

One guy at Warner said, get yourself a pair of leather pants and get hip to yourself. He stabbed the desk with his finger when he said it...getting kind of testy. I thought, what the hell are they talking about? Many years later I look back and realize I was just not a good team player. I didn't know what I was there for. I was expected to make money, for Christ's sake. What did that mean? You get your own pop act, a persona, a pair of leather pants, get hip to yourself. The guy was right. Make us some goddamn money, what the hell do you think this is? One other guy stabbed my chest and said, "You're a prima donna. Who do you think you're kidding?" I got offended. Years later I look back—the guy was right! What the hell did they have me around there for then, the question was. Then of course, that's open to speculation but...no one ever sat me down and said, "You better know that this is a money thing. This is a business. You're supposed to make money, and if you don't, get out. Go learn to do something else. Because if you're going to be in here and use up the time and use up the space, you better turn over a dollar for us."

The other thing was no one will tell you how to make good sounding records, you have to find out. That's a very hidden secret world of knowledge. Why did my stuff sound so dry, I thought. Where's the beef? Where's the pump, the bubble, that diaphanous edge that you play for. Bit by bit I figured it out. Mostly because of film recording. Thanks to Walter Hill I got to play with that and see about that. But I'm telling you, it's hard work. Looking back, I'd have fired me. But they didn't, until at some point my contract ran out and I was free to go, but at that point the record industry had changed so much it didn't matter anymore, like it doesn't now.

You held on to your values and principles as an artist. You seem to be in a position now where you can really do whatever you want.

Well sure, look at me. I mean I'm sixty-one years old, so I just say I'm going to do these things. Everything's changed, all bets are off; there is no business, it's retail. Records, radio, and retail: the three Rs, which were the pillars that held the whole thing up. Because if you had a record, then you took it to the radio, then they played it, then the people went out and bought it. It was a very simple idea, a perfect business model. Absolutely perfect. Beautiful music, for all of your emotional states, preserved forever at a price you can afford.

Now, you find me anything better than that: not shoes, not cars, not food...not anything. Even books, as much as I love books, it's rather arcane. But the record gets you...isn't this true? People even need it, for Christ's sake, or it seems like they do. They turn to it. What the hell happened? But in any case, I finally got to the point where I'm going to do what I want to do now, and it's just as good as the next guy who does what he wants to do, and we're no longer dominated by bureaucracy or a record business...it doesn't exist now, so who cares?

There's a story in this. That gave me a way to go to Lalo Guerrero and say, "Lalo, you remember *Chávez Ravine*? [2005 release]" "Of course," he says. He can sing in his old way about the times and his old place, and it comes alive. Then we add in all the old historical references and the ephemera, and the pictures of this, and I like this kind of thing...this is what interests me, are these stories and the evidence we have of it, and the way that the songs can be like that rather than stupid little songs that exist in the ether and are of no value. So let's tie it all together, it's what I like anyway. So do what you like.

So Buddy comes along. [*My Name is Buddy*, 2007 release.] So OK, Buddy's a cat. It's a simple idea, he tells you what really happened. The songs are fun and interesting, but really life is tough for the workingman. And I'll tell you what went on that day and how I got arrested and accused of being a communist from Manila and all this. But they're short stories, little paragraphs, because Buddy's just a cat, he doesn't have too much to say. And then the drawings prove that it's true...I mean there's Buddy with Hank Williams and Buddy in jail and all this stuff you know...and I was inspired by the fact that Buddy's just a simple cat with a soulful face, and he looked like a workingman on the move looking for a better life, trying to find unity, trying to find solidarity one more time, which we don't have anymore.

But then I thought, "OK, across town from Chavez Ravine, at that time, call it 1950, all of these working class white guys, so called blue collar, so called common man, they're out there working in the factories, like we were saying earlier, and they've got a story, too. It's different, but the music is a big part of it. If you just start writing these songs, you're going to run into Merle Travis everywhere you go. Everywhere you go you will hit Merle. Forget it. There's nobody living that should even try to touch that stuff, because Merle is Merle, and others were others. I mean dare I say Harlan Howard, Willie Nelson, I mean everybody. You cannot do that stuff."

So I said, "Write a story. Let's write about it. Let's hear their talk," and I started playing with that and then the songs may emerge. Having some relationship to the people in the story—I'll do better that way—rather than just trying to be Merle Travis, it's ridiculous. I can't. So that's what I was doing when I was doing *Chávez Ravine*, I started messing with the Kash Buk character. First there was the girl Donna Greva because I found a picture of her in this Temple city. This tough looking babe, twenty years old with a face like a hatchet. Really nice photograph. Wow. She's got a story; let's go see what she says. And she's complaining about this ex-husband. Who's he? Kash Buk. Let's go find out who he is. Oh, he's kind of a cool character, but then we need a softer side of Kash Buk, a kinder gentler Kash Buk.

Well, who's going to tell that story? Well, it's going to be his crippled steel guitar player, who is used to being nobody and quite happy with it. Just a guy you'd meet on the street, you wouldn't look twice. But he's got a pretty good story to tell because he's a witness. You know he wasn't proving anything like Kash Buk always was. He was just an observer like a steel player would be...sitting off to the side watching the whole thing happen. That guy I really like.

So once I started doing this, I thought, "This is great. I'm going to sit here in the morning at my word processor and type this stuff out, and let my mind go." And after two years of writing this I knew what the songs were probably going to be about. Without crashing into "Hot Rod Lincoln," well, I'll quote some of that stuff, because it's fun to quote things. There's plenty of film dialogue that's been skin-grafted into that story, let me tell you. I like it, I like to do it. I'm doing more of it now. I'm sitting and doing that.

The oral history and dialogue really lends life to the stories. It's great to see you doing more of that with this trilogy.

Well sure, it's not about philosophy or inner mind, which a novel is typically about. [The characters] don't operate that way, they just say "Hey, get me a drink" or "Let's go faster," "Or come on down to the joint and let's try and sing this song." I mean, it's more active, more physical in that way, it's easier. I'm not a novelist for heaven's sake, but I have some ear for how people talk. Because I can remember how people talk, some of the conversations you're reading in there are things people said to me when I was eight years old. I can remember a lot of that stuff. I guess in the mind, you know, information is stored but dislocated from the original context. Conversations live in there simply as sound bites. I don't know what was happening at that time, but I remember what was said. It's easy.

I've always been paying attention to people: "What are they saying?" It's neat. It's fun to listen to and it may come in handy...so the idea of the oral history, the lost tapes....Why did someone go record Kash Buk in his trailer or Donna Greva at the bar? Where do these tapes come from? And finally you learn something about that. A guy traces down the girl Roxanne out into the desert and she sort of takes care of him. So the tapes just sit in a box so to speak, because a lot of stuff has been found that way.

I had a friend who was a hyper-literal translator and she worked for twenty-five years on the Nixon tapes, hyper-literally translating every sound in his mouth, because he had a lot of code, Nixon did. All the ums and ahs meant something. It wasn't just sound that he made. This guy was hiding so much and he was so secretive and so cryptic that he, well she was telling me this, you can see over time in these tapes the development of these sounds as language. And so she had, well she's one of the two known people that does this—hyper-literal translation—I said that's interesting. Let's hyper-literally translate Kash Buk and so on. And then why do we have these tapes? Nobody knows. You know, what do they find in the trash? The Sun sessions of such and such.

One of my favourite recordings by you is "Thirteen Question Method," the Chuck Berry song.

I tried to play like that for years, do that kind of swing thing, you know? Swing guitar? Because it's hard to do. There was a fella you may know, Teddy Bunn his name is, a black guy, a 52nd Street in New York guy, before and after the war, mostly before the war. And he was in these little swing bands—six-piece bands, seven-piece bands, 52nd Street club guys. And he played with his thumb. He played f-hole jazz guitar, but he played with his thumb, real fast, and everything was done this way. And I heard these things again when I was in junior high school. Somebody laid a 78 on me, an instrumental solo by Teddy Bunn. And I knew nothing about who this guy was, and I thought uh oh, that is good...cuz this is really ripping and fluid and swinging and light, and it sounded like he was using his hands, not a pick, because I can't use a flat pick worth a damn.

I certainly learned that from watching Clarence White. I thought if he can do it, I am putting the pick down and I'm not going to pick it up again. So it's gotta be the fingers, which is fine. So I went ahead there. But this Teddy Bun mystified me on how to do it. I learned the notes and I practiced at this and I tried and tried and tried. And one day, Joachim was little, maybe seven or eight years old, and I would sit, for years—I'm talking about decades of time—trying to do this Teddy Bunn stuff as an exercise, you know?

And one day Joachim says, you're getting it! It's starting to sound good. I said oh no, you listen to this, and I put the original on. Oh, so Joachim, he's a little kid, says that's OK, he has a touch you don't have. That son of a bitch, you know. Now what? What do you do? How can you beat the rap, you know? So if my own son, as a little boy, spotted this, in minutes...in seconds...so I said you know, that's fine. Keep trying. I'm sixty-one years old, Joachim is twenty-nine, he's going to be thirty in August, now I got it. I can do it now. I got my thumb working—it's fast. It's almost as fast as those flamenco guys. It's accurate. It's back and forth stroke here; it took me thirty-five years. No, forty. Teddy Bunn was probably in his twenties when he was doing it, what the hell? But the great Terry Melcher once said to me, this was back in the sixties, "At the rate you're going, it's going to take you twenty years to get where you want to be, musically speaking." Well, he was flat wrong, it took forty. It took a lifetime.

Now Dizzy Gillespie once said, "You never stop learning your instrument." When I read I said, "Thank god, because I was starting to worry." You know, when's this going to get straightened out? But, little bit by little bit, everyone is the same. Artist friends of mine, they get up and they paint every day or they get up and do ceramics every day, or they write every day, or whatever they do. Walter Hill told me, "Keep working." There's nothing else you need to know. So, we do that, and I mean I'm happy to say I'm still feeling that way and little bits of progress and it gets better.

You know, I think Kash Buk is good; I like the way it's going. We sat and played one take, I sang live, something I never would have done. And Buddy is pretty much live singing too and playing it right and singing right and I dig it and I pick up on it and I think OK, you got there you know, it's good enough. This is what life is, so now I can look back and say, "Hey, it happened." It just took a little while, you know? And I didn't get the leather pants, I didn't get hip to myself, and now all bets are off. You can't sell a record. But, I thought if I put this story to it, and have the songs and call it a trilogy (by the way, I didn't intend to [call it a trilogy]), then people may pay attention. They may say, well, there's something to this maybe. Or they may not. They're so busy on their cellphones talking to their friends and figuring out where to have a latte or something...no offence. People are out there working three jobs. Do they have time to read Kash Buk? Probably not.

But I'm happy to do it, and I'm happy to have the opportunity, because Nonesuch puts this stuff out. I don't know that they can sell it, but they're putting it out, aren't they? If they're still around in five years I still may be doing these things. But they're records, they're not goddamn downloads. Nor is a book a download, nor is a film a download, I don't like it, I don't hold with it. And the public has been sold the Brooklyn Bridge on this whole thing, and that's all there is to it. And I'm mad about it. You've got to hold it in your hands, at least do that. And you may find, it's worth having around.

I believe there's a Vancouver connection to My Name is Buddy?

That's right, Buddy lived in Vancouver. He was the mascot in the Red Cat Records store. How I found out about this is a crazy thing. A friend of mine, a very perspicacious, observant fellow who owns a guitar store in Berkeley, California, found this death notice. It's a photograph of Buddy, who died in 2005, and then a website. And a phone number. And I thought, "Well this I need to know about, so I called the store." "Red Cat Records," the guy says. I didn't know what it was. And I said "Hello, this is Ry Cooder from LA." "Bob, is that you again?" "No it's Ry Cooder from LA." "Bob, will you stop that?" And words to that effect. So I said "Let me prove it to you. Something, something, something...." I proved it somehow; they believed me. I said, "Tell me about Buddy." "Well, he was our store cat, he lived in the store. We found him in the alley sleeping in a suitcase." I said, "Thank you, I'll get back to you in a little while."

So these songs just appeared to me all at once. All of this story: the classic progression of the dust bowl migration to LA, being out of work, running from the Klan, running from the sheriff, arrested in strikes, all of the stuff that's known. All of these Wobbly-type stories that you've heard a thousand times, and the songs that you've heard a million times: Being out of work in California, sleeping in a cardboard box, rescued by a poor farm girl.

Point being that institutions have failed, that we have to take care of each other, and Buddy the cat ought to know, because animals are very vulnerable, are they not? And the little mouse and everything, the lefty mouse, the *Jewish Daily Forward* mouse, you know these are all very vulnerable people. It's the fable. And I thought, "Isn't this terrific? Isn't this great?"

Nobody bought Buddy. "Well, you really did it that time," said Chris Strachwitz of Arhoolie Records. "That's the end." Chris, if I live to be a million, I would like to make a record that Chris Strachwitz find acceptable, but I haven't done it yet.

But Buddy was very inspirational—I was very happy about it—and meaningful to me, because these are all feelings that you have: "Where did the progressive agenda go? What happened to the workingman?" No one wants to be a workingman anymore, they want to be an SUV driver, or they want to be somebody sharp at the gym. Is that wrong? Is there something so terrible about it?

It's just something you miss in the timbre of life or the texture of society, you know? And it gets you into trouble. The unions were very good at educating the workers, so they would know when the wool was being pulled over their eyes. But the evil clowns couldn't stand that. They want to get you back to your ignorance, so you can be manipulated by the evil clowns. You think these evil clowns are going to give up power in November? Ha.

Buddy says you better watch out for your tree, cuz he has a simple view of things. You know the tree is important, it's attached to this and then this and then this, says Buddy. You know, you were asleep and they hijacked the whole country. I got good feedback from schoolteachers on that record though, and that was nice. To learn that they were reading it to their kids in class and the kids were getting into it. So I thought "terrific, mission accomplished."

Index